HANNAH ARENDT

Acknowledgements

A number of essays now included in the present volume have appeared, generally in somewhat different form, elsewhere: Ferenc Feher's 'The pariah and the citizen: on Arendt's political theory' in *Thesis Eleven*, 15 (1986: 15–29); Michael W. Jackson's 'The responsibility of judgement and the judgement of responsibility' in the *Windsor Yearbook of Access to Justice*, vol. 8, 1988; Maria Markus' 'The "anti-feminism" of Hannah Arendt' in *Thesis Eleven*, (1987: 76–77): and Agnes Heller's 'Hannah Arendt on the "vita contemplativa"' in *Philosophy and Social Criticism*, 12 (1987). In addition, Ferenc Feher's 'The pariah and the citizen: on Arendt's political theory' has also appeared in A. Heller and F. Feher *The Postmodern Political Condition* (1989). For this the permission of Polity Press and Anthony Giddens is acknowledged. For permission to quote from 'To Save the Jewish Homeland: There is Still Time' by Hannah Arendt, © 1948 by the American Jewish Committee, the editors thank Harcourt Brace Jovanovich, Inc. For permission to quote from W. H. Auden's poem 'The Cave of Making', Elizabeth K. Minnich and the editors express their gratitude to Faber and Faber, London.

HANNAH ARENDT

Thinking, Judging, Freedom

Edited by Gisela T. Kaplan and Clive S. Kessler

Sydney
ALLEN & UNWIN
Wellington London Boston

© G. T. Kaplan & C. S. Kessler 1989
This book is copyright under the Berne Convention. No reproduction without permission. All rights reserved.

First published in 1989
Allen & Unwin Australia Pty Ltd
An Unwin Hyman company
8 Napier Street, North Sydney NSW 2059 Australia

Allen & Unwin New Zealand Limited
75 Ghuznee Street, Wellington, New Zealand

Unwin Hyman Limited
15–17 Broadwick Street, London W1V 1FP England

Unwin Hyman Inc.,
8 Winchester Place, Winchester, Mass 01890 USA

National Library of Australia
Cataloguing-in-Publication entry:

Hannah Arendt: thinking, judging, freedom.

  Bibliography
  Includes index.
  ISBN 0 04 820041 7.
  ISBN 0 04 920109 3 (pbk.).

  1. Arendt, Hannah, 1906–1975. 2. Political science – Philosophy. I. Kaplan, Gisela, 1944– . II. Kessler, Clive S., 1942–   . III. Title: Thinking, judging, freedom.

320.5'092'4

Library of Congress Catalog Card Number: 89–83953

Set in 10/11pt Plantin by SRM Production Services Sdn. Bhd., Malaysia
Printed by Dah Hua Printers, Hong Kong

Contents

Preface	vi
Notes on contributors	viii
Introduction	1

I Politics, theory, and values

1 P. SPRINGBORG	Hannah Arendt and the classical republican tradition	9
2 F. FEHER	The pariah and the citizen: on Arendt's political theory	18

II History and responsibility

3 C. E. ADAMS	Hannah Arendt and the historian: Nazism and the New Order	31
4 M. W. JACKSON	The responsibility of judgement and the judgement of responsibility	42
5 M. BITTMAN	Totalitarianism: the career of a concept.	56

III Jewish identity and conscience

6 G. T. KAPLAN	Hannah Arendt: the life of a Jewish woman	71
7 C. S. KESSLER	The politics of Jewish identity: Arendt and Zionism	91
8 S. FARGANIS	The chosen people: the historical formation of identity	108

IV Feminism and anti-feminism

9 M. MARKUS	The 'anti-feminism' of Hannah Arendt	119

V Philosophy

10 E. K. MINNICH	To judge in freedom: Hannah Arendt on the relation of thinking and morality	133
11 A. HELLER	Hannah Arendt on the 'vita contemplativa'	144
References		160
Index		173

Preface

The present volume has its origins in our wish not merely to commemorate the work of Hannah Arendt, a scholar and radically self-defining actor in history, but also to signal and probe its continuing relevance. From that idea to the finalisation of the present volume, our Hannah Arendt project has taken on a certain life of its own — even a generative life, in establishing intellectual friendships and cooperation among contributors, and editors.

Before embarking upon this book we hoped that it would live up to its advance characterisation as an interdisciplinary occasion: that it would exemplify what interdisciplinary endeavour has to and can be — a mutually beneficial and richly informative dialogue or encounter between intellectual traditions and their exponents. More, we hoped to see the figure of Hannah Arendt — intellectually so versatile and diverse, and hence so often misunderstood — reconstituted in her wholeness, both as an original thinker and as an actor in the historical epoch whose origins and meanings she so insistently sought to fathom. The outcome, presented in this volume, has amply fulfilled the editors expectations.

Not only were intellectual friendships formed from the book. More, as the time needed to produce a coherent volume proved somewhat extended, the intervening period saw a number of the contributors, now dispersed far from their Australian locale, go on to new academic positions and recognition. Of these changes, none is perhaps more gratifying and appropriate than the appointment of Agnes Heller to what had previously been Arendt's own chair, now the Hannah Arendt chair of philosophy, at The New School of Social Research, New York.

Transcending our various differences of discipline and approach as well as our individual personal or temperamental reactions to our subject, the editors and contributors share a common conviction upon which the rationale for our book rests. We see Hannah Arendt as a classical thinker whose ideas are deeply grounded within a venerable philosophical tradition. We also see and understand her within and as a most self-aware product of her own turbulent times. Yet we also see her very much as a thinker of the present, of our own times. We who engage here in argument with her feel ourselves to be not only her interlocutors but also her contemporaries. Both in her attempts to 'think through' her own epoch and her relation to it and in the central questions she thereby raised—notably about the revival in the modern world of a life of active citizenship and, through commitment to such a politics, about the creation of a genuine and positive power—she provided us, now facing our own uncertain future, with a clarifying, orienting, and empowering legacy. This is the claim that her ideas and her life make upon us, and why we may profitably contemplate them.

Of the many debts of gratitude incurred in the production of this volume, we wish especially to acknowledge the support of the School of Sociology, University of New South Wales; Professor Edward Mendelson of New York, for the benefit of his expertise concerning the poetry of W. H. Auden; and Dr Daniel J. Cohen of Jerusalem for his guidance on some points of German–Jewish history. For his unfailing good humour and much tested forbearance as well as quiet efficiency in the preparation of the typescript, we record our appreciation to Karl Krebs.

GTK & CSK

Notes on contributors

CAROLE E. ADAMS was educated at Harvard University, where she was awarded her PhD in 1984, and is a lecturer in modern German history at The University of Sydney. She has just completed a study of female white collar workers, entitled *Women Clerks in Wilhelmine Germany: Issues of Class and Gender*, Cambridge University Press, 1988.

MICHAEL BITTMAN is lecturer in the School of Sociology at The University of New South Wales, where he graduated with first class honours in 1969. He has taught extensively on the sociology of Karl Marx and Max Weber, on the nature of industrial societies, and on the sociology of the family and has pursued research in those areas in England and Germany. He is co-author (with S. O. D'Alton) of *The Social Experience* (Nelson, Melbourne, 1974) and has published articles on race, capitalism, the thought of Marx and Weber, and on contemporary familial relationships. He serves on the Sydney Editorial Board of the journal *Thesis Eleven*.

SONDRA FARGANIS was educated at Brooklyn College, The New School for Social Research, and at the Australian National University where she earned her doctorate. She has taught at the City University of New York and at Vassar and Hamilton Colleges and is now Chair of the Social Sciences and Director of the Vera List Center at The New School of Social Research. Her scholarly and research interests bridge the social science disciplines; she is especially interested in the question of gender. She is the editor of *Black Revolt and Democratic Politics* (1970) and author of *Social Construction of the Feminine Characters* (1986), as well as of articles in such journals as *Ethics, New Political Science*, and *Sociological Inquiry*.

FERENC FEHER was born and educated in Budapest and was a disciple and doctoral student of the late György Lukács. As a political dissenter he was excluded from Hungarian cultural life and after prolonged unemployment left Hungary in 1978. He has been a senior research fellow at The Australian National University and lecturer in politics at La Trobe University, Melbourne. At present he is a senior lecturer in Humanities at The New School for Social Research in New York. He has published books on Dostoevsky and on Jacobinism and Sartre. His English publications include co-authorship of such works as: *Dictatorship over Needs*, Blackwell 1983; *Hungary 1956, Revisited*, Allen and Unwin 1983, *Eastern Left, Western Left*, Blackwell 1986; *Political Legitimation in Communist States* (of which he is also an editor), Macmillan 1982, and numerous scholarly articles.

AGNES HELLER was educated at Budapest University where she was a close collaborator of György Lukács. She left Hungary in 1978 and was reader in sociology for several years at La Trobe University, Melbourne. Since 1987 she has been professor and chairperson of the Philosophy Department at The New School for Social Research in New York, occupying the Hannah Arendt chair of philosophy. Her books in English include *The Theory of Need in Marx* (Allison & Busby, 1976); *Renaissance Man* (1978), *A Theory of History* (1982) and *Everyday Life* (1984), all published by Routledge & Kegan Paul; *A Theory of Feelings* (Van Gorcum, 1979); *Dictatorship over Needs* (with F. Feher and G. Markus); Blackwell, 1983; *Hungary, 1956 Revisited* (with F. Feher) George Allen & Unwin, 1983; *Radical Philosophy* (Blackwell, 1984); and, as editor, *Lukács Revalued* (Blackwell, 1983).

MICHAEL W. JACKSON teaches political theory at The University of Sydney. He was educated at Hastings College (U.S.A.) and trained at the University of Alberta (Canada). He has published more than 50 articles and one book, *Matters of Justice*. He is at work on a study of terrorism.

GISELA T. KAPLAN was raised in Berlin where she initially trained as an opera singer. After migrating to Australia in 1968 she took up studies in social sciences, European history and literature. She is a member of the Economic History Department at the University of New England, and formerly lectured at the University of New South Wales and Monash University where she gained her PhD. Her main research interests are women's studies, migrant and Jewish issues, and the sociology of culture. Among her contributions are chapters to books such as *Feminine/Masculine & Representation*, ed. A. Cranny-Francis & T. Threadgold, Allen & Unwin; *Women's Movements of the World*, Argument; *Historical Sociology: Australian Welfare*, ed.

R. Kennedy, Macmillan; and *The Australian People.*, ed. J. Jupp, Angus & Robertson. She is joint editor of *The Australian and New Zealand Journal of Sociology* and apart from having co-edited this book on Hannah Arendt is currently at work on a book on *Contemporary Western European Feminism* for Allen & Unwin.

CLIVE S. KESSLER is Professor of Sociology at The University of New South Wales, Sydney. A graduate of the University of Sydney, he received his PhD from the University of London (London School of Economics and Political Science), where he was also a lecturer. Subsequently, he taught at Barnard College, Columbia University, New York from 1970 to 1980. He has been a member in the Social Sciences Program at The Institute for Advanced Studies, Princeton, New Jersey. His teaching and research interests include social and sociological theory, both classical and contemporary, and the politics of Islam in Southeast Asia; in addition to numerous articles he is the author of *Islam and Politics in a Malay State: Kelantan 1838–1969*, (Cornell University Press, Ithaca, N.Y., 1978).

MARIA MARKUS was born in Poland and educated at the Lomonsov University in Moscow. She was research fellow at the Institute of Sociology in the Hungarian Academy of Science. A member of the so-called 'Budapest School' of Marxist philosophers and sociologists, she (together with some of her colleagues) lost her job in 1973 for political and ideological reasons. Unable to work as a sociologist, she left Hungary in 1977 and in 1978 moved to Australia, where she is now Senior Lecturer in Sociology at The University of New South Wales, Sydney. She is co-author of several books on the sociology of work and has published numerous articles in international journals in the fields of political sociology, the sociology of economics, and feminist theory. Her publications in English include contributions to such volumes as *The Humanization of Socialism: Writings of the Budapest School* (Allison and Busby, 1976); *Political Legitimation in Communist States*, (Macmillan, 1982); *Poland after Solidarity: Social Movements versus the State*, (Transaction Books, 1985); and *Feminism as Critique*, (Blackwell, 1987).

ELIZABETH K. MINNICH was educated at Sarah Lawrence College and at The New School for Social Research, New York, where she studied with Hannah Arendt and was her teaching assistant. She has also been a Fullbright fellow in India. She has held joint teaching and administrative positions at Hollins College, Virginia and at Barnard College, New York. Since 1980 she has been Professor in the Union Graduate School of The Union for Experimenting Colleges and Universities. She has published articles on feminist scholarship in *Feminist Studies* and in several edited volumes, including an essay on Hannah Arendt in C. Asher, L. DeSalvo, and S. Ruddick (editors), *Between Women* (Beacon Press, Boston, 1984).

PATRICIA SPRINGBORG was educated at the University of Canterbury, New Zealand, and Oxford University. Since 1974 she has taught political theory in the Department of Government at The University of Sydney. She has also held visiting positions at the University of Pennsylvania, Swarthmore College, and the University of California, Berkeley. Author of *The Problem of Human Needs and the Critique of Civilization*, she has published articles on Hobbes, Marxism, need theory, Aristotle, and Orientalism. She is currently engaged on two projects: an account of the legacy of pharaonic kingship in Roman and medieval political thought; and a book on *Republicanism and Despotism* (Polity Press, forthcoming), which investigates the construction of the classical republican tradition and of its foil, theories of oriental despotism.

This volume is dedicated to Charlotte and Günter Kaplan, and to the memory of Albert and Hannah Kessler.

Hannah Arendt (1906–1975)

Introduction

Though born in Hanover, Hannah Arendt was raised where her parents also had been, in Königsberg, East Prussia, a notable city closely associated with two figures symbolising the intellectual and cultural traditions that shaped her life: the German philosopher Immanuel Kant and the pioneer of the Western Jewish Enlightenment, Moses Mendelssohn.

Educated at the secondary level in Königsberg and Berlin, Arendt attended, in the peripatetic German fashion, several universities: Marburg, Freiburg and Heidelberg, studying with the three great German philosophers of the 1920s—Martin Heidegger, Edmund Husserl, and Karl Jaspers. Not long after she completed her doctoral dissertation (on Saint Augustine's concept of Love) under Jaspers, events in Germany led her to rethink her relation to and the relations between the now demonstrably unreconciled German and Jewish traditions: to reassess critically the development of the cultural symbiosis upon which the lives of her generation (and of German Jews generally since 1871) had been predicated, and which events now showed to have been entirely chimerical. She thus commenced a study of Rahel Varnhagen, a woman whose life was emblematic of those two traditions and the besetting tensions in their flawed relation. As a project of self-discovery and self-definition, Arendt was to complete that work in Paris in 1938, after her flight from Germany (following her arrest in 1933 for involvement in anti-Nazi activities), but it was published only in 1957.

In Paris during the 1930s Arendt was prominent and active in the anti-Nazi resistance and within the Jewish and political refugee communities. Impelled by the rise of Nazism from the contemplative to a politically active life—and, as a Jew, by the urgent politics of rescue into outspoken Zionism—she worked in particular during the 1930s through WIZO (the Women's International Zionist Organisation) and Youth Aliyah, rescuing Jewish children from threatened parts of Europe and organising their resettlement in Palestine. She also continued in Paris the work she had begun prior to her flight from Germany, documenting the rise of Nazism and probing the origins of modern anti-Semitism. This enquiry was to become the basis of the book that would establish her international scholarly and intellectual reputation, *The Origins of Totalitarianism* (1951), and indeed the basis of her entire work in political philosophy and her exploration of the origins of the contemporary political world.

After the collapse of France and a period of detention at Gurs she managed to move to New York in 1940, together with her husband Heinrich Blücher. She remained there for the rest of her life except for periods as a visiting professor at such leading universities as Berkeley, Princeton and Chicago. Though she never pursued an orthodox academic career (Blücher pursued an outwardly somewhat conventional one at the very unconventional Bard College), she maintained in New York a relationship as professor at the central institution of 'European culture in exile', The New School for Social Research. Arendt lived more from her writings than from her academic posts. An extraordinarily self-possessed and independent personality, her bitter experience of the intellectual capitulation to Nazism of many of Weimar's leading liberal academics prepared her well for a fastidious wariness towards the unedifying politics of the United States professoriat during the shamefully conformist McCarthy years.

In her views Hannah Arendt was at once conservative, regretting painfully throughout her work the rupture of tradition that the modern world had undergone, and also radical, expressing a fundamental intellectual and moral commitment to critical independence, even at the price of pariahdom. With this singular and generally little understood combination of conservatism and radicalism, and an abrasive impatience towards what she saw as the stupidity of thoughtlessness, she offended many people. Yet she did so out of neither spite nor stratagem, but from the imperative of keeping faith with herself and with the truth as she unflinchingly saw it. A case in point is her book on the Eichmann trial.

Meanwhile, as the conformist 1950s in the United States gave way to the turbulent 1960s and the dispirited 1970s, Arendt continued to reflect critically upon and to probe her own times. In such works as *Between Past and Future: Six Exercises in Political Thought* (1961), *On Revolution* (1965), *On Violence* (1970), and *Crises of the Republic* (1973) she persistently interrogated modern political culture and the politics of her adopted country, the United States, from the standpoint of a distinctive traditional political philosophy. She found a receptive, morally concerned audience for her searching analyses of such fateful events as the Vietnam war and the release of the Pentagon Papers, and of such dishonourable political episodes as Watergate. Her traditionally and morally informed standpoint enabled her in these analyses to see the appalling amorality of wholesale political deception for what it was, neither magnifying its pretensions nor trivialising its significance. Her views on contemporary history were now eagerly sought as well as compellingly and urgently relevant.

Hannah Arendt died suddenly in 1975 while working on *The Life of the Mind*, a philosophical trilogy—on thinking, willing, and judging—that was to draw together her fundamental and continuing intellectual concerns of the previous half-century. Two parts of that work were published posthumously under the editorship of her friend, the writer Mary McCarthy.

In many ways unfashionable and sometimes poorly understood in her own time, Arendt the thinker is perhaps even more alive now than ever. The years since her death have seen an intensification of interest in her as both a thinker and as a figure of her times. More than ever, the meaning and insistent contemporary significance of her philosophy and political thought are coming to be appreciated; to resonate throughout the politically orphaned 1980s, to offer the prospect of reliable bearings in a post-liberal world. Among the important moments in and contributions to this growing interest in Arendt and her work have been Elizabeth Young-Bruehl's painstaking and comprehensive biography, *For Love of the World* (1982); Derwent May's much smaller contribution, entitled simply *Hannah Arendt* (1986), to the Penguin Lives of Modern Women series; Bhikhu Parekh's *Hannah Arendt and the Search for a New Political Philosophy* (1981); Stephen Whitfield's *Into the Dark* (1980); George Kateb's *Hannah Arendt: Politics, Conscience, Evil* (1984); and the Arendt symposium published from the New School itself in its journal *Social Research* 1977, vol. 44.

Amidst this sudden and very welcome current flood of publications — biographies, monographs, and articles — on Hannah Arendt, the present volume nonetheless has a unique character. Not only is it interdisciplinary — bringing together historians, political theorists, philosophers, and sociologists, themselves all interdisciplinary in orientation; just as significant is the kind of intellectual encounter it offers. For while the essays here are not, as is so often the case, simply expository, nor are they hagiographic or iconoclastic, adulatory or acidly dismissive. Instead this volume offers a series of engagements with Arendt that are both fond or respectful yet also unyieldingly critical. Each of the contributors addresses Arendt as an interlocutor, at eye-level, in what is cumulatively a series of debates, conversations, or arguments across the full range of her major intellectual interests. These dialogues recognise, explore, and sometimes challenge the presuppositions and direction of her thinking.

Although in its overall approach (as well as in several of its individual essays) it concurs with and draws upon Young-Bruehl's work, this is not a biographical study. It seeks, in a way that no other account has attempted, to outline and investigate the unity of Arendt's life and work. It identifies and explores, as other works have only partially done, some of the major themes and preoccupations in Arendt's work—her understanding of politics, of citizenship and action; her views of totalitarianism and anti-Semitism, of evil and personal responsibility; of historical identity and its historical construction, especially among such outsiders as Jews and women; of Judaism and German history and culture; and concerning the nature of thought, of thinking as an activity, of thoughtfulness as a human, intellectual, and moral quality, and of the nature and vocation of philosophy itself.

This volume shows, as other studies have rarely done, the interconnectedness of the various themes that are fundamental to Arendt's writing—and the linking of these themes with the pattern and trajectory of her own life as she lived and understood it. For her distinction rests not so much in the various intellectual interests or themes that she brought together, as in the fashion in which she did so.

In contrast to the kind of selective appropriation of Arendt, for a variety of political purposes (often those that were not hers), that has made her so often and so generally misunderstood—instead of parcelling Arendt out into so many manageable if flat fragments—the essays in the present volume cumulatively piece together, in its complexity, the unity of her life and work. It is the great strength and value of Young-Bruehl's biography that it captures the totality, the coherence, the *gestalt* of Arendt's life (as also, in far briefer compass, does May's portrait). The present volume continues that same process.

More than anything else what this approach shows is that Arendt was not simply a European thinker who happened to be a Jew, nor was she merely a thinker and historian who devoted much time to probing the situation of the Jew in modern European society. What demonstrably and fundamentally unites her work as a political theorist, historian, political scientist, and philosopher is a set of concerns anchored in her own life, experience, and self-understanding as a Jew. This is not to say that Arendt's work rested on any simple personalisation of history or personal projection from her own life to the modern world at large. On the contrary, her work addressed at their own level the major crises of our time: Nazism; imperialism and totalitarianism; the collapse of the political culture of citizenship; genocide; and the failure of human responsibility in the presence of political evil. These crises did not simply happen in her time; they directly and intimately shaped her life, and the probing of their origins and meaning gave direction to her thinking. It is her personally informed yet anything but personal explorations of those connections that make her work relevant, even essential, for an understanding of our times. It is these questions and connections that are explored and, we believe, illuminated in this book.

GTK & CSK

I
Politics, theory, and values

Patricia Springborg

1 Hannah Arendt and the classical republican tradition

> If any label at all were to be pinned on her, it could only be 'Republican'—not in the sense of the American party, but in the old, eighteenth century sense of a partisan of public freedom, a companion of men like de Tocqueville, Jefferson and Machiavelli.
>
> (Canovan, 1974:15)

In her judgement upon Hannah Arendt, Margaret Canovan might have added to this republican panoply the names of Aristotle, Kant, Marx, Nietzsche, and Weber, who were her more immediate influences. For Arendt's republicanism belongs to the Germanic tradition of the resuscitation of Aristotle in the 19th century. The earlier tradition of Aristotelianism, transmitted by means of 12th century Arabic and sometimes Hebrew editions of Aristotle and by way of Aquinas, was challenged for the first time, if not by Machiavelli in the 16th century, then by the moral philosophers and political economists of the 18th century Scottish Enlightenment. They challenged the tradition of agrarian, hierarchical Aristotelian republicanism and proposed instead an exchange-based society characterised by political and social independence in a polity constituted of an aggregate of clubs, neighbourhoods, and little societies of intense personal interaction. They saw in the 'commercial republic' a reconstitution of the Roman republic and its virtues, if not of the polis itself.[1]

Proponents of the commercial republic (Machiavelli[2] as precursor and Marx as successor) were at pains to emphasise the degree to which the public realm was a product of *economic* activities—the public benefit of private vices. But Hannah Arendt redraws the classical distinction between the political and the economic with the assistance of Aristotle. Pointing out that 'the political' (from *polis*) was classically the stage for individual action among peers, Arendt defines 'the social' (perhaps in the 18th century technical sense of 'civil society') as the extension, in hierarchical order, of the patriarchal family (*oikos*) and the realm of collective housekeeping (*oeconomia*). Classically, that is to say in Aristotle, the political and the social defined the realm of freedom and the realm of necessity respectively. Membership of the polis admitted one to the public realm, the realm of excellence (*arete*, *virtus*), and to the individual virtues of the courageous man. Membership of the oikos, or family (into which one was also formally admitted rather than born, although on different criteria from admission to citizenship), put one in the power of the despotic household head. Thus the polis knows only equals, the household unequals (Arendt 1958:32–33).

Arendt claims that the modern world is a product of the expansion of the social realm, or the realm of necessity, into the political, continually diminishing the public space for action and freedom. The history of society from the early modern period traces a path from monarchy, the rule of one-man, to bureaucracy, or no-man rule, in a process paralleled, paradoxically, by the destruction of the family, which has been gradually co-opted by society (Arendt, 1958:39). Society expects of its members only manners, normalised relations, not actions. It excludes excellence, the outstanding, as a danger to it, and if its history has been to tread the path from status (monarchy and hierarchy) to equality (bureaucracy and anomie), this simply means that all subordinate groups have followed the path of the family: absorption into mass society. 'Modern equality, based on... conformism,' Arendt argues, 'is in every respect different from equality in antiquity, and notably in the Greek city-states':

> To belong to the few 'equals' (*homoioi*) meant to be permitted to live among one's peers; but the public realm itself, the *polis*, was permeated by a fiercely agonal spirit, where everybody had constantly to distinguish himself from all others, to show through unique deeds or achievements that he was the best of all (*aien aristeuein*) (Arendt, 1958:41).[3]

Arendt sees in totalitarianism a terrible outcome of the alienation and loss of sense of self that mass society produces. The expansion of empire with its accompanying arbitrary bureaucratic government, which became the norm for even the constitutionally-minded British (Canovan, 1974:26), and the search for identity based on the category of race rather than a more comprehensive nationalism, together were permitting conditions for totalitarianism. Rather than seeking out individuals, totalitarianism as an irrational onslaught in the name of nightmarish ideologies sought 'objective enemies' identified by category (Jew, Gypsy or kulak). This was a way of confirming regimes which denied all practical and economic considerations and thrived only on fantasy—Arendt points out that killing Jews or kulaks was economically costly (Arendt, 1958a:382, 433, 459, & 353).

The total dislocation of fascist movements from reality is due, Arendt maintains, to their divorce from an ongoing community, the secure basis for common sense and civility provided by the polis and its successor, the nation-state. Correspondingly, the alienation and loss of identity of the subjects of mass society stem from their loss of a public space, the stage for action which the polis provided. Marx, in forecasting the withering away of the state, merely said what had to be said, she concludes (Arendt, 1958:60).

Much though Arendt's account owes to Marx and Weber and their preoccupation with the causes of alienation and the rise of mass society, it owes a good deal to Nietzsche as well. Arendt's emphasis on the 'agonal spirit' of the polis, 'the passionate drive to show one's self in measuring up against others that underlies the concept of politics prevalent in the city-states' (Arendt, 1958:194), is reminiscent of Nietzsche's praise for the 'aristocratic commonwealths' of Greece and Venice (Nietzsche, 1966:210). It is a cruel irony of history that in the work of German philosophers from Nietzsche to Heidegger, the glorification of ancient agonistic society as compared with the mediocrity of modernity laid what theoretical basis fascism might have claimed. When appropriated by the petty bourgeoisie, this reverence for the golden age of antiquity and its virtues of courage, fearlessness and contempt for weakness produced the very antithesis of an aristocratic republic: the barbarous reign of terror with which Arendt is concerned.

Some of the more contentious features of Nietzsche's thought also appear in Arendt's work, for example, Arendt's glorification of action as opposed to mere behaviour:

> Unlike human behaviour—which the Greeks, like all civilized people, judged according to 'moral standards', taking into account motives and intentions on the one hand and aims and consequences on the other—action can be judged only by the criterion of greatness because it is in its nature to break through the commonly accepted and reach into the extraordinary, where whatever is true in common and everyday life no longer applies because everything that exists is unique and *sui generis* (Arendt, 1958:205).

This passage evokes the language of Nietzsche and his praise of daring and agonistic deeds beyond good and evil, an evocation further enforced by her quotation of Thucydides and Pericles who 'found the glory of Athens in having left behind "everywhere everlasting remembrance *[mnemeia aidia]* of their good and evil deeds"' (Arendt, 1958:206). The voluntarism of Nietzsche, Heidegger and subsequent existentialists, who invest in the deed the expression of human individuality, is echoed in Arendt as well: 'Greatness, therefore, or the specific meaning of each deed, can lie only in the performance itself and neither in its motivation nor its achievement' (Arendt, 1958:206).

The point here is not to criticise Arendt for her elitism, her reverence for Aristotle's *megalopsuchos* or Nietzsche's 'noble soul' 'who has reverence only for himself' and 'looks down' on others (Nietzsche, 1966:227–228), who walks with a slow gait, talks with a deep voice to indicate that nothing can touch him, nothing can move him (Aristotle, *Nicomachaen Ethics*, IV, iii, 1123b–1125b). This *megalopsuchia* is the virtue of the notable, the paradigm of aristocratic polis life, which Arendt explicitly upholds. She can be held to account, however, in that the polis that she thus romanticised was after all simply an agonistic male warriors' club.[4] Weber, whom she extensively quotes, was singular among German 19th and 20th century thinkers in his appreciation of the enormous waste of human life and energy that the polis entailed. The role of the *agon* (contest) as the dominant social form in the gymnasium, theatre, circus, even in Socratic dialectical contests was counterproductive to the extent that it favoured confrontational, rather than cooperative, values (Weber, 1968, vol.3, chap.16:1367–1368).

In her diagnosis of the mediocrity of modernity and the evils of totalitarianism Arendt, like the grand German social theorists to whose tradition she belongs, was concerned to lay claim to the polis as the progenitor of traditional Western political values. There are frequent veiled references to 'despotism', or what Weber termed patrimonialism, as the norm for Eastern societies (Arendt, 1958:13, 27, 32, 40–43, 203n, 221). The term *despotes* is used by Aristotle to refer to the relationship between master and slave and was, therefore, characteristic of household (*oikos*) rule. In this instance Weber uncritically adopted the stereotype of oriental despotism as rule by virtue of which the ruler treated society at large as an extension of his household (Weber, 1968, vol.3:1006–68).[5] Ironically, this characterisation of despotism had been produced by an earlier tradition of classical republicanism — that of Harrington and Montesquieu — to describe the rule of *European* absolute monarchs. References to Turks and Persians were for the benefit of the censors and for rhetorical purposes: to shock readers with an unflattering comparison between civilisation and barbarism. Whether these authors knew it or not, societies of the Eastern Mediterranean belonged for the most part to the polis type. By the time that such 19th and 20th century German theorists as Hegel, Marx, Nietzsche, and Arendt appropriated it, the image of oriental despotism had long been detached from the knowledge that it was created as an allegory of European conditions rather than as a description of oriental reality. Although Marx was also largely ignorant of the oriental world, he alone among these thinkers had certain intuitions about northern European society and its place on the spectrum from republicanism to despotism, intuitions of a kind that elude Arendt entirely.

That Marx was aware of the *political* nature of familial forms of association is evident from his account in the *Grundrisse* (1953) and his observations in *The Ethnological Notebooks* (1974). Marx and Weber were aware of what Arendt apparently was not: that the persistence of powerful traditional familial structures and forms such as tribe and clan, far from being incompatible with political society was in fact an essential feature of it (Weber, 1968, vol.3:1344–1347).

Arendt states in *The Human Condition*:

> It was not just an opinion or theory of Aristotle but a simple historical fact that the foundation of the *polis* was preceded by the destruction of all organized units resting on kinship, such as the *phratria* and the *phyle* (Arendt, 1958:24).

Arendt's claim however, is simply not true, as a careful reading of Aristotle suggests. But her opinion represents a 19th century prejudice that lasted well into the 20th; it was an assumption of 19th century writers on ancient society, such as Morgan, Maine, Toennies and others, who subscribed to the theory of progress (and the titles of their works show that they did). Consider the prejudices betrayed by Morgan's *Ancient Society, or Researches into the lines of Human Progress from Savagery, through Barbarism to Civilization* (1877)! For writers such as these the transition to civilisation, in the form of the polis, was assumed to involve the transcendence of primordial forms of association based on family, clan, and tribe, which were renounced with the creation of explicitly political forms.

Aristotle's account describes not the evolution of the city out of primordial forms which are superseded, but an amalgamation of familial, clan, tribal, and village forms which live on as parts of the greater whole. Many forms of association were based on claims to consanguinity, even if fictitious, as classicists have now demonstrated (Ferguson, 1910, 1938; Sealey, 1960), while almost all familial forms of association from earliest recorded history were *political* (Roussel, 1976; Bourriot, 1976).

/Thus the *polis/oikos* distinction drawn by Arendt, and as drawn by Morgan, Maine, Fustel de Coulanges, Glotz, Thomson, Wood and Wood, and others, has now become questionable. Much of Arendt's argument is insecurely founded upon this distinction which corresponds to the distinction between the public/private. The theory of modern society as *Volkswirtschaft*, as an extension of the *oikos* and the locus of collective housekeeping, is built upon this same distinction.

Despite its questionability, Arendt's thesis is a fertile one, suggesting that mass society is a product of the collective housekeeping of the

Germanic tribes which had never known the public space of the polis. Indeed, in the *Grundrisse* Marx had suggested that Northern European society was actually the product of decentralised feudal society. Weber's view was really not too different from this. He had argued explicitly that the modern state had its origins not in the ancient but in the medieval feudal city (Weber 1968, vol.3:1343–1359), which latter in his view nevertheless constituted a commune of the type Marx attributed to the polis. Arendt might well have accepted such a connection and its implications.

In the light of such views, Arendt's observation that the nation constituted a collection of families in the feudal West — and that the concept of *mon-archia* on which the structure of Northern European government was modelled was fundamentally antithetical to the polis — take on a new significance. She even concedes:

> This is not to deny that the nation-state and its society grew out of the medieval kingdom and feudalism, in whose framework the family and household unity have an importance unequalled in classical antiquity (Arendt, 1958:29).

Similarly, her clear insights into the organisation of guilds is consistent with a general thesis that forms of association in Northern Europe were always social and never political:

> The bringing of all human activities into the private realm and the modeling of all human relationships upon the example of the household reached far into the specifically medieval professional organizations in the cities themselves, the guilds, *confréries*, and *compagnons*, and even into the early business companies, where 'the original joint household would seem to be indicated by the very word "company" (*companis*) . . . [and] such phrases as "men who eat one bread", "men who have one bread and wine"' (Arendt, 1958:34–35).

Amendment of Arendt's thesis in this direction, although not apparently major, has significant ramifications. To begin with it involves conceding that the important differences between the classical polis and the modern nation-state are regional rather than chronological or developmental. For the polis is, in fact, an Eastern phenomenon. It had its origins in the city-states of Mesopotamia and the Levant, as Herodotus had already argued, and its successors live on in the states of the Eastern Mediterranean and the modern Middle East (Springborg, 1986). These states show all the signs of the polis society they inherited from antiquity. As we know, even in classical antiquity the Middle East was the most fertile ground for polis development. For example, Babylonia in the third millennium BC consisted of a very dense network of city-states, and in the first two centuries AD the Hellenistic kings were responsible for the foundation of an extraordinary spate of cities in the Eastern Roman provinces.

To accept that the polis is an Eastern and not a Western phenomenon, however, is to challenge the myth of classical republicanism, or at least to confront critically the purposes that the myth serves. It is not too difficult to establish the case historically for monarchy as characteristic of Western, rather than oriental systems; or that the republican, or so-called democratic, institutions (such as elective bicameral legislatures and trial by jury) long considered as hallmarks of Western states, were imports as foreign to the West as the West now considers them to be to the East. City development in the Western provinces of the Roman Empire had always lagged behind that of the Eastern provinces (Stern, 1970:32); and when, from the 11th century on, after the feudal hiatus, cities were revived, the classical republican institutions of magistracies, assembly, and courts served as models. In the Eastern provinces, however, where city life had not been interrupted to the same degree, political institutions followed an unbroken trajectory: that of increasing bureaucratic control by the *imperium* over the municipality, a process which eroded municipal autonomy to the point where few were willing to serve in the elective magistracies. Thus the Islamic kingdoms tended to be organised along the lines of the Roman governorates of the Eastern provinces.[6] While accommodating the political organisations of the typical Middle Eastern state (the brotherhoods, syndicates, and militias; and the highly politicised, participatory, militaristic and semi-anarchic social relations of polis society), this thesis does grave damage to theories of oriental despotism with which the West has comforted itself.

The desire to legitimise the Western nation-state as heir to the political institutions of Athens has been very powerful in European history, having surfaced at different times in Italy (Machiavelli), England (Harrington, Gibbon), Scotland (Smith, Ferguson), France (Montesquieu), and Germany (Nietzsche, Weber, Arendt, and perhaps Marx). The force of this desire may be largely attributed to two factors. One was the cosmopolitanism of the Roman Catholic Church which, born in the Orient, propagated the republican ideals of Greece and Rome through the work of the Church Fathers, thereby perpetuating Eastern forms of congregation and cultic organisation. Both monasticism, an Eastern institution from Babylonian times and probably transmitted through Egypt, and a variety of popular cultic traditions (of saints and martyrs, brotherhoods and sodalities) were revived by the Church. Without these imports life under the prophetic religions would have been considered dull by those accustomed to the constant round of fêting and feasting associated with cultic life (Nock, 1933). The second factor, one also related to the influence of the

Church, was that European societies since the Renaissance had educated their elites not on indigenous literature but on the classics of Greece and Rome.

That Western political evolution constituted a classical republicanism of the polis type is now questionable. Hannah Arendt among others has convincingly shown that even if, as they believe, Western nation-states once enjoyed a way of life that could be deemed political — urban, heterogeneous, entrepreneurial, face-to-face, highly participatory, and democratic — they no longer do. The impersonal, passive, homogeneous mass society of the bureaucratic state would seem to be our fate: as Arendt, in a distinguished line of German thinkers that includes Marx, Weber, Nietzsche, Heidegger, and the Frankfurt School, bleakly recognised.

Notes

1 On the commercial republic in the thought of the Scottish school, see the article by Phillipson, Pocock and Winch, in Hont and Ignatieff, 1983; and Pocock, 1985. On Aristotle and exchange based society see Springborg, 1984b and 1986.
2 Hannah Arendt did not see Machiavelli this way, since she believed him to have rediscovered the political after the feudal slumber. But Machiavelli did indeed support economic expansionism, maintaining that:

> In free countries we also see wealth increase more rapidly, both that which results from culture of the soil and that which is produced by industry and art; for everybody gladly multiplies those things, and seeks to acquire those goods the possession of which he can tranquilly enjoy. Thence men vie with each other to increase both public and private wealth, which consequently increase in an extraordinary manner. (Machiavelli, 1950:287).

3 Arendt's words were strikingly close to those of Marx in the *Grundrisse* (Marx, 1973:245) where, describing the juridical conditions for capitalism, he maintains:

> Equality and freedom as developed to this extent are exactly the opposite of freedom and equality in the world of antiquity, where developed exchange value was not their basis, but where, rather, the development of that basis destroyed them. Equality and freedom presuppose relations of production as yet unrealized in the ancient world and the Middle Ages.

(See Springborg, 1984a:546ff). The German edition of the *Grundrisse* was available to Arendt at the time of writing.
4 A considerable feminist literature presents very different views on the agonistic virtues of *gymnasia*, *ecclesia*, and *symposia*, compared with the life-preserving activities of the *oikos* and its reproductive division of labour. See Elshtain, 1982; Hartsock, 1983; Humphreys, 1977; O'Brien, 1981; Okin, 1977; Saxonhouse, 1980; and Slater, 1968.

5 It is true that Aristotle was perhaps the first to characterise absolute kingship as partrimonial rule, or an extension of the household into the public realm (Aristotle, 1981 edn., III, xiv, 1285b, 20–32:219), and at the same time talks about the natural slavishness of Asiatics who 'tolerate master-like [*despotik*] rule without resentment' (Aristotle, 1981 edn., III, xiv, 1285a, 20–25:218). Nevertheless, it is interesting to note that Aristotle characterises non-Greek rule as 'acquired by birth, exercised as by a master and subject to law', which he distinguishes from tyranny (which can also be according to law, but is rule over unwilling, as opposed to willing, subjects), and absolute monarchy, which does not involve rule of law. Moreover, Aristotle, like Plato, had considerable admiration for the Persian monarchy, which he did not consider to be partrimonial rule, but rather the judicious admixture of the principles of democracy and monarchy, at least under Cyrus (Plato, 1926 edn., III, 694:224–5; Aristotle, 1981 edn., V, x, 1310b, 31–39:335).

6 The entire issue of oriental despotism is tied up with the question whether imperial bureaucratic government is a legacy that Rome passed on to the Islamic kingdoms, or one that the oriental kingships bequeathed to Rome. Thus Millar (1977) believes that the imperial style was learned by Roman officials on duty in the Eastern provinces, while Bury (1920) maintains that 'there was a certain continuity in the fashions of monarchical courts, passing from the Ptolemies and Seleucids to the Roman Emperors, and thence coming down through the Middle Ages to modern times' (Bury, 1920:14–15). Rostovtzeff entitles the last chapter of his great work on *The Social and Economic History of the Roman Empire* (Rostovtzeff, 1957:502–27 and notes) 'The Oriental Despotism' but he means by this the cult of the Roman Emperor and Roman imperial bureaucratic government, which destroyed municipal government by forcing the notability, under the burden of taxes, to flee into the countryside, thus marking the beginnings of feudalism. We do know that the monarchies of Babylonia and Assyria were constitutional (as even Aristotle recognised), involving the promulgation of common law in the famous codes of Bililama, Lipit Ishstar, Hammurabi, and others, while recent studies suggest that the Sassanian empire flourished, like its Islamic successors, because of its tolerance of local practice and the autonomy it afforded municipalities and their confessional communities (Morony, 1984).

Ferenc Feher

2 The pariah and the citizen: on Arendt's political theory

When *The Origins of Totalitarianism* was published in an atmosphere of general acclaim, critics failed to observe the truly astonishing structure of the work. Instead of commencing her analysis with sweeping generalisations, Arendt devoted the first quarter of the book to a painstakingly detailed chronicle of Jewish emancipation and to an account of the unfolding of political anti-Semitism. Yet this strategy affords deep insight into her most profound intentions.

The pariah

The story of totalitarianism starts with the story of the 'pariah', with the 'exception' and the 'politically anomalous'. This analysis of the pariah's situation is used to explain the rest of society, rather than the other way around. In this book and elsewhere in Arendt's work, the concept of the pariah does not cover only the paradigmatic case of the Jew. It also embraces the colonial native; millions of stateless persons, whose situation may provide a better clue to understanding the nation-state than the solemn declarations such regimes promulgate of the rights of the citizen; and the slaves of the pre-Civil War period and their socially unemancipated post-Civil War descendants in the United States. Arendt even argued that, had the lunacies of certain Allied politicians towards a defeated Germany been realised, the whole German populace, after World War II, would have become the pariah of the comity of Europe.

Despite this more general application, the Jew remains for Arendt the paradigmatic example of the pariah. Her use of this term has engendered a good deal of criticism. Gershom Scholem found the term offensive, for he correctly understood the condescending tone of

Weber's analysis of the Jewish pariah which was Arendt's principal source for her own. Weber's presentation of the morphology of the pariah might have seemed impartial, but he had well and truly internalised Nietzsche's myth of the 'religion of resentment' attaching to the unsuccessful. But her theory was distinguished by a unique absence of sentimentality. For her, love and compassion had nothing to do with understanding the lot of the pariah; indeed, she viewed such sentiments as impediments to intellectual reflection.

Arendt drew only one theoretical insight from Weber: that of the absence of political community that marked the long history of the Jewish pariah in the Diaspora. With this absence also went a lack of political self-consciousness and, until it was too late, a general lack of interest in political affairs. Following Scholem's analysis of the Shabbetai Tzevi movement, Hannah Arendt saw outbursts of religious mysticism as gestures of political passion acted out in messianism. (It should be mentioned in parentheses that Arendt paradoxically does not seem to be familiar with the catastrophe which had preceded, and which triggered, the Shabbetai Tzevi movement, namely the first holocaust of Eastern Jewry suffered at the hands of Bogdan Khmelnitsky's haidamaks, an event which underscores the social and political conditions of the pariah's existence). But in Arendt's presentation the Weberian pariah, the 'man of resentment', appears as a rebel. His initially otherworldly aim gradually becomes a thisworldly strategy, thus transforming the religious or ethnic community into a 'people' or political community, though not necessarily in the framework of a nation-state.

If the pariah is a rebel, as Arendt polemically argued against the mainstream of the Enlightenment, then his emancipation is not solely a 'social' one. A merely social emancipation gives rise to the 'parvenu' who perforce pays with political excommunication for social glory, and with social excommunication for political ascendancy. Nor for Hannah Arendt is genuine emancipation simply 'human', as Marx had contended in *On the Jewish Question*. For 'human' emancipation, which is neither therefore social nor political, would only create a being without a political existence. Rather emancipation must be political, as evidenced in the establishment of a political community, a people, though again not necessarily in the form of a nation-state.

Arendt identifies four paths allegedly leading to the emancipation of the pariah, all of which she regards as utterly misguided. These are: the 'organistic', the existentialist, that of 'emancipation through willing', and that of emancipation through the redemptive act.

The organistic attempt at self-emancipation may take two forms. It can be a solely individual act without further consequences, a sudden 'liberating moment' of internal self-illumination which has no impact on one's life strategy. This is the case when the assimilated Jew recognises, during a testing period for the Jewish community, that there is 'something' in his or her emotional make-up which would render life unbearable, should the community to which he or she never belonged in any conscious way perish. Alternatively, it can also arise in the form of a sudden collective experience of 'an innate affinity', resulting in the emergence of a new nationalism. Such a result is of dubious merit for Arendt, who criticises mainstream Zionism precisely on this score.

The existentialist path is perhaps best exemplified by Sartre's thesis (in his preface to Fanon's *Wretched of the Earth*) of the colonial native's self-emancipation through 'therapeutic' violence. Arendt clearly detested Sartre's politics of 'the radicalisation of evil', his recommendation that the aborigine should 'opt for himself' through destroying others, on the grounds that violence initially glorified as 'self-therapy' must end in unfreedom.

The third and closely related scenario sees the political pariah 'will himself or herself' *qua pariah* into freedom, achieving this transformation by an act of willing alone. Arendt quotes Lafayette's dictum: 'When a nation wills itself, it is already a nation', and terms it the last vestige of a Christian politics whose central category was 'willing'. Her sharp eye also detects the remnants of a Christian politics in Rousseau's concept of 'the general will' which was to become allegorised and, even more fatefully, institutionalised, by Rousseau's greatest disciple, in the 'cult of the Supreme Being'.

As far as a redemptive politics is concerned, both historical study and philosophical inclinations sufficiently convinced Arendt that this was not an adequate response to the pariah's bondage but a sham response and, moreover, a dangerous one which would eternalise bondage in the name of emancipation.

From Arendt's understanding of the nature of genuinely emancipatory political action on the part of the pariah there ensues a conflict between the principles of *freedom* and *life*. The yield of this conflict was highly positive yet extremely problematic. If the pariah's cause is victorious everywhere, 'the human condition' in modernity must be that of a political freedom based on human rights, though not in any sense which implies the notion of a 'unified humankind'. But for this to happen a politics of need and necessity, as distinct from one of freedom, must be relegated to the background. When the social overrides the political, need overrides freedom, genuine politics is choked, and the political realm contracts. The culmination of this process is the global victory of the 'totalitarian syndrome', which means, a pariah existence for all. Arendt's almost obsessive emphasis on freedom against life is accompanied by an explicit rejection of the so-called 'Massada complex', the choice of death over unfreedom.

Calls for collective suicide she regards as a symptom of political pathology.

Arendt's emphasis on freedom also implies a much superior type of politics to that prevailing in today's 'corporatist' societies. Her passionate plea for freedom and liberties may be contrasted with Raymond Aron's sceptical understanding of a common 'human nature' allegedly underlying both Western oligarchic pluralism and Soviet totalitarianism. Or, again, we may contrast Arendt's theory with those whose pre-eminent value is equality, not freedom, and whose main concern is 'life', and thus the satisfaction of material needs. Such comparisons highlight the uniqueness and superiority of Arendt's focus on freedom. Yet this conflict between freedom and life is the source of the problems critics have pointed to in her separation of the 'social' from the 'political'.

The 'social' and the 'political'

The distinction between the 'social' and the 'political' has a specific significance in Arendt's theory. Though found throughout her work, it comes into sharpest relief in *The Human Condition*. In the ancient world, the social was identical with the world of needs. Its proper location was the household and its greatest theorist, the classic author of a *non*-political economy was Aristotle. The world of needs, located in the household, is a pre-political world. Whoever is compelled by the misfortune of birth or external circumstances to dwell in it eternally is a pariah, not a citizen, and therefore not fully human. For the prospective citizen, a mastering of the problems posed by needs is a precondition to becoming political, that is, fully human. The social therefore merges indistinguishably with the private, or, more precisely, in the ancient world their separation had yet to come about. The dubious progress of the modern age was the spatial and temporal separation of the social, the world of needs, from its initial and appropriate realm, the private. Deriving from the modern combination of technological innovation and the division of labour, this 'progress' resulted in the transformation of what had been until then a household concern into a general issue for society, thus leading to the 'socialisation of politics'. What Arendt means by this is a politics whose major and increasingly exclusive concern is no longer the issue of free self-government, an end in itself, but the 'social problem'.

In other words, economic issues as expressions of needs were elevated onto the agenda of a given body politic. The new science arising from this change is political economy, whose greatest exponent, Marx, did not invent the centrality of the social for the political. Rather, he expressed the shifts that had taken place in modernity between the social and the political. Alongside this transformation there occurred a change in the conception of 'property'. Property, Arendt contends, was initially not associated with wealth. In ancient Greece, property was a correlate of participation: ownership of one's house conferred the right to participate in the political life of the city. Wealth became synonymous with property only in modernity, with the advent of the cult of production and growth. Thus property, which had formerly belonged to the realm of the political, was now tied to wealth and, thereby, to the economic and the social. But a 'socialised politics' operates with the Hegelian dichotomy of state and civil society, which Arendt resolutely rejects as greatly inhibiting free political activity.

This dubious advance, so central to modernity itself, found concrete form in the 'liberticide' political tradition of the French Revolution. Stimulated by the Rousseauean attitude of 'compassion for misery', the Jacobins translated the 'social question' into the language of politics. According to Arendt, they abandoned the cause of freedom and the task of creating free institutions for the sake of resolving the 'social question'. This was a fatal mistake. The social question, whose proper domain was the household, could not be resolved by any revolution;[1] but in the belief that it could be, the totalitarian syndrome was born. And even when politics does not degenerate into totalitarianism, it still remains in modern times captive to the primacy of the 'social realm'. For Arendt the welfare state is therefore a contradiction in terms.

Arendt's rejection of the relevance of the social for the political does not stem from any sympathy she held for capitalism. For her, capitalism means above all expropriation, a violent act in which peasant masses were deprived of their property and freedom. Further, by its very existence and with its expansive nature, capitalism implies colonial imperialism, which provided the terrain where racism and proto-totalitarian methods of government were first tested. Moreover, she is very sceptical of the free market, which for her was an unmixed blessing only in the United States. She rejects all politics which homogenise their sphere of influences under the common denominator of the free market and then call it a 'free world'. Finally, Arendt is an explicit critic of the cult of growth and its governing universe of competition. She regards the theory and practice of boundless growth as perilous to the man–nature relationship, and she lauds the kibbutz, a collective way of life otherwise so alien to her own private nature, for fostering a new type of non-competitive human relations.

There are two principal ways of criticising Arendt's separation of the private, social, and public. The first is that of the dogmatic liberal, who believes that the trichotomy is false, corresponding to no reality, and potentially totalitarian. For such liberals, there is a public political domain, that of the state or government with its external and internal concerns, and an economic sphere, which should ideally remain private without any collective or state interference. But since Karl Polanyi we have known that this idyllic view of modern economic and social affairs derives from nothing more than the myth of the self-regulating market. In no period of modernity was 'the social' abandoned to its own, allegedly self-regulating dynamic. It was constantly controlled, checked, deflected, and supervised both by the state and public opinion.

The second criticism is radical and is well exemplified in a recent paper by Richard Bernstein. Bernstein asserts that the trichotomy should be reduced to a dichotomy of the private and the political. To interpose a third realm of the 'social' he sees as methodologically misleading and politically dangerous. Not all questions are political, Bernstein admits, for this would indeed be totalitarian. But all questions *can become* political. His example, the problem put to Arendt by her critics at a conference in 1969, is housing. Arendt declared the problem to be social, in that there is nowadays a consensus that 'everyone should have decent housing conditions'. However, as Bernstein pertinently remarks, the problem is not whether there is public agreement on the abstract principles governing housing. Rather, the problem is how this agreement is to be translated into practical results. Since the issue is publicly debated, the whole matter *becomes political. Quod erat demonstrandum*: there can be no 'social' issue in Arendt's use of the term. However, Bernstein's argument undercuts his own desire to reduce the trichotomy to a dichotomy and thus unwittingly lends weight to Arendt's conception in a modified version. The abstract principle 'everybody should have decent housing conditions' indicates that in modernity, in stark contrast to the ancient world, certain public and general principles are related to many (but certainly not all) private affairs—even when these affairs are not raised to a level of private–public debate. This area of the 'no longer entirely private' and 'not yet, or not for the time being, fully political' but rather 'only potentially political' constitutes what Arendt, in my view properly, calls the 'social domain'.

It is possible to redeem Arendt's trichotomy. To collapse Arendt's trichotomy into a dichotomy by relegating the socio-economic to the realm of the household is impossible under modern conditions. This relegation, when directly translated into the language of politics, becomes outright reactionary. Further, it would be suicidal for the citizen. In her highly original 'parallel biographies' of the American and French revolutions, Arendt locates the gradual paralysis of direct participatory democracy in America in the spatial organisation of cities. However, she fails to grasp the incomparably more important *temporal* factors that emerged to inhibit political action in the French

Revolution: the insufficient free time of working citizens to participate in the *assemblée en permanence*. In the modern body politic the majority of participants spend most of their time at work; at the same time, everyone is in principle a citizen. In order to safeguard the political, the 'social problem' therefore cannot be relegated to the private realm. Its solution has a universal significance. But how is it possible to draw a clear division between 'social' and 'political' action? The answer is that it is often impossible. Yet, the lack of a clear separation between these two domains causes problems only if we regard them as 'separate realms' or spheres. However, if we take as our point of departure the various 'capacities' of the social actor (as Agnes Heller has argued in her essay 'The Great Republic') and refuse to form unambiguously separable realms or spheres, the gravity of the problem is alleviated.

Against Marx, Arendt argued strongly that the political realm, which is not simply identical with 'the state', must neither be 'abolished' nor should it 'wither away'. It must be maintained, and it must have primacy. If political action is either reduced to achieving certain economic targets or if political freedom is sacrificed to promote growth and alleviate misery, we would certainly lose our freedom without necessarily eliminating poverty. This is the point of Arendt's statement that revolutions can never solve the social question.

Revolutions, these 'new beginnings', certainly cannot solve the 'social question', particularly not the problem of poverty, but the actors of free institutions, the citizens of 'the republic', can and should seek to do so, if only in a provisional sense. There is no 'end of history' in the 'social realm' either. The citizen should act to solve the social question for three reasons. It is a scandal of liberty to tolerate misery in the cultural and biological sense of the word. Moreover, the perpetuation of poverty can only lead to the suicide of liberty: from mass poverty only elites and mobs can emerge, not free actors. Finally, to divide the world into acts pertaining to freedom that are totally divorced from material demands and needs and into acts which satisfy needs but which therefore pertain only to the realm of necessity is a false spiritualisation of liberty.

The republic

Throughout her work Arendt, an enemy of natural law theory, continually emphasised that freedom is never 'natural'. This is true of freedom in both its senses: of 'liberties' and of 'freedom', of 'negative' and 'positive' freedom. She critically contrasts the French tradition, with its Declaration which speaks of 'man' *born* free, to the Greek and American traditions that assert (in the latter variant by its 'spirit' rather than in its fundamental texts) that we are born neither free nor unfree but we *create* and *establish* our freedom in and by the institution of the republic. Arendt's central concept of 'the revolutionary tradition' and her abiding interest in it can only be understood in the light of this *non-natural*, created, and re-created conception of freedom. Arendt unequivocally rejects both evolutionism and the Hegelian understanding of universal history as a process governed by the unfolding of historical 'laws'. Marx, the greatest of Hegelians, had firmly believed in evolution and the processual character of universal history, with historical 'laws' as its indispensable accessories. Arendt, an anti-Hegelian, adopts a less persuasive account of historical development and thus leaves a great many relevant questions open.

Were freedom and liberties merely natural endowments of the human condition, it would be truly impossible to understand why revolutions break out, why freedom is re-created by them to the extent it is, and, even more, why they break out in particular periods. Of course, with Arendt there is no causal explanation of revolutions, for freedom never has a 'sufficient cause' and it can never be fully deduced from any external event. These two negative and critical theses are the premises of her ambivalent campaign against Marx. Arendt's criticism of Marx is ambivalent in that she accuses Marx of abandoning the centrality of freedom through politicising economics and through introducing the 'social problem', a substantive issue, into the problem of freedom, which can only be an end in itself. This is, of course, a misguided accusation. Marx remained throughout the whole of his life a philosopher of freedom, even to a degree that was unacceptable to Arendt. He hated authorities of all kinds, so much so that he wanted to abolish the state together with all gods. Yet Arendt rightly points to the particular feature which gives Marxian theory its very seductive explanatory power.

Her conception of 'the revolutionary tradition' furnishes an important clue to the understanding of modernity. But it would have been more convincing had she combined, instead of rigidly separating and even contrasting, the 'social' and the 'political'. In her theory revolution is a modern phenomenon *par excellence*, unprecedented in earlier social and political upheavals. Revolution implies a 'new beginning' coupled with the publicly avowed aim of creating freedom, a self-conscious act of *foundation*.

The revolutionary tradition has three branches. The French Revolution, the most spectacular episode within this tradition, in fact introduced a most problematic, even fateful, development. It initiated the 'socialisation' of the issue of political freedom, a process in which both social liberation (a notion of which Arendt herself was extremely sceptical) and political freedom suffer a resounding defeat. Unfortunately, this variant with its erosion of freedom survived and attracted many followers and imitators. What grew out of this variant may not always have been a blatantly proto-totalitarian system. At the very best, however, it resulted in democracy, not a 'republic'.

A second branch of the 'revolutionary tradition', the American, was providential. From the dedicated work of the American founding fathers, the American Revolution established the most accomplished form of political freedom yet known. However, for reasons which Arendt does not address adequately, the American example was a dual failure. It remained without followers and it failed to realise the greatest of revolutionary promises, a republic which actualises freedom at all levels of society and practises it day by day.

The filling of this gap remains the task of the third, as yet incomplete and, in a manner of speaking, 'underground' branch of the 'revolutionary tradition': the often anonymous and collective struggles for direct democracy. The allegedly participatory system which reigned supreme in the Paris sections in 1793–4, the Paris Commune, the Russian revolutionary soviets of 1905 and 1917, and finally the Hungarian Revolution of 1956, whose historic greatness and wisdom Arendt never ceased to admire, were the main junctures in this still continuing long march. However long misused and oppressed by both revolutionaries and counter-revolutionaries, this trend when it prevails will result in a genuinely free republic.

Arendt's sharp contrast between democracy and republic still remains remarkably insightful. This is particularly evident when we consider what this contrast does not imply. For instance, it has little to do with the technical meaning of the term 'democracy': for her, both the British monarchy and the French Republic are democracies. Second, in distinguishing between 'republic' and 'democracy', she is not concerned with the central problem of liberal theory: the dilemma of positive and negative freedom. For Arendt, any freedom which is purely negative is perforce a mere transient phase of 'liberation' which must give way either to its establishment in a more positive form or to tyranny. Further, in her understanding, neither republic nor democracy should be interpreted in terms of the Tocquevillean reading of democracy in America (upon which, by contrast, Aron's whole theory rests), which has at its centre the key concept of 'equality'.

What then are the features of democracy which account for Arendt's suspicion towards it? It means, first, the rule of consensus (or rather, one which leads, at least tendentially, towards consensus) and for Arendt such a goal is inevitably tyrannical. Second, majority rule means the oppression of minorities, either in the form of a systematic social discrimination against or the political silencing of the dissenting minority. Far from being consensual, opinions are irreducibly pluralistic, and all opinions should be given a voice in a free political community. Third, consensus can only be achieved through, and result in, a homogeneous will, the ominous Rousseauean–Robespierrean 'une volonté une' which transforms the free political process into a system of tyranny and organized witchhunts. Fourth, democracy rests on the ingenious but highly questionable French institution of 'popular sovereignty'.

In Arendt's extremely debatable understanding of the American system, which of all political systems remains closest to her republican ideal, the concept of popular sovereignty was never an issue. She claims that in America there had been no sovereign prior to the constitution, only an internally free political community in the colonies (though, of course, there had been a sovereign in the colonies against which the new American body politic was devised, namely the British). By contrast, in France, the new political system built upon the key concepts of *peuple* and *nation* was so devised as to replace an absolute sovereign. She does not deny that even the best conceived republic, the American (let alone the 'mere democracies'), has degenerated into an oligarchy of a kind in which the so-called 'political elite' rules and the 'people' practise their freedom only on the day of periodic elections. As a result, 'government' has been transformed into 'administration' which is termed by Arendt 'the rule of nobody' because of the anonymity of decisions and the lack of personal responsibility. But if this is so, the concept of popular sovereignty retains its cogency and relevance and serves as a point of departure for all who remain critical of the present state of affairs.

The final feature of a democracy of which Arendt is wary concerns the character of *power*, which she claims is fundamentally different in a 'democracy' than in a 'republic'. Under democracy it is identical with the *state monopoly of violence*, a Weberian conception she resolutely rejected, pointing out the strange coincidence between Weber's and Trotsky's views on this matter. In the republic, power means *participation*. The fundamental principles of 'the republic' gain their enduring validity from the act of foundation. And this enduring quality (of traditions, institutions, laws) is for Arendt one of the distinctive features of the republic — in sharp contrast to the reckless spirit of perpetual change so characteristic of democracy, with its unceasing metamorphoses of all laws and principles following an ever changing 'popular will'. This conclusion lends a certain conservative touch to Arendt's basically radical theory of the republic. Without being able to answer Jefferson's initial dilemma, she reformulates it. Jefferson had asked whether a free people does not possess the freedom to revise its own constitutive principles whenever it so wishes, but then also asked whether constant revision would not lead to a self-inflicted devaluation of those same constitutive principles.

The dichotomy 'democracy–republic' does not denote in Arendt two different sets of existing or 'desirable' institutions. Rather, the republic serves for her as a Kantian regulative theoretical idea of the free commonwealth of which modern democracy is but a very imperfect realisation. However, even if by definition they can never be 'realised', regulative theoretical ideas must descend from the heaven of theory to the earth of our political struggles. The actor in whom this descent is embodied and by whom it is realised is the *citizen*. Arendt, a passionate and often biased critic of Marx, retains the Marxian dichotomy of 'citizen versus bourgeois' in full. She regards the victory of the bourgeois, the competitive private person, over the citizen as the single major catastrophe that befell political man and woman in the 19th century. Indeed, this catastrophic victory set the scene for the triumph of the 'totalitarian syndrome'.

Notes

1 Yet this claim seems absurd in the light of Arendt's own theory that one of the distinctive features of modernity is the replacement of the household economy by socialised production, consumption, and distribution.

II
History and responsibility

Carole E. Adams

3 Hannah Arendt and the historian: *Nazism and the New Order*

Hannah Arendt stated in *The Human Condition* that her purpose was to 'think what we are doing' (1958:5). Invoking the historian's craft to 'think what we are doing' — to explore Arendt's vision of the modern age, in particular the nightmare of totalitarianism that according to her could arise only in contemporary times — this essay argues that Arendt's vision is far too bleak: it presents totalitarianism as a completely novel system against which humans are virtually powerless. Yet this interpretation emerges from the presentation of static typologies of human activity in the modern age and from her interpretation of history as mere process, which leads Arendt to overlook moments of political action on the part of human agents.

Hannah Arendt might well question whether historians 'think what we are doing'. For she has harsh words to say about the discipline of history. She groups it with the natural sciences and argues that both fields present the world and its human inhabitants as determined by processes functioning according to laws (Arendt, 1961:48–50 and 57–63; cf. Shklar, 1963:287, 289; Jay, 1978:354–5; and Pitkin, 1981:340–41). This leads to the belief that human beings are powerless to act, to be agents in the realm of freedom. Both history and natural science are therefore intellectual preconditions for the modern use of ideologies as totalitarian instruments for the destruction of human beings and their world (Arendt, 1958:320ff and 1961:50–63). Her emphasis on history and science is significant, for the two totalitarian ideologies that she criticises are based on Marxist historical determinism and on pseudo-scientific race laws.

Arendt's view of history is problematic. Although many historians do accept that history is a process, for most it is not a seamless web of necessity. There is no inevitable development, no predetermined end.

There is room for human agency, space for human freedom. Further, despite her suspicion of the modern practice of history, Arendt herself relies on historical modes of interpretation in her study of the modern age. Yet it is precisely her acceptance of history as process that leads her to such a pessimistic picture of the modern world. It is worth exploring whether either that picture or her pessimism are warranted.

Hannah Arendt views her project as one of political theory; her primary concern is to establish the conditions in human communities within which political action and thereby freedom are possible. Her method combines abstract definition and historical analysis (cf. O'Sullivan, 1975:246; Heather and Stolz, 1979:11, 13). In *The Human Condition* Arendt describes the three types of activities in which, to her mind, human beings engage: labour, work, and action. She argues that in early modern times Europe was dominated by the worker, *homo faber*; the modern age is dominated by *animal laborans* — the 'job-holder'. This has occurred as labour was elevated in status and as abundance, its fruit, became the highest human goal.

Arendt is ambivalent about the potential of this labourer for political action (cf. Canovan, 1978:5). She suggests that freedom from necessity is essential to political action and that the labourer is incapable of action and speech. She also asserts that *animal laborans* lives in a social realm which engenders conformity and sameness, rendering such persons 'basically antipolitical'. Yet she acknowledges that for the previous hundred years political action had been carried out by labourers, describing the role of the labour movement as 'glorious' (1958a:214, 215). Even so, she notes that such political action rarely succeeded. For Arendt, the French Revolution and all others that followed went astray because the 'social question', the eternal problem of human poverty, became a central concern (Arendt, 1973:60ff). The demands of the poor for social and economic equality took precedence over truly political questions such as establishing a constitution. This fact is related to her contention in *The Human Condition* that the modern age has given rise to the social realm, which has largely replaced the political: politics has become mere housekeeping, economic management, and administration. The public space for true political action has disappeared (Arendt, 1958a:28ff; Arendt, 1979:316–319; Canovan, 1974:85–89; O'Sullivan, 1975:237–238; Jay, 1978:361–363; Pitkin, 1981:333–336).

Margaret Canovan has noted the tension between Arendt's elitist and her democratic views (1978:1). Arguably, this is at the same time a tension between typological and historical thinking. Insofar as she establishes categories, Arendt creates a series of discrete pigeonholes to which the human beings of the past are consigned. The modern age is one of labourers; they are part of society; therefore they cannot be political actors. Yet, recognising historical fact, Arendt acknowledges that indeed labourers have engaged in political acts.

For Arendt the emergence of the social realm is related to a far greater danger to political action and human freedom. That danger is totalitarianism, a new form of government invented in the 20th century as the levelling of classes—themselves a danger to political action because they represent specific group interests—created 'mass man'. Arendt defines the masses as 'people who either because of sheer numbers, or indifference, or a combination of both, cannot be integrated into any organization based on common interest, into political parties or municipal governments or professional organizations or trade unions' (1958a:311). She suggests that masses originated in modern society, where human beings defined themselves as jobholders alone; that is, in which labour was deemed the only worthwhile human activity (1958a:338; O'Sullivan, 1973:190; Kateb, 1983:67–69). These masses, atomised and lonely and without a common world or a political space and seized by 'blind hostility...against the existing world' (1958a:380), were receptive to ideologies that restructured reality, removing uncertainty and serving as a substitute for a now unobtainable freedom and plurality (1958a:348ff; 478).

For Arendt, ideologies are 'isms which to the satisfaction of their adherents can explain everything and every occurrence by deducing it from a single premise', since 'ideologies pretend to know the mysteries of the whole historical process' (1958a:468, 469). Important for the acceptance of these ideologies was the apparent consistency of experience they afforded, for that gave security to 'masses who had lost their faith in the world and now were prepared to be reintegrated into eternal, all-dominating forces which by themselves would bear man ... [to] safety' (1958a:350). Within the world of ideology, distinctions between fact and fiction, truth and falsehood no longer exist, and mass man is no longer able to think or to distinguish reality (1958a:474; Nelson, 1978:274–275).

In their susceptibility to ideologies, the masses open the way for totalitarian movements to succeed. Arendt insists that totalitarian regimes are something new that could only arise in the modern age. For her, totalitarianism is not the same as tyranny, which she visualises as a pyramid with the ruler on top and the subjects all together on the bottom, while a totalitarian regime resembles an onion with the ruler in the centre surrounded by front organisations. Each layer of the onion represents a different degree of ideological militancy, so that those in each layer can accept that the movement fits the real world. A tyranny, moreover, is lawless; a totalitarian regime terroristic, enclosing people in iron bands that destroy the possibility of freedom, so that 'human nature as such' is at stake (Arendt, 1958a:459; O'Sullivan, 1973:190–91; Canovan, 1974:17–21; O'Sullivan, 1975:239–244; Nelson, 1978:273; Heather and Stolz, 1979:14–15; Kateb, 1983:75–79). Those two features—ideology and terror—are for Arendt the distinguishing characteristics of totalitarianism. In particular, she insists upon the anti-utilitarian and all-encompassing nature of totalitarian ideology, which, allied with terror, both attracts the masses and maintains their passivity.

Arendt has complained that modern historians are capable only of uncovering patterns, which they then take for meaning (Arendt, 1961:48–50). The same charge can in fact be made against Arendt herself, for in her analysis of totalitarianism human agency and political action are largely lost from sight (Canovan, 1974:40–41, 47). A consideration of the example of Nazism serves to challenge her pessimism about the modern age and her belief that totalitarianism is distinct from tyranny, rather than simply tyranny in modern guise. This exercise will further serve to establish a place for the modern discipline of history as one concerned with more than mere process and as one hostile rather than conducive to ideology.

Central to Hannah Arendt's explanation of the origins of totalitarianism is her notion of the masses, who emerged when classes disintegrated at the end of the 19th century. Classes themselves had limited the human potential for political action, because they emphasised group interest and the social question rather than general human, political concerns. But they were at least a commonality, whereas mass society is characterised by separateness and loneliness. It is the masses to whom ideology appeals, and it is ideology that attracts the masses to totalitarian movements.

This scenario for the success of Nazism is simply not true.[1] Arendt herself seems at times aware of this when she explains that totalitarianism creates masses, in which case the existence of masses could not have been a precondition for a totalitarian power seizure. Germany in the 1920s was not a mass society.[2] To a greater extent than was the case in England or the United States, Germany both before and after World War I was a society in which men and women organised themselves on the basis of class or occupation in order to defend their interests. The working class was organised into trade unions and socialist political parties that made both socio-economic and political demands, including civil rights and suffrage reform. Many members of the middle class—white-collar workers, artisans, retailers, farmers, and a variety of middle-class professionals—were also organised into associations to defend their socio-economic interests. Many of the individual groups sent members to sit on municipal councils and to participate in a variety of reform societies. They also attempted to work with political parties and to influence legislation.

In Arendt's terms much of the activity of these groups was not political. The people were participating in interest groups that represented their members rather than in political groups that transcended individual or group interest. Further, their aims, even many of those which they themselves would have defined as political, fall largely into Arendt's category of social, for they were concerned with securing legislation to solve aspects of the social question. If the acts were not political, however, neither were they activities of the masses, who by Arendt's definition do not join parties, unions, and associations.

Central to Arendt's analysis is the claim that the masses were prepared to accept an all-encompassing ideology that promised nothing more specific than to overcome reality. The Nazis, she asserts, only made general ideological pronouncements, they did not make concrete claims or appeal to particular groups. This is, however, not the case. The Nazis themselves recognised the existence and importance of organised interest groups. Rather than stressing a general, all-encompassing ideology in their electoral campaigns, the Nazis after 1928 aimed their propaganda very narrowly, for earlier attempts to woo the entire population by creating a 'People's Party', and in particular to win working-class support, had failed. The Nazi leadership therefore shifted its policy and began to address the particular concerns of very discrete segments of the middle class. They addressed immediate social and economic needs: homeowners were told about Nazi mortgage policy; farmers were promised credit and secure land tenure (Allen 1984; Childers, 1983).

This is not to say that the Nazis did not ever appeal to nationalism, or launch into tirades against Jews or Communists. However, these issues were offered on the level of slogans, as were statements praising Nazism as a party of youth and movement. They were presented less as aspects of an all-encompassing ideology than because they served to provide scapegoats for current economic and political problems: Jews, Communists, and Allies were to blame, or the Jews alone (since they were both, Communists and international capitalists). Similarly, a racial *Volksgemeinschaft* (folk community) was held up as the future ideal in which social, economic, and political problems would be solved.

In the context of the 1920s, recourse to such general appeals was not surprising: Germans at the end of the decade were facing economic depression, and their government seemed incapable of taking appropriate measures. Behind these immediate concerns lay the belief held by many that their economic plight could be traced back to the Treaty of Versailles, with its onerous reparations clause which, in the eyes of most Germans, was responsible both for the inflation of 1923 and for the current crisis. Nazi voters, and even some Party members, appear to have been attracted by the concrete promises concerning social and economic needs and foreign policy goals rather than by the vision of Hitler's racial ideology. It was the Nazis' claim to be able to solve specific problems, rather than their claim to have unlocked the secret of historical race law, that won them votes.

If neither the masses nor ideology in fact played the roles Arendt assigns to them in the Nazi movement's rise to power, what of afterwards? Both the masses and ideology play a special role in Arendt's analysis of totalitarian rule, for she sees terror and ideology as means to reduce the masses to passivity. Terror either transforms classes into masses or maintains them in a herdlike condition in which everyone is both isolated and yet so compressed that neither public space nor the potential for freedom is possible (Arendt, 1958a:421), 438; 1965:127). The image Arendt creates is of an abstract entity in which all human beings are caught up, whether as victims or executioners, in an inexorable process defined by ideology, leading to antiutilitarian goals and ultimately to human destruction. Executioners commit great crimes because they do not think, because they are private men, jobholders. Executioners and victims alike cease to be actors. Evil is banal (Arendt, 1965:24, 31–33, 48–49, 252).

Arendt is correct to insist that the 20th century replaced the nihilistic 'all is permitted' with 'all is possible'. The crimes of the Nazis *were* unprecedented; the deliberate murder of millions of human beings, using modern science and technology and bureaucratic organisation, *was* evil. The sense of urgency and outrage that permeates *The Origins of Totalitarianism* is an appropriate response. But at issue is not Arendt's moral judgement, but the correctness of her historical and political analysis: whether hers is the correct warning to give to the world. I think not. Despite her many brilliant insights into Nazi rule, Arendt misreads both the role of the masses and the power of terror, and mistakes the role of ideology in the regime. This reading leads her to disregard the continued existence of political action in Nazi Germany, and to fail to recognize totalitarianism as tyranny in 20th century garb.

Classes continued to exist in the Third Reich, although the Nazis used restrictions on public life as well as terror in their attempt to reduce the population to the level of atomised masses. The Nazi 'coordination' (*Gleichschaltung*) of society forced the dissolution of all public associations in Germany, from political parties and trade unions to leisure groups, limiting Germans to membership in nazified organisations. Neighbourhoods and even families were infiltrated by Nazi spies — statements made to friends and children could land the speaker in a concentration camp. All public and many private activities therefore were watched over by the Nazis (Allen, 1984).

But neither class-based activities nor political action succumbed totally to coordination and terror. One class, at least, certainly maintained its identity and a sense of its particular class interests: German workers. While elections were still held for plant positions, Nazi candidates had difficulty in securing election. The Nazi German Labour Front, which represented employers as well as employees, found that it had to press the interests of the workers against those of the employers or face a degree of worker hostility that they feared would undermine the stability of the regime (Broszat, 1981). After full employment was reached in the late 1930s, Gestapo agents also found that they had to tolerate certain worker demands, for instance for overtime, or lose irreplaceable workers (Mason, 1966).

In addition, many workers went further than merely pressing economic demands; they entered the political realm and established resistance groups. Most were broken by the Gestapo. Others survived by confining themselves to small acts of courage, rather than grand gestures—reporting BBC news broadcasts to each other, for instance, or hiding 'undesirables' (Reichhardt, 1970). And when the war ended in 1945, so-called 'anti-fascist fronts' sprang up spontaneously throughout Germany—an indication that the capacity for political action was not totally eradicated during the years of Nazi rule. These predominantly working-class groups sought to work with the Allies in establishing a new form of government in Germany. In Hannah Arendt's definition, acts of resistance and renewal, which these were, are certainly political, as she herself indicates in the preface to *Between Past and Future* (1961:3).

Recognition of the political rather than merely social nature of resistance, even when initiated by specific interest groups, must also hold true of the upper-class 'conservative' opposition to Hitler that led to the attempt on his life in July 1944. Arendt claims that this group was not motivated by moral concerns, but by its fear that Hitler was mad and would bring Germany to ruin (1965:97–101). This is a strange objection, for the thrust of Arendt's political theory is to separate morality from political action. The point is surely that these conspirators did engage in political action, unlike the mass men Arendt postulates as inhabiting Germany.

The role Arendt assigns to ideology is also questionable. From examination of police reports of popular opinion in the Third Reich, the primary sources of the regime's popularity appear to have been interest-based rather than ideological. There was grumbling about the Nazi regime; many leaders were held to be either incompetent or corrupt. Largely exempt from any criticism, however, was Hitler, who appeared in the reports as a mythic, charismatic figure ignorant of the venality, inefficiency, and injustice around him. Nevertheless, the source of his popularity lay not in his relation to or fulfilment of Nazi ideology, but in his concrete, mundane achievements. He had rid Germany of the Versailles Treaty, stood up to the Allies, ended the

Depression and its massive unemployment, and created prosperity. His popularity, in other words, rested on the belief that he was serving popular interests (Kershaw, 1981a; Kettenacker, 1985).

Many Germans believed the ideological claim that Hitler had ended class divisions and had created a true *Volksgemeinschaft*. Such people ignored the realities of Nazi society and praised Hitler for this newfound harmony and equality, despite the continuation of social and economic trends that had started in the 1920s or before: the expansion of big business, the decline of the lower middle class, the unchanged distribution of wealth and education in the population, and the lack of upward mobility (Schoenbaum, 1967). This might appear to support Arendt's contention that what mattered to the masses was an ideology that gave them a place, whether it fitted reality or not. The problem, however, is that such commonplace values differ from Arendt's definition of ideology. Germans might have gloried in patriotic pride or sought the bonds of community, but it is hard to differentiate such sentiments from views held by members of Western democratic nations. Few Germans felt caught up in an all-embracing world-historical plan, or destined for world domination (indeed, one source of Hitler's popularity throughout the 1930s was the prevalent belief that he would keep the nation out of war).

Hitler and other leading Nazis clearly recognised that the regime had to meet certain concrete needs of the people in order to remain in power. Even rearmament planning required consideration of this. Despite Hitler's plans to wage large-scale aggressive war, a fully mobilised 'total war' economy was never instituted, even after Stalingrad. A war economy, of course, would have meant longer working hours, rationing, and the disappearance of many consumer goods. Some historians even attribute the German fixation on *Blitzkrieg* to Hitler's insistence that the German standard of living not be allowed to deteriorate — Blitzkrieg meant war on the cheap, without an in-depth war economy (Carroll, 1968).

What, then, of anti-Semitism and the holocaust? Anti-Semitic tirades and actions characterised Hitler and the Nazis from the outset and, from the moment the Nazis seized power, official acts of anti-Semitism were central to their regime and its policies. Many Germans accepted the anti-Semitic statements, acts, policies, and legislation of the Nazis, and German Jews were driven from their homes and workplaces with nary a protest. A majority of Germans was willing to accept stereotypical images of German Jews that made them the scapegoats for all of Germany's problems (Kershaw, 1981b).

Yet to say this is not to accept Arendt's analysis of the role of ideology in the Nazi order. For Arendt, the masses believed and needed an all-encompassing ideology based on race law. Her definition of ideology goes far beyond an assertion that the mass of Germans

Nazism and the New Order

believed that Jews were to blame for social, economic, and political dislocation and that the Nazis would make Germany great and powerful again. In her view they also believed that they were a superior Aryan race, that Jews were subhuman, and that the Germans would undertake a mission in accordance with the laws of race-history to establish their domination of the world over the coming millennia. But anti-Semitism and racial ideology did not at all fulfil that role in the Nazi state. Popular opinion appears to have been largely satisfied with the belief that the Third Reich provided security, harmony, prosperity, and greatness (Kershaw, 1981a and 1981b).

As with her categories of the *vita activa*, Arendt has here created a typology of totalitarianism in which human agents are lost and contradictory explanations abound. Arendt describes an historical process in which a system appears with no responsible actors. Masses are attracted by ideologies; functionaries carry out lawless orders; concentration camps serve as laboratories. But who evolved and used the ideology? Who gave the orders? Who wanted to test human behaviour in the camps? Most important, what propels the juggernaut? Arendt does not answer this. She presents the leader at the centre of the totalitarian onion, dependent upon the masses rather than leading them as a tyrant does. The greatest degree of militancy exists at the centre of the onion and yet she also asserts that ideological belief is strongest at the outer layers, so that as one approaches the centre cynicism increasingly replaces gullibility and ideological belief (1958a:382). These images suggest human beings who are propelled, rather than humans who propel or who determine acts. She argues that Himmler sought jobholders and family men for the SS, and the SS weeded out brutal or sadistic members; she presents Eichmann as a cynic, who is at the same time a careerist, a jobholder (Arendt, 1965:105; Dossa, 1980).

In this view, it is strangely the masses with their great susceptibility and attachment to ideology, not the cynical higher functionaries of the regime, who are responsible for the excesses to which ideology leads. It is their lost ability to think and act, not the readiness of the functionaries to act without thinking, to which totalitarian atrocities are in this deterministic view to be attributed.

Moreover, to argue that all Germans, leaders and masses alike, were simply caught up in a machine of ideology and terror cannot explain why some tenets—aggressive war and murder—were adopted as political objectives rather than the far more popular and benign tenet of creating a popular community. It does not explain why it was the anti-utilitarian tenets that were adopted, and it cannot, unless Arendt meant to argue that according to some innate law, a structure can propel itself to its own destruction, regardless of the wishes of its leaders.

In fact, however, Arendt's analysis needs to be reversed and some notion of human agency introduced. Ideology was not situated at the outer layers of the onion but was directed from the centre. Those furthest from the centre thus needed and used Nazi ideology least. They may have supported individual tenets of the ideology that served their needs; they gave lip service to others, either because of the constant drone of propaganda or because of the threat of terror.

To understand fully the role of ideology in the Third Reich, we must consider Hitler's role.[3] It was he who believed in an all-encompassing ideology based on pseudo-scientific racial laws and in his own providential mission to fulfil it by destroying the Jewish people and leading the Germans, a superior race, into an aggressive war for the domination of Europe, if not the world. Unless one recognises that Hitler was no cynic or mere passive jobholder, but an ideologue who initiated and sustained political action, the Nazi movement and the Nazi state appear contradictory or unfathomable (cf. O'Sullivan, 1975:245). Accept it, and it is possible to comprehend how an anti-utilitarian or destructive ideology can be brought to fulfilment. Are we not then back to tyranny, but a tyranny in which the ruler has a madness in his method, seeking power because he—especially he—believes in an ideology that is all-encompassing?

By emphasising Hitler's role as ruler, we strengthen many of Arendt's brilliant insights into the structure and functioning of the Third Reich. She has noted the dynamism inherent in the system, which propelled it toward greater radicalism. But that dynamism took the direction it did because Hitler had particular ends in mind. This also affected individual Nazi leaders. Some actually believed the ideology as Hitler did; others cynically pressed its realisation in order to strengthen their position with Hitler or to maintain the dynamism of the movement (Broszat, 1981:346–361; Kershaw, 1985; Koch, 1985).

Anti-utilitarian aims, particularly policies directed against Jews, were those most easily enacted, not because the German population firmly held to Nazi ideology, but because, at the top, Hitler approved, while at the base, no vested class interests opposed those policies.

Arendt herself seems uncomfortable at times with the omission of human agency in her writing on totalitarianism. At the end of *Eichmann in Jerusalem* (1965:232–233) and in her preface to Bernd Naumann's book on trials of SS men (1966b), she affirms human agency, writing of individuals who took action to save the lives of others. There is a further inconsistency here. Arendt insists that it is the anti-utilitarian character of its ideology that distinguishes totalitarianism from tyranny. Yet she also defines totalitarianism as having an ultimate aim, namely absolute domination. This implies a degree of rationality and purpose and the existence of a leader seeking power— all of which are indices also of tyranny.

Hannah Arendt has provided insights into the terror, and into the functioning of a modern state that seeks to establish total control over its subjects. She has shown how radical acts can result from attempts to maintain the dynamism of a mass movement. But this leaves open the question whether totalitarianism is something new, or whether Nazism is simply 'tyranny with new technocratic methods'. If the latter is the case, human societies should, as always, beware of the power of those methods and should fear tyranny now as never before, but without being compelled to despair of the end of human nature as we know it or of the possibility of human action.

It is ironic that a political theorist of freedom and a critic of undue emphasis on process in history should herself present a picture of the modern age in which a doom-laden pattern unfolds. Margaret Canovan argues that Arendt's pessimism — indeed, despair — lessened after the 1956 Hungarian Revolution and as a result of the student movement of the 1960s (1978:12, 21). But if the Hungarian Revolution led her to rethink the possibility of political action in the 20th century, it did not lead her to rethink totalitarianism. For her, the modern age, with its processes of history and natural science, its glorification of a life of labour and necessity, and its ubiquitous masses, is rarely capable of generating successful political action. How much more must this be so in a society dominated by terror and ideology? Certainly Arendt felt a sense of the fragility of action (Canovan, 1978). Yet this sense led her to posit an inexorable historical process that denies an historical reality, a reality of individual and class-based political action, of which she herself was aware.

Notes

1 A related set of criticism of Arendt's view of Nazism is found in O'Sullivan (1973:192, 193). For a reading of Nazism more sympathetic to Arendt's analysis, see Crick (1977).
2 For general works on Germany in the 1920s and 1930s, see Bracher (1973); Craig (1978); and Kershaw (1985).
3 For interpretations of Hitler, see Bullock (1962:806–808); Fest (1974: esp. 89–106); and Kershaw (1985).

Michael W. Jackson

4 The responsibility of judgement and the judgement of responsibility

> The sad truth ... is that most evil is done by people who never made up their minds to ... do evil or good.
> (Arendt, 1978, I:180).

At his trial Eichmann was portrayed as an inhuman monster. Since then his own claim to have been a simple bureaucrat has been widely accepted. Most people, in fact, see him in one or other of these two quite simplistic ways: for example, 80 per cent of respondents to one survey classed Eichmann as either the monster or the bureaucrat (Glock, Selznick, and Spaetch, 1966:61). But if either were the case, there would be little point in reflecting upon Eichmann today. If he was a monster, then the evil of Nazism was 'fallen as lightning from heaven' (*Luke* 10:18). We cannot learn why it happened, where and when it happened. We cannot learn to prevent it. Moreover, the monster stereotype implicitly absolves all those who participate in evil, but who know themselves not to be monsters (Rogat, 1961:11 and Draenos, 1982:14). If, however, Eichmann was the inevitable outcome of bureaucracy, then we admit Eichmann's own claim that he was not responsible for what he in fact did do. The bureaucratic stereotype explicitly absolves all those who participate in evil, provided only that the organisation of that evil be bureaucratic.

There is also a third implicit stereotype. It is that the Eichmanns of this world represent a certain personality type — the authoritarian personality of the cultural archetype of the obedient German. Though there is no need to discuss this stereotype directly, it should be clear that it is as unacceptable as the first two. It lulls one into thinking: it could not happen to me, because I am not an authoritarian personality, and it could not happen here, because we are not obedient Germans. Comforting as these thoughts are, the truth is that Eichmannism was and is a general phenomenon. It is not limited to monsters, to bureaucrats, to authoritarians, or to Germans. Part of the purpose in directly challenging the monster and bureaucrat stereotypes is to draw attention to the generality of Eichmannism. To anticipate what will be explained later in detail, Eichmannism is the refusal to make moral judgements, not because bureaucratic duty makes one amoral and not because a monster is immoral, but because an Eichmann is unable to think and so unable to judge. This is Hannah Arendt's explanation, and the one followed here.

In *The Origins of Totalitarianism* in 1951, Arendt described Nazism as 'radical evil', but in *Eichmann in Jerusalem* in 1963, having changed her mind, she called it 'banal evil'. In *Eichmann in Jerusalem* and in other later writings, Arendt attributed the undoubted evil of Nazism to ordinary men and women; not to monstrous individuals, though they certainly played a sizeable part, nor to a dehumanising system called bureaucracy, though it was a contributing factor of great importance. For Arendt, Eichmann represented the ordinary people who ensured the smooth running of society and state under German Nazism, as well as Italian Fascism, Soviet Stalinism, and other no less evil situations such as the Algerian revolution, Argentina under the generals, and the United States during the Vietnam War. Without the compliance of so many ordinary people neither the monsters nor the bureaucracy would have been so effective.

It is one of the most common assumptions in political science in general and in political theory in particular that political power can only be exercised with the voluntary support of at least some of the governed, even if only of a praetorian guard. David Hume called this a first principle of government, as did A. V. Dicey (Hume, n.d.:110 and Dicey, 1905:2). Thus, much research in political science examines the support that rulers enjoy, be it through elections, class interests, conspiracies, or alliances. Similarly, a good deal of teaching rebuts the command model of politics that sees the leader as giving orders to everyone else; instead, students are taught to look for those who benefit from a certain leader. A good many writers who seek to explain 20th century totalitarianism have accepted this first principle. Consequently, they have tried to explain how evil regimes received this voluntary support. In addition to repeating the three stereotypes identified above, some novelists offered their own explanations, which have found a wider audience and escaped the criticism that social, scientific, and historical explanations have received. Ignazio Silone took the absurdity of fascism as obvious and attributed its success to fear (Silone, 1962:233). Meanwhile, George Orwell saw in the kind of compartmentalisation that Max Weber thought was characteristic of bureaucracy a source of this readiness to comply. To be sure, the denizens of Airstrip One were afraid but they hid fear from themselves by double-think in which war was peace (Orwell, 1984:186).[1] These self-deluded citizens then voluntarily supported Big Brother.

By contrast, Arendt's analysis of Eichmann's ordinariness implies that a regime does not need the voluntary support of anyone, not even a praetorian guard. Though coercion, fear, and double-think have their uses, the inertia of ordinary men and women when they do not think or judge suffices to sustain even the most barbaric regime. The result of this inertia is a compliance with the system but not a voluntary support for the regime. In the end nearly all citizens could thus truthfully say that they did not support the regime but, nonetheless, the regime persisted. It is not double-think, fear, and coercion that oil the wheels of totalitarianism, but no-think.

After setting aside the monster and bureaucrat stereotypes that have deprived the judgement of Eichmann of meaning, this discussion will explore Arendt's preoccupation with no-think and the promise it holds for future evils. In what follows, part 1 deals with the monster stereotype, part 2 reviews the bureaucratic stereotype, and part 3 outlines Arendt's diagnosis of Eichmannism.

Eichmann the monster

Eichmann's defence at Jerusalem followed the example of General Alfred Jodl at Nuremberg. Jodl denied all responsibility for his actions. He said that it is 'not the task of a soldier to act as *judge* over his supreme commander. Let history do that or God in Heaven' (International Military Tribunal, 1950:517). Exculpation on the grounds of obedience to superior orders was a defence discouraged by the Nuremberg charter (Wasserstrom, 1974:140–41). The tribunal itself admitted the plea where duress could be shown, but it only applied to mitigation. The tribunal did not entertain the plea from high ranking officials who were regarded as the policy-makers and programme designers.

As a matter of fact, Jodl's plea did not sit well with existing German law and precedent. A German Supreme Court in 1921 had heard and rejected this very plea from two submarine officers who had obeyed orders to massacre the survivors of a sinking ship. This judgement had never been repudiated (Lord Russell, 1962:310). Moreover, the German Army field manual declared each soldier responsible for his own conduct, a standard provision to discourage indiscipline, pillage, and rapine. No soldier in the army Jodl commanded had the duty of blind obedience he claimed for himself. Judgement was not left either to God or history but to a tribunal and the result was definitive. Jodl and the others received capital sentences. That Eichmann should choose a line of defence which had already proved so unsuccessful indicates not only his desperation but also his bad judgement (Van Lang, 1984).

Eichmann described himself as a petty factotum. Throughout his interrogation and testimony, he alleged that he had decided nothing. Every decision he had referred to his superiors. 'Pity me,' he said, 'I was a tool in the hands of the strong and powerful' (Lord Russell, 1962:231).

Since the plea of blind obedience was not an acceptable defence on the precedent of Nuremberg, the prosecution at Jerusalem might have charged Eichmann with crimes committed as a dutiful bureaucrat, but the prosecution did not. Instead, he was vilified as evil incarnate (Hausner, 1966:4).[2] He was portrayed as a fanatical Nazi and a thoroughgoing anti-Semite. In his absence at Nuremberg, other defendants depicted him as that, the better to shift attention from themselves (International Military Tribunal, 1950:76).[3] The severe sentences meted out to these defendants indicate that the Nuremberg Tribunal did not conclude that Eichmann was responsible for everything others attributed to him. Nonetheless, his reputation preceded him and in Jerusalem the assumption seems to have been that only a monster could have committed such monstrous crimes. Hence, a good part of the prosecution's efforts was directed at Eichmann's intentions and beliefs as well as to what he had done.

But even the most committed demonologist found it hard to reconcile this satanic characterisation with Eichmann. He was small, grey, and insignificant in more than stature. The disproportion between Eichmann's crimes and Eichmann was obvious. Everyone who observed the trial remarked upon it. They rejected the self-evident fact that Eichmann was a pygmy (Canovan, 1974:46), opting for intellectual consistency at the expense of the facts. If his crimes required skill and dedication to be accomplished, they reasoned, then he must have or have had skills and dedication, all appearance to the contrary notwithstanding (Trevor-Roper, 1961; O'Donovan, 1961; or Crossmann, 1963).[4] This is the fallacy of affirming the consequent: if Eichmann were an evil man, he would have committed these crimes. He committed these crimes. Therefore, he is an evil man. But the conclusion does not follow.

Alone among those who observed the trial, Hannah Arendt 'took seriously Eichmann's own understanding of himself as a man without base motives, a man who had conscientiously done his duty' (Young-Bruehl, 1982:382).[5] Then she asked: 'What's wrong with this man? Didn't he have any ability to tell right from wrong?' (Denneny, 1979:254). Arendt argues that Eichmann was neither the demonic anti-Semite asserted by the prosecution nor the archetype of the bureaucrat asserted by Eichmann himself. Rather he was a man devoid of the ability to make a judgement or even to see that a judgement was needed. This is what she described as the banality of evil.[6] Her Eichmann is a much less satisfying villain than Robert Shaw's in *The Man in the Glass Booth* or Friedrich Duerrenmatt's in *The Quarry*. Though her book *Eichmann in Jerusalem* aroused a storm of protest, most of the controversy settled on her interpretation and judgement of the role Jews played in their own destruction.[7] Her interpretation of Eichmann as anything but an inhuman monster received criticism, but mainly because it seemed to many people to imply that the Jews were responsible for their own destruction. As will be shown below, her interpretation of Eichmann has also been wrongly taken as authorising the bureaucratic stereotype.

Eichmann had neither the strong beliefs nor the will-power to be a consistent anti-Semite or anything else. He was vain, weak, supercilious, a man who very often tried to get along with everyone by telling them what he thought they would like to hear. He was also very stupid; his perception of the desires of others was none too keen. The essential point is that it was not that the bureaucratic system had prevented him from exercising what Immanuel Kant had called 'reflective judgement' to distinguish right from wrong. He lacked that ability in the first place.

Arendt makes clear exactly what kind of man Eichmann was. He was very unintelligent, with almost no education (Arendt, 1964:133). His testimony shows that he had little or no grasp of the routines of his office (Lord Russell, 1962:203). His speech was prolix. Asked to name the day he arrived in Vienna to take up a post, his reply took 180 words (Arendt, 1965:121). His language was riddled with neologisms, malapropisms, and euphemisms. When challenged to be concrete, he replied: 'officialese is my only language' (Arendt, 1965:43–44). One of the Israeli police officers who interrogated Eichmann made the same point (Less, 1983:45). To Arendt, he seemed incapable of uttering 'a single sentence that was not a cliché' (Arendt, 1965:44 and 50). Others had already perceived him to be a liar and a braggart (Lord Russell, 1962:224). These traits Arendt, too, saw (Arendt, 1965:40–41). He made ridiculous claims of saving Jews by the thousands in the face of the evidence that he had done nothing of the kind (Arendt, 1965:172).[8]

Eichmann went to some pains to suppress the 'normal knowledge' that Jews were human beings (Arendt, 1965:86; cf. Dossa, 1980:314). When he visited the death camps at Chelmo, Minsk, and Treblinka he was horrified, but he strove to quell his own innate repugnance towards his crimes (Arendt, 1965:93). After all, 'he could see no one, no one at all, who was actively against the Final Solution' (Arendt, 1965:116).

Eichmann did not become as Arendt and others saw him as a result of long years of bureaucratic service in some government office, working his way up from a clerk. Far from it. In fact, it is not accurate to speak of him as a bureaucrat at all. He was never a public servant, but a low ranking officer in the SS. He had joined the SS in the hope of finding a career. Whatever influence he had on decision-making, he did not rise in rank. The SS, if it needs to be said, was not just another government department and no model of bureaucratic functioning, either internally or externally (Kogan, 1978; cf. Kent, 1973; Newman, 1942; and Friedrich and Brzezinski, 1966).

Admittedly, during his SS career and later at his trial, Eichmann demonstrated a shrewd native cunning and he was completely self-serving. His consuming interest was promotion and pay, not duty or anti-Semitism. These qualities sufficed to make him useful to others and he was a survivor—though, ultimately, not a successful one like Albert Speer.[9]

Of course, there are difficulties in Arendt's taking Eichmann at his own word. Perhaps the most serious problem is that Eichmann in Jerusalem may have become a different man from Eichmann in Berlin and Vienna. Defeat and imprisonment change a person. Observing the trial of Pierre Laval, Simone de Beauvoir found it difficult to reconcile the tired, meek, and mild defendant with the sleek, confident, and masterful collaborator she had hated (de Beauvoir, 1946:823).

Eichmann the bureaucrat

Adolf Eichmann has been depicted as the archetype of the bureaucrat: industrious, obedient, committed, and efficient (Browning, 1983:146). He has also been described as a loyal 'organisation man' (Banks, 1983:109). Consequently, it is said that he 'believed...disobedience to his superiors would have been a worse crime than killing Jews' (Scott and Hart, 1979:156). What is described as Eichmann's 'insensitivity' is attributed mainly to his 'bureaucratic mentality' (Kamenka and Tay, 1979:128). Robert B. Denhardt has gone so far as to declare that the logic of bureaucracy itself implies that Eichmann had only to obey superior orders (Denhardt, 1980:84). A slightly more sophisticated interpretation can be inferred from Albert Hirschmann's notion of an unconscious loyalist, even though it is presented by an unconvincing analogy to visual perception (Hirschmann, 1970:93). In these references, his horrible crimes are taken to prove the evil potential of the reification we call bureaucracy.

To assume that Eichmann was a bureaucrat does a disservice to our comprehension of bureaucracy. Max Weber defined bureaucracy as the application of rules, the realm of Kant's 'determinative judgement' (Kant, 1952). But nothing in Weber's famous list of the ten features of bureaucracy implies that each and every rule is beyond reflective judgement of right and wrong and is an end in itself (Weber, 1947:333-34). In addition, there is plenty of reason to doubt that the SS fulfilled Weber's ten criteria. Nor are there empirical grounds for supposing that bureaucracies slavishly apply rules without the slightest exercise of discretion, or that such rules are in fact 'a hundred per cent prescription' (Thompson, 1975:13). There is plenty of evidence to the contrary (Hall, 1963). Eichmann does not represent some necessary consequence of bureaucracy. One need look no further than the resistance to Nazis. As M. R. D. Foote has noted, there are numberless occasions when resistance came from those who had spent a lifetime in some government office filing papers, in other words, the clerks (Foote, 1978:13). These, the most stereotyped of all bureaucrats, were certainly not any less capable than anyone else of reflecting and resisting. For Arendt, evil results less from premeditation than from 'thoughtlessness' (Arendt, 1978, I:5).

Elsewhere, in *The Pentagon Papers*, Arendt considers a good deal of evidence that shows that even the most bureaucratic of systems is not necessarily dishonest, amoral, and self-serving. Arendt is generally inclined to name bureaucracy, by which she usually means impersonal rule, as one of the two great misfortunes of modern life (Hill, 1979:321). In that particular case, however, she admitted, albeit reluctantly, 'that the evils of bureaucracy' do not 'suffice as an explanation' for the thoughtlessness of American conduct of the Vietnam war (Arendt, 1972:22). The failure was in the people and not in the system. Evidence was simply ignored and, even more remarkable, dissent was 'domesticated', in the phrase of J.C. Thomson (1968:49). Dissenters became devil's advocates, or like the fool at a royal court. In the years since the war, many closet dissenters have declared themselves, but Daniel Ellsberg was the first and almost the only bureaucratic or political office-bearer to resign.

There is no sure safeguard against the evil of banality. Arendt concluded that the collapse of a decent society is not retarded by the faithful of any noble creed. 'Those who are reliable in such circumstances are not those who cherish values and hold fast to moral norms and standards', she observes. 'Much more reliable will be the doubters and sceptics' — not because scepticism is good or doubting wholesome, but because such people 'are used to examining things for themselves thoroughly and making up their own minds' (Arendt, 1965:185). Yet the sceptic and doubter can certainly perform the functions required by a bureaucratic system, and many have.

Arendt has been reproached by Florence Miale and Michael Selzer for failing 'to reflect on the psychologically aberrant nature of an adult person who defines good and evil merely as synonyms for obedience and disobedience to one's superiors' (Miale and Selzer, 1975:6). But she does not argue that Eichmann thought about good and evil and decided to equate them to obedience and disobedience. Her point is that Eichmann could not and did not think at all. In this, he represents a general phenomenon in our century.

Judging

The difficulty in judging Eichmann is that ordinary crime is the individual's failure to live according to existing laws, but in Eichmann's case the laws themselves were criminal. So it was that Eichmann could argue that had he not obeyed, 'his conscience would have bothered him at the time' for disobeying the laws (Denneny, 1979:255). Somehow conscience and law, morality and society, became set in opposition in Eichmann and this, in Arendt's view, is the moral collapse of 20th century Europe.

Of course, not all were conscience-bound in the way that Eichmann was:

> Those few who were still able to tell right from wrong went really only by their own judgements, and did so freely; there were no rules to be abided by, under which the particular cases with which they were confronted could be subsumed. They had to decide each instance as it arose, because no rules existed for the unprecedented (Arendt, 1965:295).

But how can an individual judge right and wrong without reliance on rules? How can one judge a particular without reference to a universal rule? My students are always morally disturbed by the Nuremberg War Crimes Trials. Invariably, these students conclude that the Nuremberg Trials judged particulars without the grace of a prior universal, *nulla poena sine lege*. Needless to say, it is the budding law students who are the most sensitive to this point. The Nuremberg Tribunal, of course, invited this sort of response from anyone because it anticipated this criticism and made feeble efforts to justify itself by reference to some prior rules of a moral and legal character, as even this essay did earlier regarding General Jodl. Law students do not find these justifications very satisfying. Nor did Arendt, though for different reasons. Arendt returned to these questions at the end of her life, a decade after the publication of *Eichmann in Jerusalem*. She was sure that these were radical questions.

For Arendt, the life of the mind consisted of three autonomous but interactive functions: thinking, willing, and judging. Socrates was the thinker par excellence. Since Socrates, Western philosophy has judged particulars by reference to universals. The judgement of a particular is determined by a universal. When a man was called courageous, Socrates asked: 'What is courage?' He did not say: 'Tell me this man's story'. Socrates taught that to call something beautiful, we must have a prior idea of what beauty is, whether we are aware of it or not. The realisation of those ideas became the programme of Western philosophy. But in Arendt's view, Socrates' two-world theory — particular things and universal ideas — collapsed intellectually in the 19th century and morally in the 20th (Arendt, 1961:17).[10] We lost our universals but not the habit of thinking in terms of universals, or to be more precise, the habit of thinking that the only rational way to think of particulars was by reference to universals. Today, we still want to think in terms of universals to which we can relate particulars, but we have lost faith in our universals. The result is thoughtless willing. For Arendt, Eichmann was the paradigmatic example of the un-thinking, un-judging person. Without the thought to imagine other people, without judgement in common with them, he had only himself. Willing is private for Arendt if it is not aimed at a judgement, which in turn is informed by thinking. In addition to thoughtless willing, another common response to the loss of faith in universals as a secure foundation for thinking is to call for a return to lost faiths, be they religious or ideological.

The universals that used to be accepted as limits are lost: tradition, nature, God, natural law, nation, or ideology. These transcendent values have given way to the impermanence of individuals in Arendt's telling. The transitoriness of individual life is now the measure of all things. This 20th century reversal is partly due to the accelerated rate of change experienced in our time. It is also partly due to the fragility of the world. Once we imagined it would take a wrathful God to destroy the world with fire and flood, but now we imagine that a person just like ourselves could destroy the world by accident. In such a world, neither tradition, nor God, nor nation any longer offers firm ground for the judgement of human action.

The loss of universals is readily discernible in the pervasive relativism of our time. To offer a moral judgement is anathema to most people. The more highly educated people are, the more reluctant they often are to make moral judgements. Yet, they may approve of extreme political action such as that of revolution or terrorism. For such people, it is sensible to say: 'I will silence, even kill you in order to assert my values', but not to say: 'You are wrong'. To these people, the latter is hopelessly naive and irrational, as well as impolite, in its assumption that there is a right and wrong, let alone that any of us may confidently ascertain and assert right and wrong. But to these same people, the first statement is intellectually honest in its amorality. For Arendt, the ethics of individuals without universals has become 'might makes right' and that is no ethics at all. Embracing a set of rules, be it the Führer's word or an ideology, is no alternative because the rules may be wrong in themselves, inappropriate, or misapplied.

The alternative is judgement. As Erich Auerbach has remarked regarding Montaigne, judgement is making oneself at home in a world without fixed points of reference, without universals (Auerbach, 1953:311). Judgement is the assertion of values that are no longer underwritten by a transcendent reality. This loss of transcendent universals began when we learned to distrust our senses, thanks to Galileo's telescope. The Cartesian divide between *res extensa* and *res cogitans* resulted. Since that division, moral life and philosophy have oscillated between the equally fruitless poles of objectivity and subjectivity.

Arendt concluded that the only thinkers who escaped the prison of this Cartesian dualism were those concerned with taste. Taste is the faculty that perceives realities that are neither objective nor subjective, yet exist all the same. It is Immanuel Kant's *Critique of Judgement* to which she turned to find how one can judge value that is neither an objective fact nor subjective assertion; that is neither a determinative judgement such as Eichmann applied in following given rules, nor a subjective preference akin, for example, to my liking chocolate. Can one judge the particular without reference to a general concept or universal rule, and can that judgement have any validity beyond the judging subject i.e. for other people?

A reflective judgement is one without an absolute rule. We make such a judgement of taste when we say: 'This is beautiful'. A judgement is aesthetic precisely because it is a direct experience. No one can judge the beauty of an unseen object, but one can judge the truth of a scientific proposition without direct experience. In Kant's words: 'The judgement of taste is not based on concepts; for if it were, it would be open to dispute (decision by means of proofs)' (1928:198).[11] The example T. D. Weldon gives is wine tasting (Weldon, 1953:160; cf. Oakeshott, 1962).

Risking a legal analogy to the common law tradition unknown to Kant and ignored by Arendt, a reflective judgement is made when a jury pronounces what is just in a case though no juror knows what justice itself is. Justice develops through cases as taste develops through a study of exemplary models. However vague the processes are, one thing is certain. Judgements such as: 'The Final Solution to the Jewish Question was evil' command far greater comprehension and agreement than any scientific proposition (Phillips, 1983:183). It is clear that (i) we *can* and *do* make particular judgements all the time, whether we know what courage is, what beauty is, what justice is, or what evil is. Furthermore, (ii) these judgements are no less intelligible or persuasive than scientific propositions (which for the sake of this argument are taken to be the very models of Socratic thought, moving as they do from universals to particulars).

Now, philosophers since Socrates have been unable to explain how we make such judgements and why we understand and agree to them when other people make them. So philosophers ignore them. The phrase generally used of contentions (i) and (ii) above is that they are not 'philosophically relevant'. In ethics, what is philosophically relevant is, for example, a proof that evil is conceptually impossible or that theft is self-contradictory. The fact that people murder and steal all the same is not philosophically relevant. Arendt was not one who respected such 'philosophical relevance', and the price that she paid for that irreverence has been the scorn of professional philosophers.[12]

According to Kant, when we are confronted with an object, we respond subjectively by saying: 'This pleases me' rather than objectively by saying: 'This is good'. A subjective statement such as 'this pleases me' or such equivalents as 'it seems to me' make no demand on others. However, to say: 'This is beautiful' does make a demand on others. In this statement, we mean not only that is pleases me, but that it will and should please others or everyone. There is no contradiction if I say of something: 'This pleases me' and you say of it: 'It does not please me'. But there is a contradiction if I say something is beautiful and you say that it is not. In this case, we require a judgement of beauty. In making this judgement, we take the perspective of others or of everyone, but we do not judge as others would or as we think others would (Arendt, 1961:220ff.). That would be empathy rather than judgement.

If an object pleases me independently of my particular subjective situation, then it ought to please others too, independently of their subjective situations. Arendt does not go so far as to require a veil of ignorance *pace* John Rawls' *A Theory of Justice*, but that veil expresses the disinterestedness and generality of the moral community of judgement that she requires (Rawls, 1971:136–142). She would demur from Rawls' faith in the application of the veil as a universal rule of judgement.

By not judging, Eichmann was the essentially private person devoted to making a good life for his family. He willed his private desires, which dictated his public duties. The dominance of private motives is, of course, not limited to the Eichmanns of this world. The private dominates the public realm when personal grievances are politicised as some political theorists recommend (Pitkin, 1981:348). To Arendt, the private person 'has driven the dichotomy of private and public ... so far' that there is no longer any connection between the two. The private person not only leaves the moral community, but destroys it. When a public occupation forces such a private person to murder, the person does not regard himself as a murderer because he has not done it out of personal motives but in a professional capacity. 'Out of sheer passion, he would never do harm to a fly' (Arendt, 1945a:234).

Eichmann did not think and, consequently, could not judge. The 'desk murderer' Eichmann was a 'sleepwalker' (Arendt, 1978, I:191).

One of the most common excuses made for domesticated dissenters or near-Eichmanns is the plea of the lesser evil. But Arendt insists that those who justify to themselves and others their immoral deeds as lesser evils 'forget quickly that they chose evil' (Arendt, 1964:186). No moral idea is more liable to abuse with the result that 'good men do the worst' (Young-Bruehl, 1982:374). To say that the end justifies the means is another thoughtless way to escape from making judgements, but it is not a way to escape being judged. A plea of the lesser evil creates a situation where those who took part in an evil policy could charge those who refused to take part with irresponsibility (Kateb, 1983:87). This is the attempted extenuation of the claim that: 'We who appear guilty today are in fact those who stayed on the job in order to prevent worse things from happening'. The refusal to collaborate with evil, even where this meant great risks, occurred 'not because the world would then be changed for the better, but because only on this condition could they [those who refused to collaborate] go on living with themselves' (Arendt, 1965:186). Here, Arendt differs from her mentor Karl Jaspers who insisted on a utilitarian justification of resistance (Jaspers, 1947:32 and 71).

One can 'judge particulars [such as Eichmann] without subsuming them under those general rules which can be taught and learned until they grow into habits' (Arendt, 1971:446). Eichmann wholly lacked the ability to judge, because he was unable to think (Kateb, 1983:38). There is no recipe for judging. Hence, it is mistaken to criticise Arendt for equating reason and morality, as Joseph Beatty does (1976:273). Arendt described the reflective procedure in this way:

> In judging, you say spontaneously, without any derivation from general rules, this man has courage. If you were a Greek, you would have 'in the depth of your mind' the experience of Achilles. Imagination is again necessary: you must have present Achilles though he is certainly absent. If we say of someone he is good, we have in the back of our minds the example of St. Francis or Jesus of Nazareth. The judgement has *exemplary validity* to the extent that the example is rightly chosen (Young-Bruehl, 1982:300–301).

We do not spontaneously see the general in the particular, contrary to Socrates. It is precisely when the determinative rules of judgement disappear, either because they do not exist or because they are wrong, as Eichmann's were, that the faculty of judgement comes into its own (Arendt, 1953:391).

The spontaneous appeal to examples depends on a prior choice of examples. That earlier choice is stimulated by thinking. A person is prepared to make particular judgements spontaneously by having thought about the questions What is courage? What is justice? What is beauty? and What is goodness? When Arendt asked What is thinking?

she settled on Socrates as her example (Young-Bruehl, 1982a:302). Arendt once said that 'in the last analysis... our decisions about right and wrong will depend upon our choice of company, with whom we wish to spend our lives. And this company is chosen through thinking of examples from history, from literature, from experience' (Beiner, 1982:113). Arendt chose Achilles and Socrates for company. The gift of thought to judgement is these examples in the depth of the mind. 'Thinking is "good for nothing" in the world, but in the mind, it is good for guidance' — not the universal rules of law (Young-Bruehl, 1982a:302).

If judgement is not exercised, it atrophies. Arendt wrote:

> The argument that we cannot judge if we were not present and involved ourselves seems to convince everyone everywhere, although it seems obvious that if it were true, neither the administration of justice nor the writing of history would ever be possible (Arendt, 1965:295–96).

The reflection that one might also have done wrong under the circumstances may kindle forgiveness but that conclusion follows judgement, it does not replace it. 'The sad irony is that this atrophy of the faculty of judgement was precisely what had made Eichmann's monstrous crimes possible in the first place' (Beiner, 1982:99). Eichmann's no-think enables us to explain, rather than is explained by, totalitarianism.

Conclusion

For Arendt society is a community of judgement. It consists of thinking individuals who, like Socrates, are not alone when without company. Because Socrates thought, he was never alone; he always had several points of view present in his mind's imagination. Winston Smith's memory in *1984* played the same role. Because he did not think, Eichmann was always alone.

The community of judgement also includes the example of those one esteems, however unconsciously. While thinking can be done alone, judging cannot. Judgement is 'inherently social because our aesthetic judgements make reference to a commonly shared world' (Beiner, 1982:119). The particulars judged, like Eichmann in Jerusalem, are held in common. Judgement is a boundary principle for a moral community in Arendt's telling of the story of the life of the mind. When various Eichmanns refused to judge or neglected to judge, they left the moral community, if ever they were in it. The boundary of the moral community is not shared universal rules, but the common experience of particulars to be judged.

Judgement requires thinking, thinking makes judgement possible, but thinking is not judgement. The paradox is that although judgement is an inescapably social act, in order to render judgement a person must withdraw from the company of others, to contemplate and to reflect. Judgement is social in another sense, too. I never judge for myself alone. A judgement is a communication to others. Persuading others of the validity of the judgement is the *raison d'être* of judging. General Jodl could not have been more wrong. History does not judge; we do.

Notes

1 This is an explanation reminiscent of Thucydides' description of the revolt in Corcyra (1954:208-209).
2 Hausner was the Israeli attorney-general who conducted the prosecution.
3 One of the legal officers attached to the Tribunal emphasises the same point, Neave (1978:310).
4 Other examples of demonology include Donovan (1960:90) and Reynolds (1960:3ff.).
5 She was not quite alone since François Bondy independently described Eichmann in the same way (1961, pp.32-54) and she won a persuasive ally in Bruno Bettleheim (1963/1964:23-33).
6 A thesis confirmed by Jesse Glenn Gray's interviews with German POWs (Young-Bruehl, 1982:370, and Nash, 1980:62-79). Similar findings from other interviews are reported by Dicks (1972) and J. A. M. Meerloo (1969:609-614).
7 She is dismissed in a footnote by Lucy Dawidowicz (1975:514N).
8 There is a moving account of a moral S.S. officer in Friedlander (1969).
9 On Speer see the perceptive remarks of John K. Galbraith (1980:217-218) and Matthias Schmidt (1984).
10 If the existentialists are right, and we are all free, but refuse to recognise it because we fear the responsibility, then the bureaucracy is the perfect embodiment of that escape from freedom. The point is: the bureaucracy answers to that need; it does not create it.
11 Arendt's appropriation of Kant has been challenged by R. J. Dostal (1984:725-755).
12 The aristocratic disdain is palpable in Anthony Quinton's biography of her (1983:19).

Michael Bittman

5 Totalitarianism: *the career of a concept*

Ideas, we now realise, often display a paradoxical relation to social context—both the contexts from which they arise and those into which they are subsequently injected. This is certainly true of Arendt's concept of totalitarianism. Born of her attempt to understand the genocidal policies of Nazi Germany, it was appropriated in its own time, the immediate postwar period, to legitimate the anticommunist crusade of the Cold War—a crusade, moreover, as Arendt acknowledged in a footnote to later editions of *The Origins of Totalitarianism*, that itself had 'totalitarian tendencies' (1958:356n).[1] In its development the concept of totalitarianism came to have a career of its own, quite independent of Arendt's authorship and even remarkably at odds with her own understanding of it.

In order to follow the vicissitudes of the concept of totalitarianism, it is necessary to comprehend some of the special circumstances surrounding its formulation and its subsequent elaboration. A reconstruction of its history may reveal whether it was not certain inconsistencies in Arendt's own thinking that inadvertently allowed her analysis of the 'radical evil' of totalitarianism to be perverted during the Cold War into a justification for a crusade with 'totalitarian tendencies'.

The term 'totalitarianism' did not originate with Arendt. Whitfield (1980:8–24) suggests that since its inception in the 1930s the concept has passed through a number of phases which can be distinguished according to changes in its denotation. In its first phase it was used primarily as a description (and incidentally, in Mussolini's case, a positive goal) of the political organisation of fascist states during the

1930s. Arendt and others writing in the 1950s subsequently employed the concept to denote features common to both Stalin's and Hitler's regime. A third phase was initiated by the mid-1950s, establishing a conventional usage which counterposed 'totalitarian' one-party (and especially communist) regimes to the pluralist democracies such as the United States (Friedrich and Brzezinski, 1961; Brzezinski, 1956; Aron, 1965; Schapiro, 1972).

Since that time, the concept has not altered greatly in meaning, although it has been widely attacked as being more polemical than meaningful (see Spiro, 1968; Friedrich et al, 1969) and has lost the almost universal academic endorsement it enjoyed during the fifties.[2] Perhaps the most widely accepted definition of totalitarianism is given by Friedrich, who lists the following features:

(1) a totalist ideology;
(2) a single party committed to this ideology and led by one man, the dictator;
(3) a fully developed secret police; and three kinds of monopoly or, more precisely monopolistic control: namely that of
   (a) mass communications;
   (b) operational weapons;
   (c) all organisations, including economic ones, thus involving a centrally planned economy (1969:126).

A brief summary of these shifts in the referent does not convey the significant changes in the hold that the concept of totalitarianism exercised over the popular imagination, nor the role played by Arendt's boldly original work in this process.

While academics may have groped for new concepts to comprehend political events in Europe in the 1930s and 1940s, combating totalitarianism was not the popular justification for hostilities. The Allies justified participation in World War II in much more mundane terms—as a response to aggression. What provided the specific context for the reception of Arendt's work was the impact, at the very end of the war, of the Allies' discovery of the Nazi death camps and the liberation of the camp survivors. The disclosures about the death camps provided compelling retrospective reasons for the war against Hitler. In particular, they made it easy for the Americans, who had entered the war in Europe so reluctantly, to justify their participation. Now it was easy to say what was hateful about the Nazis and why it had been imperative to stop them. It was a peculiar time in which a stunned world came to the realisation that the fight had been against madmen, who had diverted themselves from their war effort in order to commit atrocious genocide. The death camps were now revealed as the ultimate project of the Nazis and as a symbol of what the victory of the Axis powers would have meant.

The monstrosity and lunacy of the death camps cried out for explanation. Arendt was quick to recognise the compelling need to fathom the implications of their existence. For many in the English-speaking world, she represented the first intellectual to give a serious account of these events and to attempt to draw the 'lessons of the war' for the generations that followed. The result was her justly celebrated study, *The Origins of Totalitarianism*.

However, Arendt did not merely rail against the insane malevolence of a defeated enemy. She employed the concept of totalitarianism, to describe the logic not only of Hitler's regime but of Stalin's as well. This analysis justified, after the event, the inescapable logical necessity of fighting Hitler. At the same time it acted as a giant conducting rod, capturing this lightning flash of militance and directing it against the political system of the USSR. The limitless dread aroused by the evidence of Nazi atrocities passed from Hitler's now defunct regime to the United States' newly emerging rival in world affairs.

The concept of civilian mobilisation is important here. The fundamental changes that have occurred in the conduct of war during this century were those that shaped the character of the Cold War. During World War I, when the contending societies were increasingly driven to engage all the human resources available to them, the distinction between the civilian and military populations of nations at war became blurred. That civilian mobilisation had become a critical element in modern warfare is nowhere more clearly illustrated than in the bombing of centres of civilian population behind the so-called 'lines'. The deliberate 'saturation bombing' of places of domicile, which happened for the first time on a large scale in World War II, was an attempt to disrupt this civilian mobilisation.

Just as the European conflagration had been preceded by a so-called 'Phoney War', so too it was followed by a Cold War. After World War II, as nations remained militarily prepared for hostilities, there arose a need to sustain and also to legitimise continuing civilian mobilisation. In the absence of an actual 'shooting war', this mobilisation was accomplished by ideological means. While Arendt's analysis of totalitarianism certainly cannot be held responsible for the Cold War, her concept was enlisted to harness this surplus mobilisation and direct it into the service of an anti-Soviet crusade.

Arendt's work thus represents the break from the concept's initial usage, during Whitfield's abovementioned 'first phase', in which it was used to refer simply and exclusively to fascist regimes of the right. The continuity between her use of the concept and that of the third phase typified by the work of Friedrich, however, is more apparent than real. Writers of this third phase paid tribute, often elaborate, to Arendt's work. Their emphasis on the significance attached to totalitarian ideology and on the concentration of power in the hands of the leader, as well as their acknowledgement of the importance of terror and the elimination of plurality, would all seem to echo Arendt's concerns. As a group these writers appear to think of themselves as Arendt's intellectual heirs, engaged merely in refining her concepts by eliminating rhetorical excesses.

Yet in one of the paradoxical developments that always seem to have surrounded Arendt, she signalled her distance from this later usage by endorsing the views of those who criticised the fashioning from the concept of totalitarianism of an instrument for the ideological crusade against the Soviet Union. This support is evident not only in her criticism of McCarthyism in the United States, but also in the closing remarks of her 1966 preface to *The Origins of Totalitarianism*:

> Stalin, like Hitler, died in the midst of a horrifying unfinished business. And when this happened, the story this book had to tell, and the events it tries to understand and come to terms with, came to at least a provisional end (1966c:xl).

To understand Arendt's position and how it differs from that of her self-proclaimed intellectual heirs requires a more detailed examination of her argument in *The Origins of Totalitarianism*.

The Origins of Totalitarianism attempts to fulfil at least three aims: to explain why specifically the Jews were singled out for mass slaughter by the Nazis; to give an account of the genesis of totalitarianism; and finally to describe and, more importantly, to explain the logic of development of totalitarianism. The transitions between her pursuit of these varying aims within her exposition are not always smooth, as Arendt herself acknowledged (Whitfield 1980:5). These awkward transitions in turn give rise to certain inconsistencies in her text that lie behind the differences that were to emerge between Arendt and those who claimed to be her followers. Authors of the third phase rely heavily on the final section of Arendt's book, constructing a concept of totalitarianism as the typological converse of pluralism, while showing—unlike Arendt—little interest in the genesis of the phenomenon.

Although Arendt's explanation of why the Jews were selected for extinction appears self-contained, it is intended as a more general revelation of the nature of totalitarianism. The concept of totalitarianism which superseded Arendt's stressed the role of terror as an expression of the regime's desire for 'monolithic homogeneity': as the means of eliminating obstacles to unanimity (Friedrich, 1969:145–6; Burch, 1964:179). By contrast, Arendt emphasised the paradox that anti-Semitism became most lethal at the very point at which any influence that formerly privileged Jews might have enjoyed at European courts was in decline. Their unique position previously had allowed them to render financial and diplomatic services to the state because they were neither industrialists nor landholders.

In a profound sociological observation on the conditions of the legitimacy of authority and economic privilege, Arendt notes that as long as aristocrats held the power to oppress, they were 'not only tolerated but respected' but as soon as they represented wealth without visible function they became intolerable (1973:4). As with the aristocrats, so with the Jews. Summing up these developments Arendt concludes:

> In an imperialist age Jewish wealth had become insignificant; to a Europe with no sense of balance of power between its nations and of inter-European solidarity, the non-national, inter-European Jewish element became an object of hate because of its useless wealth and contempt because of its lack of power (1958a:15).

The first aim of Arendt's book merges with the second. In addition to an explanation of why they should be selected as victims, her narrative about the fate of the Jews requires an account of why any victim was necessary at all. What makes Arendt's work on totalitarianism far more interesting than most of the political sociology that followed it is this attempt to give a genetic account of totalitarianism. By comparison, later theories are either ahistorical or argue that autocracies such as Calvin's Geneva, the Roman Empire in the reign of Diocletian, even Plato's ideal republic, should not be identified by means of the term because contemporary totalitarianism is 'developed and employed with the aid of modern technical devices' (Friedrich, 1969:135).

Arendt, however, sees the origins of totalitarianism in the superfluous population created by mature capitalism. Mature capitalism produced superfluous capital with no opportunity for domestic investment, superfluous workers who could not be employed in times of capitalist crisis, and a decline in the status of some small propertyholders who had sunk to the lowest social levels. They were joined by a number of other groups dislocated by capitalism—aristocrats without a function, displaced peasantry and so on. These developments had two consequences: first, superfluous capital sought opportunities for expansion abroad; and second, it created a 'mob'.

The seeking of opportunities for expansion abroad caused the bourgeoisie initially to develop a political interest in the state as the guarantor of colonial expansion and, further, to develop the state as a national instrument of power. For these purposes capital entered into a political alliance with the mob. This in turn had dual consequences: it destroyed the 'comity of nations', that friendly relation between nations in which each recognises and respects the laws of the other; at the same time it promoted the idea that the most salient feature of any nation was its capacity for power.

That scramble for African colonies which preceded World War I resulted in two experiences that were also disastrous in their effects. The first was the encounter with people different from Europeans under conditions of exploitation. This experience, while it did little for the European ruling class, taught underprivileged Europeans and the mob that through sheer violence they could create a group lower than themselves. The second experience was that of colonial administration, the governing of a population not recognised as part of civil society. This subjugation of colonised peoples involved denial of the principle of the universality of law. Colonial regimes were founded upon ideas of the 'white man's burden', the conviction that racial domination was justified by historic destiny.

These developments, together with the frustrated colonial ambitions of land-locked Russia and Austro-Hungary, subverted the trinity of people–territory–state. Under the influence of Pan-Germanism and Pan-Slavism, nationality became a 'tribal' movement beyond the territorial limits of the state. The state, which had formerly been regarded as the guarantor of civil liberties, now became an instrument of the nation. Where nation, people, and territory no longer coincided, 'national sovereignty... lost its original connotation of freedom of the people and was being surrounded by a pseudomystical aura of lawless arbitrariness' (1973:231). The nation-state was no longer capable of solving the political issues of the time. This was nowhere more clearly illustrated than in the growing numbers of people who were stateless and hence without protection or rights.

The confluence of these developments—the destruction of legal and political community, the collapse of the traditional nation state, the rise of the déclassé 'mob', and the development of movements in the place of parties based on economic interest—all provided the basic soil of totalitarianism. The full development of totalitarianism according to Arendt requires that the processes which lead to the development of the mob should create the conditions for the development of a mass movement. The relation between the mob and the mass in Arendt's theory is ambiguous but the difference seems to be that, whereas the mob was politically the result of an alliance with the bourgeoisie and hence shared (perhaps in perverted form) some of its values, the mass is totally detached from all class relations and alliances—a radically atomised aggregation of individuals usually uninterested in political participation. The one social tie that remains open to this mass in revolt against an arbitrary, hypocritical world is belonging to a movement.

Arendt explicitly distinguishes between one-party states and the regimes initiated by totalitarian movements. The idea of the movement is central to Arendt's conception of totalitarianism. The seizure of power by means of violence is only a transitional stage, never an end in itself. 'The practical goal of the movement,' says Arendt, 'is to organize as many people as possible within its framework and to set and keep them in motion; a political goal that would constitute the end of the movement simply does not exist' (1958a:326). This explains why Arendt, in opposition to prevailing opinion, thought propaganda a relatively unimportant aspect of totalitarianism. What she finds interesting is the complete lack of content in any political programme. To the already deeply cynical masses these movements offer the fiction of conspiracies, for example, the world-wide Jewish conspiracy or the Trotskyite conspiracy within the Party. Simply because they are conspiracies and must therefore happen in secret, these fictions cannot be contradicted by experience. Totalitarian ideologies, as distinct from the propaganda intended for consumption by the non-totalitarian world, promise eventual relief to those who feel oppressed as a project of millennia, so that defeat becomes a temporary setback on the path to eventual victory.

In summary then: 'The true goal of totalitarian propaganda is not persuasion but organization' (1958a:361). The chief disability of this mode of organisation is the need for consistency in these ideological fictions because, where reference to experience is precluded such consistency is the only validation which can have bearing on the credibility of such claims (1958a:477):

> Before mass leaders seize the power to fit reality to their lies their propaganda is marked by its extreme contempt for facts as such, for in their opinion fact depends entirely on the power of the man who can fabricate it. The assertion that the Moscow subway is the only one in the world is a lie only so long as the Bolsheviks have not the power to destroy all others (1958a:350).

In contradistinction to the popular notion, Arendt sees the totalitarian leader's rule not in terms of personal charisma but as a function of the movement itself. Totalitarian movements are in their organisational structure 'secret societies established in broad daylight', with a core group of 'sworn blood brothers', surrounded and protected from a profane and hostile world by multiple layers of buffer groups, front groups, and sympathisers (1958a:376). The leader stands at the centre of the movement and owes his position to his ability to spin intrigues and to constantly change personnel (1958a:373).

Totalitarianism enters a new phase once it seizes power. Once in power the movement is confronted with the twin dangers of (i) its global claim becoming reconciled with the prevailing environment of non-totalitarian states and (ii) its government ossifying into a stable structure and thus becoming more conventional. According to Arendt, totalitarianism avoids the first danger by refusing to acknowledge that its claims to government might not be absolute. Hence totalitarianism is 'inherently' expansionist and seeks the elimination of every competing non-totalitarian reality (1958a:392).

Totalitarianism evades the second danger through a bewildering proliferation of offices and authorities which prevent the establishment of any hierarchy of authority. Arendt very firmly points out that it is a mistake to consider that totalitarianism has anything to do with authoritarianism. She further denies that this proliferation of offices expresses the omnipresence of the leader's authority. In Arendt's view this is what makes it so misleading to talk about a totalitarian state, since it is not a system of particularly centralised constitutional arrangements, or the merging of party and state, but a 'shapeless' arrangement which destroys responsibility and competence and ensures perpetual motion. Power remains inside the movement and strictly separated from the state. The resulting confusion of ostensible and real power turns the state into a front organisation and organises the population as sympathisers. Thus rule becomes progressively more secretive and there is an expansion of the secret police, who become 'the true executive branch of government', the 'only openly ruling class', whose 'standards and scale of values permeate the entire texture of totalitarian society' (1958a:430).

But what distinguishes the role of the secret police under totalitarianism from their role under other forms of government is their use for total domination. Unlike *agents provocateurs* the totalitarian secret police do not have any initiative of their own, since the victims of their terror are 'objective enemies' (1958a:422). What for Arendt is distinctive in totalitarianism is the development of terror beyond the function of the elimination of opposition, or even those suspected of opposition, and its application to constantly growing lists of 'objective enemies', such as the Jews or the kulaks. Under totalitarian regimes terror increases in inverse proportion to the existence of opposition. For this reason Arendt excludes all other forms of despotism and one-party rule, including the fascist dictatorship of Mussolini, from the category of totalitarianism. Arendt never tires of citing accounts of the concentration camps which all comment on the similarity between victim and persecutor, and how both experience loss of individuality, spontaneity, and sense of agency. Arendt comments:

The introduction of purely objective criteria into the selective system of the SS troops was Himmler's great organizational invention: he selected the candidates from photographs according to purely racial criteria. Nature itself decided, not only who was to be eliminated, but also who was to be trained as executioner (1958a:468).

The 'iron band' of terror becomes the instrument through which totalitarianism executes the 'laws of nature', or the 'laws of history'. 'In these ideologies, the term "law" itself changed its meaning', says Arendt. 'From expressing the framework of stability within which human actions and motions can take place, it became the expression of motion itself' (1958a:464). Born of the desperate isolation of superfluous men and women since the industrial revolution, totalitarianism not only destroys 'the public realm of life... [it] destroys the private life as well' (1958a:475). It eliminates plurality amongst humans, it reduces humans beyond solitude to absolute loneliness, it destroys their capacities for thought, experience, and action.

The preceding discussion makes clear why Arendt would have distanced herself from her purported followers among the third phase theorists of totalitarianism. They have not merely misconstrued important nuances of Arendt's concept but have missed her overall point. They have attempted to domesticate her vision of a 'radical evil' — 'crimes that men can neither punish nor forgive' (459) — by confusing it with commoner types of tyranny, autocracy, and despotism, novel merely because of their use of technically modern means. This confusion was accomplished by means of a series of substitutions exemplified in Friedrich's definition. Instead of Arendt's emphasis on the anti-utilitarian character of totalitarian regimes, we are told that it is the denial of the free market and its replacement by central planning that is indicative of the totalitarian road to serfdom. Our attention is directed towards the monopolistic nature of control over the mass media of communication, rather than to the function of this control. Yet the idea of an independent 'free press' in the non-totalitarian world is rather naively assumed and certainly not sociologically examined.

Max Weber's definition of the state — the organisation embodying the exclusive claim to the legitimate use of the organised means of violence — is held somehow to distinguish totalitarian regimes. Arendt's emphasis on movement rather than party is sacrificed for the more readily observable characteristic of party organisation, specifically whether one can identify one or two parties. The corresponding confusion about what can be classified as totalitarianism and what is merely some older form of government no doubt follows from this.

The treating of terror as no more than the mere suppression of opposition fails to explain why Jews and Gypsies perished in their millions. Nor on the basis of this simple reductionism can one comprehend the significance of Arendt's claims about the ultimate similarity of victim and persecutor. In place of an anti-human logicality of ideas that subordinates behaviour to an objective outcome of a supra-human law, we are offered the suggestion that totalitarian ideology is distinctive simply because (i) it is revolutionary (ii) it purports to explain everything, and (iii) it is taken seriously by the rulers of the system. The chasm which separates this latter theory—with its echoes of the 'end of ideology thesis', implying that not taking politics too seriously is what keeps the 'free' world free—and Arendt's own celebration of active participation in the political is vast indeed.

All these differences between Arendt and those who claimed to be her followers can be related to the latters' fundamental reluctance to accept as significant the problem she poses concerning the genesis of totalitarianism. Totalitarianism was not, according to Arendt, a summation of the differences between the properties of the organisational vehicles of one's own political persuasion and those of one's political opponents, but a radical evil unleashed by the social havoc of the industrial revolution. It is a possibility that dwells in the heart of all modern societies. It is towards this aspect of her theory of totalitarianism that we must now turn.

If Arendt's work is to found a tradition of political sociology aimed at understanding the conditions under which totalitarianism may arise, then one is obliged to note that the principles of her genetic explanation stand in some tension with her analytic description of the phenomenon. One might describe the purpose of the genetic explanation as ideographic, that is, constructed in terms of explaining particularities. On the other hand, her description of the phenomenon might be described as nomothetic, or establishing generalities, since she deliberately abstracts in order to cover not one but two cases—Stalin and Hitler.

The tension between these two principles is most clearly evident in the transition between the first two sections of her book and the final one. Her explanation of Why the Jews? is not easily capable of extension to Why the kulaks?. That both groups were victims of systematic terror, 'objective enemies', there can be no doubt. But it is difficult to argue that they were both equally wealthy but 'without visible function'. Nor is Pan-Slavism as easily related to the fate of the kulaks as anti-Semitism is to that of the Jews. The parallel appears to be one more of form than of explanatory substance. This does not, of course, make the explanation of Why the Jews? any less acceptable in its particularity but demonstrates the difficulty of expanding her analysis without supplementation into a general explanation of why certain groups became the victims of totalitarianism.

Similarly the second part of the book dealing with the social conditions giving rise to totalitarianism also suffers from this tension. Of particular interest is a no doubt deliberate ambiguity concerning these circumstances. Although the explanation is explicitly couched in terms of a process that occurred throughout Europe, it is not clear why totalitarianism has occurred only in Germany and Russia. Rather than a failure, this seems to be a problem of ideographic explanation in each case. While this tension doubtless corresponds to Arendt's desire that we remain alert to the possibility of the recurrence of totalitarianism (1958a:478), it does not assist us in predicting the possibility of such a recurrence. With regard to Russia, Arendt herself seems to suggest that the explanation is incomplete. She argues that Stalin himself artificially created an atomised, mass society (1958a:318). If this is possible, then the elaborate explanatory structure of the first two parts of the book is largely irrelevant as a warning of the circumstances in which totalitarianism may arise. In this case, too, the desire to abstract is at cross-purposes with the desire to particularise.

If one examines more closely the structure of Part 3 of *Origins*, it can be seen that Arendt has difficulty in maintaining the abstracting, nomothetic momentum in her analysis. So that the abstraction may succeed she is obliged to give examples from both Stalin's Russia and Hitler's Germany for each aspect of the general pattern of totalitarianism that she discovers. Yet there is a preponderance of examples drawn from the Nazi period, which is understandable given the sources available at the time. But these difficulties of comparison cannot be avoided altogether, as consideration of the idea of movement illustrates. This idea operates on a number of different levels. It represents (i) the idea of inhuman agents in the service of a suprahuman law of motion; (ii) a description of the restless ever-changing forms of organisation; and (iii) on a still lower level of abstraction, a concrete social movement which precedes totalitarianism proper. While she finds similarities to sustain the parallel between the German and Russian cases on the first two levels, on this third level almost all the illustrations come from the Nazi example. In contrast, Stalin, by virtue of his 'attention to detail' (1958a:373–374), simply inherited from Lenin and Trotsky a movement that already held sway. That movement called 'Bolshevism' must therefore, by implication, have had a quite different character before Stalin, an implication that her argument does not however recognise or address.

While the parallel holds up on the second level, since Stalin like Hitler was surrounded by a confusingly fluid succession of secret organisations and moribund party and state forms, there is a further difficulty of correspondence at the first level. Arendt attempted to demonstrate the underlying similarities between a racist ideology of 'those fit to survive', which claims derivation from a quasi-Darwinian notion of the laws of nature, and an ideology constructed around the impersonal workings of the laws of history. However, while she seems to imply that this applies to Marxism in general and therefore presumably to the Bolshevism which preceded Stalin (463–466), the rest of the text suggests that it was specific to Stalin's regime. All this uncertainty indicates that Stalin's case has a dynamic quite distinct from the Nazi case, and one perhaps requiring separate treatment. Pointing out these dissimilarities does no damage to the parallels in relation to the use of terror, but it does contribute to the feeling that Arendt's abstracting moment is a little contrived.

These failings become more pronounced when Arendt attempts to confront de-Stalinisation and the 'thaw'. The Preface to the revised edition of *Origins* in 1966 acknowledges that Stalin's death had altered the nature of the Soviet regime. In a surprisingly steadfast way she uses the invasion of Hungary in 1956 to demonstrate this shift. She argues that the use of the army and not the secret police to assert control, the lack of mass deportations or of any attempt to depopulate the country, as well as the aid sent to prevent starvation were all signs of a change that vindicated the precision of her categories of analysis (xxxvi). This is true insofar as it demonstrates that her categories can distinguish between those regimes which are strictly totalitarian and those which are not. But in terms of the genetic plane of the explanation it deepens the puzzle. Why should totalitarianism perish with Stalin?[3] Arendt's concept of mortality may give us grounds to believe that 'everything done in history is doomed' (Arendt, 1958a:246), including Stalin's creations. Arendt's concept of natality, of fresh beginnings with each birth, may provide the ontological basis for hope (1958a:247). But surely there need to be mediations between statement of these general principles of the human condition and explanation of specific historical changes.

The absence of these mediations and the difficulties of reconciling the genetic and analytic moments of her argument must have contributed to the feeling among those who selectively appropriated her ideas that such a separation was desirable. Once Arendt's concern with the nature of totalitarianism was removed from the context of the dynamic of modernity, it is easy to see how her interest in the conditions which make free human action possible might be considered so much unnecessary philosophical baggage, cluttering up the business of producing an accurate description of the techniques of domination. Such considerations may have been powerful influences on the reception of her concept and its later modifications, but they are not sufficient in themselves to explain its ideological appropriation. Important circumstances extrinsic to the theory itself, which are haltingly perceived but never thoroughly incorporated in it, must also be acknowledged.

Arendt had recognised that 'every fully-fledged ideology has been created and improved as a political weapon and not as a theoretical doctrine' (1958a:159) and that 'the survivors of the trenches did not become pacifists' (1958a:328). Yet she failed to take sufficient notice of the thoroughly militarised nature of modern industrial states (see Giddens, 1985) and of the fact that no real demobilisation accompanied the end of the Second World War. As a result, the concept of totalitarianism escaped her control and the dread she had so vividly captured in her work was appropriated in the service of civilian mobilisation. The fiction of the world-wide communist conspiracy was translated in the United States into the ostracism and persecution of the 'enemies' of the free world. That this self-styled 'anti-totalitarian' movement should have reached its zenith after Stalin's death must for Arendt have been a supreme moment of historical irony.

Notes

1 In a footnote to the revised version of her book she was moved to comment: 'the totalitarian tendencies of McCarthyism in the United States showed most glaringly in the attempt not merely to persecute Communists, but to force every citizen to furnish proof of not being a Communist' (356).
2 Typical of this response is the entry in the Macmillan *Student Encyclopedia of Sociology* under the heading of 'Totalitarianism':

> The term 'totalitarian' was first used by Mussolini... Subsequently it came to be used by political sociologists to characterize features common to the political systems of Hitler's Germany and Stalin's Russia... it was popularized during the Cold War period... As an explanatory concept totalitarianism fails, as an image of frightening possibilities... it offers a salutary warning (Mann, 1983:399).

3 Clearly the application of the concept of totalitarianism to Soviet societies and its periodisation continues to bedevil analysts. Agnes Heller, in *Dictatorship over Needs* attempts, rather controversially, to resolve these difficulties by adopting Mussolini's first phase definition of totalitarianism to cover most of the history of the USSR, including the present, while distinguishing Stalin's regime under the label 'terroristic totalitarianism' clearly inspired by Arendt (Feher, Heller, & Markus, 1983:137–217).

III
Jewish identity and conscience

Gisela T. Kaplan

6 Hannah Arendt: the life of a Jewish woman

The story of Hannah Arendt cannot be told in the way in which she herself was able to recount Rahel Varnhagen's life: as a story 'as she herself might have told it' (Arendt, 1974:xv). Hannah Arendt had two lives: the German–Jewish one and that of her new world citizenship in the United States.

This paper will concentrate on Hannah Arendt's German–Jewishness, specifically on the socio-historical context of that condition. It is the first part of her life, however, to which a German, even a German–Jewish, writer of a post-World War II generation can only barely gain access. A gulf so vast separates Hannah Arendt's youth from the post-holocaust era that imaginings are scarcely able to recreate the culture, life, or *zeitgeist* of her German–Jewish upbringing. There is no road to that past of her childhood in Königsberg via a subjective understanding from the other side of the abyss, modern West Germany. Every access has been bombed, destroyed, or distorted. The Nazi regime and the holocaust together have created unusually sharp fractures—fractures not like those in prisms but like those caused by earthquakes. There was, after all, a zero hour (*Stunde Null*) in Germany,[1] at least for those social groups that were irretrievably wiped out, among them a German–Jewish middle class to which Hannah Arendt's family belonged.

The handful of Jews remaining in modern West Germany today have little if anything in common with the cultural, social, and political existence of the German Jews of the prewar era i.e. with the kind of environment and self-understanding (*selbstverständnis*) of Hannah Arendt's generation. It is worthwhile expanding on the postwar period. In West Germany today, the ghosts of the past keep reappearing, as Merz so poignantly argues: 'There are too many dead

Jews alive in Germany today — even if fewer anti-Semites are about' (Merz, 1974:291). Those few of Hannah Arendt's generation who survived the holocaust and stayed in Germany are burnt-out cases, psychologically destroyed (*seelisch endgelöst*), as Broder notes. They live a shadow existence and generally do not enter into debates on German–Jewish issues (Broder 1979:85). Others of the same generation who live in West Germany today often trace their family histories back to Eastern Europe. They are not transmitters of the German–Jewish tradition, nor would they want to be. Tragically, the same generation when and where it escaped the holocaust has often not fared much better outside Germany. Unlike Hannah Arendt, they endure a home-sickness for a Germany that no longer exists which makes them oddly out of place anywhere in the world. The publication *Heimat ist anderswo* (Home is Elsewhere, 1983) written by *Yekkes* (German Jews) in Israel is an exemplification of the problem. Alice Schwarz-Gardos, the editor, calls the contributors split and truly contradictory personalities who live with a sense of homelessness and yearn for their places of childhood.

Then there are those whom Broder calls contemptuously the so-called *Berufsjuden* (professional Jews) who will speak on certain official occasions like the Week of Brotherhood — at times without any discernible mandate from the Jewish communities — but who remain non-committal otherwise (Broder, 1979:11). Official representatives of Jewish organisations have likewise played highly ambiguous roles in the public arena because of their self-imposed programme of recon-ciliation with Germans. Then there are those who are forever just about to leave West Germany but never do — aptly called the *Kofferjuden* (suitcase Jews). West Germany for them is and remains a temporary abode with permanent residency status: they are uprooted in their own country, staying but not living in it, occupying a house but not a home, speaking the language but not communicating; fence-sitters (*Zaungäste*) as well as émigrés, people whose internal emigration makes them foreigners in their own country (Brandt, 1979:71).

The younger generations born after the war have a profile all their own, as any younger generation has, but it often is not one constructed in positive ways. Their Jewishness is either discarded, or affirmed in a semi-alienating way. The martyrdom of the parents lives on. Through the distortion of time the question of identity cannot be answered by the parents, as Lea Fleischmann argues in *Dies ist nicht mein Land* (This is not My Land, 1981) (see also Brandt, 1979:72). Moreover, the present fragmentation and the small numbers of Jews in West Germany today (a mere 0.1 per cent of the population as against 0.8 per cent in prewar Germany) has implications of almost existentialist dimensions. Goral puts this most cogently when, in pondering upon his identity and place in modern German society, he states that he lives 'in a Germany without Jews and in so far then I live here without myself' (Goral, 1979:220).

However, the Jewish question has been kept alive, not just through the tasks of *Wiedergutmachung* (compensation) but through the existence of Israel. The existence of Israel has had considerable impact on the postwar West German climate. This climate, so Bernstein argues, is and has remained an unhealthy one. The *Unbefangenheit* (unselfconsciousness) has gone once and for all (Bernstein, 1979:39). Moreover, the problem with conciliation is also a problem of audience. In West Germany today there are performances staged, but for what and for whom?[2] Bernd Engelmann's book of 1979 on the Jewish issue could not have had a more apt title than *Deutschland ohne Juden* (Germany without Jews) for the debates are held without the victims, without those German citizens who were betrayed and deprived of their civil rights. The speeches sound hollow in an 'aryanised' space. Goral (1979:207) speaks of his written monologue, sent on a voyage into no-man's sea (*Eine Flaschenpost ins Niemandsmeer*), addressee unknown, so Brand argues, because Jews in West Germany are a 'state of affairs without future' (Brandt, 1979:75). The Jewish question today then is, as Goral rightly says, much more a German question than a Jewish one (Goral, 1979:220).

In other words, the German Jews of the prewar period are no more, many of them buried in 'the grave of the winds', as Celan wrote in the haunting poem 'Death Fugue'. Although Hannah Arendt possibly did not conceive of the extent of the barbaric final solution that was to come, she already knew when she fled Germany in 1933, aged 27, that the German–Jewish question and with it the German–Jewish experience was relegated to history. This knowledge justified her writing of Rahel Varnhagen's life[3] as a statement of history that had come to an end; a history unique both within the annals of Germany and throughout the wanderings of Jews in the Diaspora (Arendt, 1974:xvii).

It is equally justifiable to attempt to draw a bridge between Hannah Arendt and Rahel Varnhagen's German–Jewishness as something historically significant and unresolved. Rahel Varnhagen (1771–1833) and Hannah Arendt (1906–1975) belong to a very small group of exceptional German–Jewish women whose lives, compelling on their own account, provide important historical insights as well. They represent start and end points in the history of German–Jewish relationships: Rahel Varnhagen strives for entry into German society and culture; Hannah Arendt, who fully achieved this, is forced to make her exit from that society.

For Hannah Arendt, the study of Rahel Varnhagen's life was at once a search for identity, a process of self-identification, and an opportunity to study German and Jewish history. She was less interested in the processes of that history than in the individual human being in that process. How did Rahel respond and how did she make her world, what were her strengths and how were they asserted in contexts often so unconducive to individual Jewish self-confidence and action? *Rahel Varnhagen: The Life of a Jewess* was almost completed by the time Hannah Arendt left Germany. It is an important work in so far as she clarifies several elements of that uneasy relationship between Germans and Jews which ended so suddenly and drastically in 1933. Moreover, through her study of Rahel Varnhagen, she began the process of *dis*similation which was partly prepared by the Blumenfeld circle (see Kessler, in this volume).

The politicisation of Hannah Arendt took little time to complete. She saw earlier than most German Jews that national socialism spelt impending disaster for Jews and she decided quite rightly to leave early (in 1933), not without promising herself that she would devote her future energies to Jewish causes. She argued already then:

> When one is attacked as a Jew, one must defend oneself *as a Jew*. Not as a German, not as a world citizen, not as an upholder of the Rights of Man (Young-Bruehl, 1982:109).

In the story of Rahel Varnhagen Hannah Arendt first develops her concepts of the 'pariah' and the 'parvenu' betokening 'legitimate' and 'illegitimate' ways of dealing with outsider status. The parvenu, social climber, assimilationist, must deny self in order to make an individual and personal success of life. The parvenu is seen by Arendt as one of the most loathsome of creatures. It is as if even the reader is bathed in her scorn:

> The parvenu's overestimation of himself, which often seems quite mad, arises out of the tremendous effort, and the straining of all his forces and talents, which are incumbent upon him if he is to climb only a few steps up the social ladder. The smallest success, so hardwon, necessarily dazzles him with an illusory: everything is possible; the smallest failure instantly sends him hurtling back into the depths of his social nullity, misleads him into the shabbiest kind of worship of success (Arendt, 1974:201–202).

The pariah, on the other hand, draws strength from separateness, neither denying it nor apologising for it, but insisting on the uniqueness of individuals as an ubiquitous phenomenon, and one on which formal equality must be based (see Markus in this volume).

There are obvious costs to being a pariah and no one could have been a better judge of these than Rahel Varnhagen. In Varnhagen's letter of 1810 to Alexander von der Marwitz (the existence of which Hannah Arendt was in all likelihood not aware)[4] she comments:

That's why I like that quote in *Wilhelm Meister* so much... 'O, how strange it is that human beings are denied not just the impossible but all too often that which is possible!' This is the basis and subtext and the whole terrible joke with which the pulse of our life is put into action from the start. This is a thinking observation ... and it has always made me very quiet.[5]

However, in the same letter she encapsulates much of what Hannah Arendt was to say later of the pariah. In response to Marwitz's letter and his complaint about his career — although a member of the aristocracy he was an outsider and in sharp disagreement with predominant ideology on several issues — she writes:

> But what do you want? You want to become a major, a general, a minister, a professor in a world you don't like; which you cannot change as a major, general, minister, and professor; more than that: in which you cannot become any of these as long as you remain a worthwhile person.[6]

Finally she entreats him with the words: 'Don't leave yourself!' (*Verlassen Sie sich nicht selbst!*), meaning that he was not to be disloyal to himself, not to put at ransom what he believed and represented.[7]

Hannah Arendt's concept of the pariah may have been indebted to Varnhagen, or to Nietzsche and Weber, but it is important to note here that it was developed by her as a 20th century woman. And once it is pronounced from the vantage point of someone like Arendt — whose 'misfortune' it was to have been born a Jew and a woman and who, later, was forced to become a refugee and an immigrant — the concept of pariah becomes fundamentally modern and pertinent. Every single one of the labels she wore is potentially and in reality a marker for discrimination and oppression. Ironically, we only know this since the notion of civil equality has appeared, as Arendt argues in *The Origins of Totalitarianism* (Arendt, 1951:54). When basic equality is supposed to be a right but is not translated into daily life, the contrasts between reality and myth, experience and ideal, become all the more apparent and the labels, as a justification for discrimination, all the more obnoxious. However, Hannah Arendt derives from her concept the strength to consciously adopt the position of the pariah, a stance that can be used as rebellion, as a starting point for thought, judgement, political action and ultimately for freedom, a freedom not for the isolated individual but for all. Unlike Hannah Arendt's later work, the book on Rahel Varnhagen is written with marked personal compassion and love, just the qualities that Arendt had valued in Varnhagen.

Rahel Varnhagen, born as Rahel Levin in 1771, lived in a period in which the discovery of the humanness of all members of the human species was just beginning to be interpreted as logically requiring some recognition in law and civil treatment. Yet although notions of fraternity and equality echoed from the days of the French Revolution, Rahel was never a recipient of the most basic civil rights. Her undoubted importance in literary and cultural life was never translated into citizenship rights—not until she married Varnhagen.

Her life spanned a decisive period of political upheaval and one of the most important German cultural epochs. Rahel was five years old when the United States proclaimed its independence, 15 years old when Moses Mendelssohn died in Berlin, 18 years old at the beginning of the French Revolution and a mere 20 years old when her salon in the *Jägerstrasse* in Berlin became one of the focal points of German intellectual life. In 1806, the ramshackle Holy Roman Empire of German Nations finally collapsed, and with it her circle at the salon.[8] The spirit of openness and humanity, the cosmopolitanism of the Enlightenment and the Weimar classical period gave way to a new closed-mindedness in which militarism and certain unsavoury trends of German nationalism were able to thrive.[9] After a number of unhappy love affairs and engagements Rahel was finally baptised and married at the age of 43, at the beginning of the Congress of Vienna (1814). She died in 1833.

Throughout her life she had been able to attract the company and friendship of famous men, engaging with them in debate and in extensive correspondence. Her early correspondence was still in Yiddish but she later wrote only in German. She was not rich. In fact, her social and economic situation gradually deteriorated, and at times became desperate, especially after her mother's death in 1809. Nor was she particularly 'cultivated' or beautiful (Arendt, 1974:6). She completed her life as the wife of a Prussian chargé d'affaires, a baptised Jewess, isolated but economically secure. Rahel Varnhagen witnessed during her lifetime not only the first attempted reforms in the status of Jews but also their rescission by 1819, followed by a new wave of anti-Semitism and pogroms. Legal equality of Jews was not achieved until the formation of the German Empire in 1871, almost 40 years after her death. The few Jews who, up to 1871, lived well and in relative peace were privileged or what Hannah Arendt called 'exception' Jews.

All the elements of the problems of Jewish emancipation in 19th century Germany are embodied in the life of Rahel Varnhagen. For Germans and Jews alike the concept of emancipation was a double-edged sword. To those Germans defending the spirit of Enlightenment and advocating dramatic social change, the visible court Jew, as a supporter of kings and governments, appeared as a representative of the old order, an order which needed to be torn down. On the other hand, this same spirit dictated that Jews be as free to choose the kind of life that they wished to lead as any other human being.

Of the Jewish population a few wanted emancipation, but for different reasons. Of the many who did not want it, some shunned it because of their fear of a disintegration of Jewish communities; others, from the well-to-do group of 'exception Jews', preferred to keep their privileges; still others, like Rahel Varnhagen, were fiercely against emancipation because, as Hannah Arendt sensed, they thought that it was probably going to be even harder to escape from reformed Judaism than from orthodoxy (Arendt, 1974:125). For many, as for Rahel, escape was the only wish (ibid:7). Moreover, the emancipatory movements in German territories neither coincided with processes of democratisation, to allude here to Rürup's thesis, nor had they evolved from grass roots origins via a revolution.

Thus the emancipation of Jews was a superimposed, haphazardly expedient, and half-heartedly pursued process that for Jews, as Hannah Arendt rightly says, first presupposed wealth and second, for a short period at least, was of interest only to the nobility and rulers. Hannah Arendt argues that Rahel Varnhagen's — and for that matter also Henriette Herzl's — success in Berlin as an 'idyll of mixed society' was a brief chance constellation 'in an era of social transition' and nothing more (Arendt, 1974:57).

It was deeply distasteful to Arendt that Jews chose to attune themselves to the changed environment of the 19th century not as a group but as individuals, as social climbers, as parvenus. The Jewish reaction to the new demands showed no signs of solidarity, consensus, or communal attempts at political action. The Jews were joining enemy camps, sometimes becoming openly anti-Semitic themselves and, like Rahel Varnhagen, referring to their own fellow Jews as a 'scattered, neglected and more than all that, a deservedly despised nation' (Arendt, 1974:220).

People like Rahel Varnhagen had to learn to reinterpret their station of birth in a new way. Those who turned away from Judaism were not saved, for they had to exchange a secure religious identity, consolidated by the tradition of Judaism, for a new tag of Jewishness. Jewish history was seen by many as the sordid product of the ghetto, and Jews began to confess their own inferiority (Arendt, 1974:8). As Hannah Arendt explains, Rahel's life, at least in its early decades, was bound by this inferiority. Rahel Varnhagen was so obsessed with the curse of her Jewishness that no personal behaviour, thought or wish could eliminate it. At the age of 20 she wrote: 'I shall never be convinced that I am a Shlemihl and a Jewess... that's why I am still living' (1974:9).[10] The fight against her Jewishness became a fight against herself (1974:13). She was overcome by intense shame, unable to forget that shame for a single second. She said: 'The Jew must be extirpated from us... even if life were uprooted in the process' (Arendt, 1974:120).

It is when she discusses Rahel Varnhagen's self-effacing remarks and self-recriminations that Hannah Arendt's very different position as an emancipated Jewess of the 20th century surfaces, sometimes as impatience and sometimes in rather unfair judgements. Unfair in the sense that she dwells too little on the constant barrage of hostility and contempt that surrounded the Jew from *birth* making the label, indeed, unbearable. When Rahel declares in the letter to Marwitz (mentioned above) that she is an 'infamous demoiselle', she is making oblique reference to the views held by German gentiles in general. And while she wishes that she were not called by those names, there are passages to indicate that she herself does not and cannot quite believe that they are true as descriptions of herself.

The German negativity towards Rahel Varnhagen's identity as a Jewess can perhaps best be gauged by the remarks of benevolent and well-intentioned 'friends' who visited her. Thus, Wilhelm von Humboldt, one of the most noted enlightened aristocrats—but also one of the 'keenest and most malicious gossips of his age' (Arendt, 1974:201)—speaks of Rahel Varnhagen in a letter to his wife as the 'little Levin girl' (Rahel was 38 years old then). He explains that the reputation of 'the little one' (*der Kleinen*) had not exactly improved, describing her as an 'eternal socialite'—but he called in twice to see her during his travel on that occasion (Vigliero, 1987:54).

The problem of self-recrimination, even of absorbing some of the anti-Semitism surrounding Jews, is one only too familiar to Jews who lived through German or other fascist nightmares, as Sibylle Krause-Burger argued recently in her film *Dies ist und bleibt mein Land* (This is and remains my country, 1981). But it cannot be valid for a person of Hannah Arendt's generation and upbringing at the crucial moment in German–Jewish history, one hundred years after Rahel Varnhagen, and before the systematic extermination of Jews in central and Eastern Europe.

The Franco-Russian war of 1812–14, in which Prussia was involved, gave those Jews who had just obtained citizenship rights (in 1812) an opportunity to demonstrate their patriotism. Hannah Arendt expresses contempt and annoyance at Rahel's patriotic behaviour which she calls 'abominable as all philanthropic ladies' and 'thoroughly stupid and commonplace' (Arendt, 1974:196). Yet she admits that the Jews' ostentatious readiness for self-sacrifice during this war merely exemplified 'how insecure they felt despite the edict' (1974:194). Such a sense of insecurity was indeed more than justified, for by 1819 the edict was withdrawn and new pogroms swept across Prussia and shouts of 'Down with the Jews' could be heard everywhere. 'How loathsome it is always to establish one's identity first. That alone is enough to make it so repulsive to be a Jew', wrote Rahel Varnhagen despondently in those years (Arendt, 1974:219). Her marriage to Varnhagen protected her and exposed her simultaneously. Despite her baptism, she was still a Jew. Or, as Hannah Arendt tellingly remarks: 'Having assimilated to her enemies without being accepted by them, without being received to the point where the past was forgotten' (1974:220), she 'tumbled into the hands of enemies who rejoiced in having for once caught a wholly isolated Jew, an abstract Jew, a case which they could treat now as the very essence of Jewishness' (Arendt, 1974:221).

In Hannah Arendt's view, Rahel Varnhagen nevertheless emerges as a great woman, despite her false and desperate struggle to be accepted in non-Jewish society and to be seen as being legitimately at home in German secular culture. Perhaps Rahel Varnhagen was lucky at least in her ability to explore personal relationships. Her many love affairs during the brief spell of liberation in the name of Romanticism (popularised by Schlegel's *Lucinde* and the cult of the Saint-Simonians, advocating sensuality, even free love) could be weathered much better at that time than would have been possible several decades earlier or later. Even these love affairs were symptomatic of her yearning to belong. As Elisabeth Young-Bruehl put it so beautifully, Rahel Varnhagen's life 'was a woman's search for a homeland of friendship' (Young-Bruehl, 1982:86).

Rahel was a woman with whom Arendt felt a great affinity. She shared with Rahel Varnhagen, so Elisabeth Young-Bruehl writes, the unspoilt and unconventional intelligence combined with an absorbing interest in people and a truly passionate nature. Rahel had a sensibility and vulnerability very like Hannah Arendt's own (Young-Bruehl, 1982:56). Arendt admired Rahel's originality, her hunger for knowledge, her way of sustaining herself through her dark doubts about her own identity and position. Most important, so Hannah Arendt claims, Rahel understood that total assimilation also meant assimilating anti-Semitism, and this Rahel was not willing to do. She therefore became a pariah, a woman of strength of character who was prepared to face her origins again. At the end of her life Rahel Varnhagen says the famous words:

> The thing which all my life seemed to me the greatest shame, which was the misery and misfortune of my life — having been born a Jewess — this I should on no account now wish to have missed (Arendt, 1974:3).

In turning now to a comparison of Rahel Varnhagen's life with Hannah Arendt's own upbringing and social position, it may be all too tempting to exaggerate the improvements that had been achieved for Jews and for women in the span of less than one hundred years. While some of the differences are remarkable, one needs to keep in mind that concurrent with the 'liberation' of Jews came backlashes of a severe and potentially horrific kind. Barely a decade after the unification of Germany in 1871 anti-Semitic leagues and associations were formed. Historians like Treitschke identified Jews with the 'twin dangers' of internationalism and liberalism (Sachar, 1977:224). Men like Fritsch were able to publish and gain support for newspapers and journals like *Antisemitische Correspondenz* (founded 1885). By 1893, explicitly anti-Semitic politics had entered into parliament and union movements (see Rürup, 1975:109). Books like K. E. Dühring's *Die Judenfrage als Frage des Racencharakters und seiner Schädlichkeiten für Völkerexistenz, Sitte and Cultur* (The Jewish Question as a Question of Racial Character and its Harmfulness for the Existence, Morals and Culture of Nations, 1880) were extremely popular. This text had gone through its fifth edition by 1901. Under the cloak of serious scholarship the ideas of race, often in the most racist terms, were debated and approved nationally and internationally. The idea of life as 'devoid of value' (*Menschenunwert*) sprung up in debates on eugenics concerning handicapped, retarded, psychologically unstable people, and 'inferior races' like Jews and Negroes, Slavs and Gypsies (Chorover, 1979:95–96).

In other words, by the time Hannah Arendt was born in 1906, there existed a well-entrenched new anti-Semitism and a lively racist debate on eugenics. Theories circulated about the superiority of the 'nordic race' and political activism was geared to raise anti-Semitism to national acceptability. Accordingly, there was a manifest so-called 'Jewish question'. Theodor Herzl's tract *The Jewish State* of 1896, now a classic of Zionism, added another dimension and new sets of demands.

Amongst the best known Jewish writers and activists there was no consensus on how to solve the Jewish question, and the question of who they were themselves was answered very differently in each case (cf. Mosse, 1985). Some advocated Zionism, some socialism, some urged greater assimilation and some proposed a return to the ghetto in order to rethink Jewish values there. The scale of commitment to their own Jewishness, as Bieber argues, ranged 'from strict orthodoxy to a complete break with Judaism, from mildly German allegiance to complete assimilationist and ultra German nationalism'. There were 'no common denominators of interest in the concept of a Jew and its unreflected application became problematic' (Bieber, 1979:35). It became problematic not just for German Jews as a group but for the individual as well. Ernst Toller for instance who, like others, wanted to escape his Jewishness moved from a position of assimilatory ultranationalism and super-patriotism to cosmopolitanism and socialism (Pomeranz Carmely, 1981:84).

The new pressure of defining German Jewishness created psychological and intellectual crises and spawned strangely chimeric ideas and utopias. With such original thinkers as Bloch and Benjamin for instance it gave rise to Jewish ideas without Judaism, as Rabinbach argues, such as modern Jewish messianism (Rabinbach, 1985). Ritual murders of Jews made sombre news (Mosse, 1978:107) and political murders of Jewish people such as Liebknecht, Rosa Luxemburg, or Walther Rathenau, the foreign minister, increased (all during Hannah Arendt's youth). Jewish assimilationists despaired chiefly because such events undeniably showed that their own assimilationist goals were far from being appreciated by German society. Thus Jacob Wassermann commented on the death of Rathenau:

> Just as I did he had felt like a German, just as I he felt rejected, misunderstood and unappreciated by Germans and unrewarded for all the subordination and willingness for self-sacrifice.[11]

Of the non-assimilationists of German language background, Kafka probably gave the most cynical answer:

> One only recognises the correctness or incorrectness of a path when one has arrived. At least we are going now. We are moving, thus we are living. Around us, anti-Semitism is growing but this is good. The Talmud says that we Jews are like olives. We give our best when we are being squashed and crushed...[12]

It is into this climate that Hannah Arendt was born, but she was also born into the historical moment when full legal rights for Jews and to some extent for women were a reality. Strong political women's movements had come into existence, led by women such as Gertrud Bäumer, Helene Lange and Clara Zetkin. German–Jewish women had just organised themselves into a separate association, realising that they were not only at a disadvantage in being Jews but in being women as well (Kaplan, 1981:153–81).

With the proclamation of the Weimar Republic in 1918 began the one and 'only span of fifteen years of the German–Jewish symbiosis[13] in which those Jews who had adhered to their faith actually had the same personal opportunities assured as any other group' (Gamm, 1979:95). Arendt was born with full citizenship rights and by the time she was 12 years old, in 1918, women were enfranchised. Neither as a woman nor as a Jew did she have to face serious legal or political discrimination. Even social discrimination, in her case, was minimal. The family, assimilated and well-regarded in fairly enlightened Königsberg, had ways of dealing with social discrimination. There were, as Hannah Arendt's biographer quotes her as saying, definite rules of conduct which ensured that 'her dignity was protected, absolutely protected' (Young-Bruehl, 1982:12).

Hannah Arendt never suffered from early identity crises. The family was sure that all of its members were Germans and they saw no need for making special excuses for being Reform Jews either. The grandfather Max 'would hear of nothing that cast his Germanness into doubt' (Young-Bruehl, 1982:8). Schools were open to her and universities had opened their doors to women in Germany just a little more than a decade before she entered them. Moreover, she was very attractive, could channel her intelligence in ways that were socially acceptable, and had no difficulties in attracting friends. In the transitional, open, even frantic atmosphere of the 1920s she could engage in a series of love affairs and still marry the 'right Jewish boy', Günter Stern (later Günter Anders), whose parents had become famous for their joint work called *The Psychology of Early Childhood* (Young-Bruehl, 1982:77).

Hannah Arendt and her generation represent both the highest point of Jewish emancipation and liberation on German soil and also their end. She, as the daughter of assimilated Reform Jews (but Jews nonetheless), had learned not to fear, had no need for these terrible recriminations and masochistic attacks of inferiority that marked Rahel Varnhagen's life. Ghetto Jews were unknown to her, the Jewish question bored her intensely as a young girl and all the talk about Zionism was of little interest (Young-Bruehl, 1982:91). Her self-concept was not thwarted by a multitude of legalised oppressions. She was first of all Hannah Arendt, then a German and then a Jew. Elisabeth Young-Bruehl describes her character as 'bristling with obstinacy' (1982:xii), 'headstrong, frighteningly intelligent and far too independent' (1982:29); she depicts her as adventurous, loving life in a wilful romantic manner, smoking cigars and being 'assertively unconventional' (1982:101). Apparently she remained so all her life. Despite personal tragedy—she lost her father when she was very young—she grew up in an environment that fostered inner strength and the development of a secure identity. In short, Hannah Arendt was handed the fruits of women's and Jewish emancipation on a platter.

A pinnacle of women's liberation seemed to have been reached in the 1920s, before women were swamped by a new and virulent outbreak of a national socialist variant of the 'kinder, küche, kirche' (children, kitchen, church) ideology (Kaplan and Adams, 1988). A pinnacle of Jewish emancipation was reached at the same time with full legal, social, and political rights for all Jews of German nationality and not just the excepted few (Bach, 1984:216), before anti-Semitism reached heights that destroyed even the most optimistic hopes for any future coexistence of Jews and Germans.

It is with this kind of 'baggage' that Hannah Arendt faced increasing anti-Semitism, national socialist propaganda, and harassment. Fortunately for her, her mother and family had never obliterated their Jewishness. Fortunately also for her, she had been exposed to discussions and disputes on the Jewish question, at first especially through the Blumenfeld debates which had given her some concept of Jewishness. She and her family were therefore not amongst those German Jews of her time who had denied their Jewish heritage completely to themselves and to their children, and who were extremely vulnerable and ultimately crushed when asked to accept a Jewish identity and ridiculed for thinking that they were Germans.

Hannah Arendt's background also says something about the German middle class. Despite her mother's interest and moderate involvement in politics (social democracy), Hannah grew up as an apolitical German, as she later confessed in a letter to Gershom Scholem (Young-Bruehl, 1982:104). Politics and history continued to be marginal for her, even during her student days. In her study of Rahel Varnhagen she describes Rahel as intensely apolitical and unworldly, despite her wide correspondence with people of renown, and she criticises Rahel for becoming aware of political conditions only when they affected her own small personal world (Arendt, 1974:21). One must assume that such criticism was, to a large measure, self-criticism on Hannah Arendt's part. Arendt's transformation into political awareness was partly foisted upon her by circumstances, by the indisputable fact that her environment thought her a Jew and that such Jewishness increasingly had a number of consequences.

She left Germany as a person intact in her identity, and her attitude to persecution and oppression could well be described by quoting a saying of Rabbi Hillel which also signifies long entrenched Jewish tradition:

Im ein ani li mi li
ukeshe ani leatzmi ma ani
Ve'im lo achshav eimatai.[14]

If I am not for myself, who is for me? But if I am only for myself, what am I? And if not now, then when? These are questions Hannah Arendt might have asked. They contain a whole philosophy of identity and action (Fleischauer and Klein, 1978:32–33). From this view springs the strength necessary for fighting back.

Hannah Arendt's enforced 'consciousness-raising' experience — that one could choose or reject Judaism but could not run away from Jewishness because it was an existential given which was inescapable (Feldman, 1978:20) — made her investigate in exile why it was so difficult to rouse Jews to some concerned political action. In her various analyses she attempted to trace the causes of what she perceived as the docility, apathy, and political stupidity that allowed Jews to be led to their own slaughter without much of a protest.[15] This is the one question that Hannah Arendt, the prewar emancipated

German Jewess, has to some extent in common with the postwar generations who also asked why this could have happened.

Yehuda Bauer explains it in this way:

> The unique quality of Nazi Jew-hate was something so surprising, so outside of the experience of the civilized world, that the Jewish leadership as well as the Jewish people could not comprehend it. Unbelievably, and therefore outwitted at every turn of the Nazi screw, they stood by and watched with ever-increasing despair as Nazi policy moved from one phase to the next. The post-holocaust generation has difficulty understanding this basic psychological barrier to action on the part of Jews—and non-Jews—during the Nazi period. We already know what happened, and that mass murder was possible; they, who lived at the time, did not. For them it was a totally new reality that was unfolding before their shocked eyes and paralyzed minds (Bauer, 1978:7).

Hannah Arendt, instead, chooses to give a global explanation. One of her tenets is spelt out in the first pages of the *Origins of Totalitarianism* where she says:

> Jewish history offers the extraordinary spectacle of a people, unique in this respect, which began its history with a well-defined concept of history... and then, without giving up this concept avoided all political action for two thousand years (Arendt, 1951:8).

She is, of course, not quite right in this view. There had been uprisings and attempts at political action. She herself conceded for instance that the Sabbatian movement in the 17th century was, at heart, a great political movement of real popular dimension which had an exclusive concern with reality and action (Arendt, 1978:104). But after this movement failed, she claims, European Jewry 'retired from the public scene of history' (ibid). The 18th and 19th centuries were marked by individual Jewish attempts to gain acceptance and fame wherever possible. The kind of Jewish influx into the arts and sciences, she argues, 'resulted in the development of a truly international society whose basis was inter-European, non-national and worldless'. And 'worldlessness, alas, is always a form of barbarism' (in Feldman, 1978:26–27).

In some ways, Arendt seems to echo the words of the philosopher Moses Mendelssohn, the most illustrious protégé of Frederick II of Prussia (Kampmann, 1981:98ff), who had said, somewhat more apologetically than Hannah Arendt would have done:

> The long oppression to which we have been condemned by a prejudice too well established lies like a dead weight on the wings of the spirit and makes them incapable of ever attempting the high flight of those who are born free. It is not our fault, yet we cannot deny that this has made us abandon all activity. It has changed into

a monk's virtue and only manifests itself in prayer and suffering, not in action.[16]

Furthermore, so Hannah Arendt argues, the processes of assimilation spelt the end of traditional Jewish communities: the change from Judaism to Jewishness, in the form in which this transformation occurred, changed Jewishness into a psychological quality rather than into a potentially political one (in Feldman, 1978:43).

Hannah Arendt's thesis on the apolitical nature of Jews and their worldlessness and lack of a national history is of particular interest in comparison with German history. The German bourgeoisie in the 18th and the better part of the 19th century was largely condemned to an apolitical role in the world. It too lacked a national history and, in 1806, was made keenly aware that the last pretences to political unity had vanished. The Jewish emancipation laws were beginning to be implemented at a time when German prospects for political unity, let alone nationhood, were far from clear. Germany did not exist. Its fragmented history, intertwined in complicated ways with histories of other nations like Sweden or France, was a history of territories. The sovereignty of princes, even of the smallest principalities, was assured, not only in 1648 but again in 1815 and even later (Kaplan, 1984:44–48). Economic, cultural and social developments differed vastly between territories.

In a sense, German territories were also 'worldless' and their citizens either had the choice of suffocating in the smallness of petty sovereignties (the Mehring thesis)[17] or to consider themselves citizens of the world. Thus Kant, as a world citizen—although he never left Königsberg—is as much a product of that environment as the hopeless philistine about whom the poet and political observer Heinrich Heine (Rahel Varnhagen's youthful friend) had a good deal to say.

Her thesis that 'worldlessness' can fall back into barbarism might have been supported by Thomas Mann, the German Nobel prize winner for literature of 1929, who had to leave Germany just a year after Hannah Arendt did. In his speech 'Germany and the Germans', which he delivered in 1945 at Princeton University as an American citizen, he made a number of remarks concerning barbarism. He says that Germans (at the same time as Jews) were concerned with the idea of freedom. The concept should have been understood as a moral, innerpolitical concept but the Germans, unhappily, chose to understand it as a psychological one, to be displayed only in foreign policy.

Why, he asks, must the German desire for freedom always end in inner unfreedom? His answer is that Germany never had a revolution and had never learnt to combine the concept of the nation with that of freedom—a view that Walter Grab would probably share. Thus, Thomas Mann continues, the German concept of freedom was always 'anti-European, *"völkisch"* and close to barbarism' (1974:169–170): the emphasis was always on political unity at the price of individual liberty, and on conformity for the sake of national identity, and on an assertion of that identity at the expense of individual difference. There was little chance of democratisation and liberalisation.

The weak, politically inexperienced, and immature German bourgeoisie was finally defeated in 1848. Thomas Mann's insights support Rürup's thesis that the strands of political development were inimical to emancipation (including Jewish emancipation).

When the catastrophe of the new Nazi Jew-hatred actually happened and unfolded, Hannah Arendt, the refugee and German–Jewish exile, was adamant that Jewish existence should be acknowledged as such and not be obfuscated by considerations of national identities, as she so poignantly and passionately argued in 1943 in her article 'We Refugees':

> If we should start telling the truth that we are nothing but Jews, it would mean that we expose ourselves to the fate of human beings who, unprotected by any specific law or political convention, are nothing but human beings (Arendt, 1943:65).

Arendt despised the inactivity, the 'monk's virtue of prayer and suffering' as Moses Mendelssohn had called it, the wailing for Germanness that was not to be, the lack of understanding that no superpatriotism was going to sway the Germans' view that all Jews, assimilated or not, were really nothing but Jews. She made vicious jokes about the Mr Cohens who thought that, having been 150 per cent Germans, they could then become convinced Czechs, thereafter loyal Austrians, and, when circumstances required their departure to France, suddenly transform themselves into extremely loyal and patriotic Frenchmen. She said then that so many Jews were 'willing to become loyal Hottentots, only to hide the fact that we are Jews' (1943:63).

In a curious way, Thomas Mann seemed to agree with Hannah Arendt. When he spoke at Princeton, he stressed that his kind of Germanness was best looked after (*aufgehoben*) in the United States.[18] Here he was a citizen of the world. Before that he had been granted Czech citizenship, which made no 'rhyme or reason' and would have resulted in a narrowness and certain alienation of his existence, in just the same way as if he had accidentally turned French or Italian (1945:162). Hannah Arendt was granted American citizenship only in 1951, years after Thomas Mann. What neither Hannah Arendt nor Thomas Mann says, but both imply, is that a New World country like the United States was capable of separating the rights to citizenship from a range of other criteria that belong to the realm of personal identity and being.

For Germans the forfeiting of individual difference was the first precondition for national identity. In European countries—including Germany—linguistic unity, cultural conformity, territorial and racial homogeneity, and even religious and political confluence were often seen as preconditions for claims to nationality and national identity. The idea that someone might diverge in language, religion, or even race and still be a legitimate citizen is one that, with very few exceptions (such as the Habsburg Empire), belongs to modern pluralistic societies. German Jews, on the whole, did not comprehend this option and neither did the Germans; probably they still do not to this day.

Thomas Mann and Hannah Arendt were both grateful to America for giving them political freedom through citizenship without demanding the price of assimilation at a personal level (Young-Bruehl, 1982:xiv). For Hannah Arendt, Mann's notion of world-citizenship was still too close to the notion of Kant's world-citizenship, born out of German territorialism, which she dismissed as 'nonsense' (Arendt, 1944:75). She became instead an American of German language,[19] a *citizen* but not a *national* in the European sense, and could therefore remain Hannah Arendt and a German Jew.

One might conclude by drawing attention to Hannah Arendt's assessment of Rahel Varnhagen's status: 'Exile was not a distinction, and unhappiness no merit. Yet exile and unhappiness had made her what she was' (Arendt, 1974:174). And then one is grateful to be able to add that, unlike Rahel Varnhagen, Hannah Arendt was able to transcend the stages of exile and allowed to have a voice, a very weighty one indeed, a voice that incorporated her past training, experience, and intellectual development.

Hannah Arendt claims that there has only ever been one outstanding genuine German Jew who was as German as he was Jewish, denying neither. That was Heinrich Heine (Arendt, 1944:74). In a sense, Hannah Arendt herself is that rare balance as well. Like Heine she had to leave Germany. Like him she never denied her Germanness or her love for the German language even after the holocaust ('after all it wasn't the German language that went crazy'), her indebtedness to the culture, her education, and to her friends (such as Karl Jaspers). But she was also not afraid of defending herself as a Jew and giving the Jewish crises her urgent attention.

Rahel Varnhagen was Hannah Arendt's closest friend. She could claim such friendship partly because Hannah Arendt stood in one and the same historical tradition with her famous predecessor. For post-holocaust generations the continuum has gone. Her German–Jewish experience is now a 'foreign country' where things were done and thought differently. What she salvaged across the ocean and the abyss of history for future generations of Jews is her strength of conviction, her strong self-assertion as a conscious pariah to which present day citizens can relate much more readily than to the crushing self-denial of a Rahel Varnhagen.

Notes

1 The issue of a 'zero hour' has been debated at great length, particularly in terms of continuities and discontinuities of ideas, values, cultural and literary practices, and expressions after 1945 cf. for instance Hans Mayer *Zur deutschen Literatur der Zeit*; Reinbeck bei Hamburg, 1967 or Heinrich Vormweg, 'Deutsche Literatur 1945-1960. Keine Stunde Null', in Manfred Durzak (ed) *Die deutsche Literatur der Gegenwart*, Stuttgart, 1971, pp. 13-30. Those who dispute the zero hour concept do so by focusing on German ideas and society. The German-Jewish tradition and existence is a different problem however.
2 All translations are by the author of this paper unless otherwise stated. In cases of historical source material the original German version will be rendered in the endnotes in order to preserve the authenticity of the text.
3 The name Rahel Varnhagen will be used throughout this paper, although she changed names several times during her life. She was born Rahel Levin, after her mother's death she called herself Rahel Robert and after the marriage to Varnhagen she became Antonie Frederike Varnhagen. Rahel Varnhagen is the name under which she became famous — due largely to the collation and pulication of her correspondence posthumously. It is also the name which best reflects her German-Jewish identity.
4 Until 1987, this letter was known only as a fragment, and a small excerpt at that. This fragment was reprinted by Helmut Rogge in his article 'Kleist und Rahel' in *Jahrbuch der Kleist-Gesellschaft 1923-1924*, Berlin, 1925, pp. 127-134. But it was omitted by another publication of the same year, edited by Heinrich Meisner, called *Rahel und Alexander von der Marwitz. Ein Bild aus der Zeit der Romantiker*, Gotha/Stuttgart. Hannah Arendt used the latter for her study of Rahel Varnhagen. The entire letter has been recovered by Consolina Vigliero; see Vigliero, C., 'Ein ungedruckter Brief von Rahel Levin' in *Leo Baeck Institute Bulletin*, New York, Jerusalem, Frankfurt/Main, 1987, pp.49-71.
5 Original text:

Darum gefällt mir ja der eine Text im Wilhelm Meister so! (Als Wilhelm zur aufgerissenen Aurelia endlich sagt): 'O, wie sonderbar ist es, daß dem Menschen nicht allein das Unmögliche, sondern auch so manches Mögliche versagt ist!' Dieses ist auch der Grundtext und der ganze furchtbare Witz, womit der Pulsschlag unseres Lebens von vornherein in Gang gebracht wird. Das ist ein denkendes Wort, (wenn auch Meister es oberflächlich gemeint hat), und hat mich immer sehr still gemacht (Cit. in Vigliero, op. cit., p. 51).

6 Original text:

Aber was wollen Sie denn? Ein Major, ein General, ein Minister, ein Professor werden, in einer Welt, die Ihnen nicht gefällt, die Sie weder als

Major, General, Minister oder Professor ändern können; ja in der Sie das alles gar nicht werden können, so lange sie taugen! (Cit. in Vigliero, p. 50).

7 Original text:

Ich meine werden Sie nie untreu! Gehen Sie nicht nach außen! Verlassen Sie sich nicht selbst! Ich kann Ihnen dann nicht mehr folgen und der Tod ist zwischen uns (Cited in Vigliero, p. 52).

8 The salon in the Jägerstraße was not the only one in Rahel's life. Once she had married Varnhagen and had moved back to Berlin, the Varnhagens together entertained in their salon from 1821–1832.

9 The kind of new world that Fichte announced in which 'the pillars of the new world were to be the whole nation rather than a class privileged by birth and by history' (Arendt, 1974:130), however, was not only fully endorsed by Rahel Varnhagen; it was actually a nationalism which she wholeheartedly embraced. Fichte's conception gave her hope for a new social order in which there might be a place for her. However, strands of German nationalism which built their claims for unity mainly on racial/ethnic categories excluded her and her fellow Jews.

10 To my knowledge, the term 'shlemihl' has not altered appreciably (or at all) since Rahel Varnhagen's time. In Heine's *Romanzero*, book 3 ('Hebraic Melodies') he introduces a Schlemihl ben Zuri Schadday, recognisably referring to the leader of the Simeons mentioned in the bible called Shelumiheel ben Zurishaddai, whom Heine allows to be killed by accident in a case of revenge with which he had nothing to do ('Jehuda ben Halevy', book 4). The shlemihl there and today denotes an unlucky, unfortunate person, a born loser (sometimes also social misfit), the awkward, clumsy but trusting fool. A Yiddish proverb says: 'The shlemihl falls on his back and breaks his nose'. Cf. also Arendt, 1944, in Feldman, 1978, especially pp. 69–73.

11 Original text:

Genau wie ich fühlte er sich als Deutscher, genau wie ich fühlte er sich von den Deutschen zurückgestoßen, verkannt und für alle Hingebung und Opferbereitschaft unbelohnt. (*Lebensdienst* cit. in Pomeranz Carmely, 1981:55).

12 Original text:

Die Richtigkeit oder Unrichtigkeit des Weges erkennt man immer erst am Ziel. Jedenfalls gehen wir jetzt. Wir bewegen uns, also leben wir jetzt. Um uns wächst der Antisemitismus, aber das ist gut. Der Talmud sagt, daß wir Juden wie die Olive unser Bestes geben, wenn wir zermalmt werden (Cit. in Pomeranz Carmely, 1981:166).

13 The idea that there existed a German–Jewish symbiosis was by no means generally held and accepted as Gamm implies. Cf. for instance Gershom Scholem's essay 'Against the Myth of the German–Jewish Dialogue' in his selected essays, ed. by Dannhauser, pp. 61–64.

14 An older version, replacing line two, says instead: ve'im ani rak li ma ani?

(and if I am only for myself what am I?). But this does not alter the argument.
15 Arendt, 1948 in Feldman, 1978:104. Her argument has always aroused a good deal of criticism. The many acts of protest, and the many forms of resistance of Jews against the Nazis, are not acknowledged by Arendt: as for instance the very dramatic and desperate struggle of the inhabitants of the Warsaw ghetto, some 40 000 hopelessly under-equipped Jews, who made a final bid of resistance in April 1943; all but a few perished. For a brief introduction see 'Where the Jews fought back' in Sachar, 1977, pp. 451–455. More recent research by Konrad Kwiet (1986, 1988).
16 Original text:

Die bürgerliche Unterdrückung, zu welcher uns ein zu sehr eingerissenes Vorurteil verdammt, liegt wie eine tote Last auf den Schwingen des Geistes, und macht sie unfähig, den hohen Flug der Freigeborenen jemals zu versuchen. Es ist nicht unsere Schuld, allein wir können nicht leugnen, daß der natürliche Trieb zur Freiheit in uns alle Tätigkeit verloren hat. Er hat sich in eine Mönchstugend verändert und äußert sich bloß im Beten und Leiden, nicht im Wirken (Cited in Sellenthin, 1959, p.24).

17 Franz Mehring's *Die Lessing Legende* was completed in 1893 and is a sharply polemic work against Prussian 'right-wing' historiography and literary scholarship. It is an extremely comprehensive, well researched piece of writing on Lessing's life and on 18th century German i.e. Prussian reality, against which Mehring rallied with unrelenting scorn to the last page of this nearly 600-page oevre.
18 Thomas Mann's use of the word 'aufgehoben' is cleverly ambivalent. 'Aufheben' means several things, depending on context. It means to pick up, but also to cancel or to suspend, while 'gut aufgehoben sein' means being well looked after, cared for, in good hands. Thus, his German nationality which he gave up or lost was at once 'cancelled' and 'well looked after' by his becoming an American citizen.
19 This is true despite Hannah Arendt's acid irony about 'Americans of German language' when they were nothing but Jews (Arendt, 1943 in Feldman, 1978: 55). The point here is a different one. Her reference is to those Jews who still tried to hide the fact that they were Jewish. The reference in this paper is to Hannah Arendt's *status* as a citizen which did not require self-denial.

Clive S. Kessler

7 The politics of Jewish identity: *Arendt and Zionism*

There is a poignant irony in Hannah Arendt's life as a Jew. In her momentous times — encompassing the rise of Hitler, the attempted implementation of the Final Solution, and the creation and subsequent rise to regional military ascendancy of the state of Israel — she became a Jewish figure who was both representative and reviled, a pioneer and also a 'pariah'.

Arendt was a representative figure not simply because the major forces of modern Jewish history flowed through and shaped her personal biography. Beyond simply suffering history, she probed its meaning and fashioned for herself responses — ways of understanding and acting — that were to be of general significance: that were to be rediscovered, when they had become more timely, by others. More than merely experiencing personally those conjunctions of historical forces, she analysed them, thought through their impact and implications, and crystallised a response to them that was historically informed and political. In her own life she accordingly anticipated political developments and dilemmas that were later to become central to a growing worldwide Jewish politics — an assertive politics of Jews as Jews — in the holocaust and post-holocaust era. By being ahead of her time she became, as a thinker and activist, a representative Jewish figure of her time.

But, exemplar though she was, she was also resented and reviled. This was not simply for her precociousness in anticipating what others would only more haltingly and often less discerningly come to understand and accept — namely, the intrinsically political origins and character of the modern Jewish situation, and therefore also of any effective response to it. Even more, she was resented because she identified well in advance of their historical actualisation the inherent political and moral dilemmas within the dominant or 'official' Zionist solution to the contemporary Jewish problem.

The resentment of those who would later follow along the path that she had pioneered was not simply some laggards' resentment of an uncomfortably 'premature' political Zionist. It was also the bitterness towards a seeming renegade: one whose passionate, eloquent, and troubled warnings concerning the implications, within the actual geopolitical situation of the Middle East, of any narrow Israeli statehood or exclusivist nationalism branded her, among the zealots, as an anti-Zionist. Moreover, since these warnings, contained in her writings of the years from 1945 to 1948, were offered in the tumultuous period immediately prior to the establishment of the state of Israel, she was — to those in a Zionist political 'establishment' from which she was to become increasingly estranged — not merely an anti-Zionist, but indeed one no less precocious and 'premature' in this conviction than she had been in the 1930s as a political (as distinct from merely a religious or cultural or humanist or humanitarian) Zionist.

It is this very untimeliness that so connects Arendt to the fateful Jewish politics of her time. Yet Arendt's understanding of the Jewish situation and her complicated involvement, both creative and critical, with Zionism are central to an understanding of her thought and politics. More, in an era when the Palestinian uprising of the 1980s begins to echo the Jewish revolt of the 1940s against the British mandate, Arendt's relentless yet passionate analysis of the inherent dilemmas of 'mainstream' Zionism, of avoidable tragedy, is perhaps more timely than ever.

Hannah Arendt's central, hard-earned understanding was that to be human, properly human, is to think and that thinking implies plurality, the existence of others with different views. Difference and plurality, which thinking by its nature presumes, are of the public realm, which is the site of the political: an arena of free human engagement for the full realisation of personality, the negotiation and affirmation of difference. Thinking presupposes free dialogue and therefore freedom, which is upheld in action by politics. Our humanity, grounded in our capacity for thought, is thus inextricably political.

Not something she inherited or came to naturally, this understanding was hard-won. For she had always wanted to understand rather than to do, to pursue the life of the mind, not action (Arendt, 1979:303, 306). Yet, as the public realm and access to it came under Nazi assault, she was forced to recognise that thinking depends upon freedom which is of the public realm and hence political. Arendt was thus impelled, reluctantly diverted even, from 'pure thought' into politics and action by what she might mordantly have called 'an outbreak of history' (Young-Bruehl, 1979:4) — or, rather, by the irruption of that history into her personal and intellectual life. She who had never felt the need to commit herself was thus awakened to realities by a hammer blow to the head, as she put it (Arendt, 1979:306). 'The only group that I ever belonged to were the Zionists [and] this was only because of Hitler' (Arendt, 1979:334).

Arendt, who in this way rudely learnt the inherently political nature of thinking itself, thus discovered politics as a Jew — a circumstance that was to be central to her character and thought. Yet Arendt was not one of those proud, enlightened Germans who needed Hitler to remind them that they were after all Jews. She was someone avowedly both German and Jewish, who by that doomed conjunction was instructed in the ineluctably political nature and formation of Jewish identity in the modern world — and in the unavoidably political nature of any necessary action upon it.

The rise of Nazism impelled her, soon after completing her doctoral dissertation, to rethink the discordant relations between the German and Jewish traditions that the Mendelssohnian project had sought to harmonise. It also required her to reassess, if not philosophy itself, the philosophers and other thinkers. In particular, the self-deceiving and wishful readiness of both German and Jewish intellectuals to accommodate to the 'new realities' affected her profoundly. Heidegger, her former teacher and lover, made that accommodation: at Freiburg he succeeded to the rectorship when, in 1933, his predecessor, a Social Democrat, was dismissed for refusing to implement the so-called Jew Notice excluding Jews from universities. Heidegger soon marked his accession with an address lauding the 'greatness' and 'nobility' of the Nazi 'national awakening' (Young-Bruehl, 1982:108) (though he did subsequently beat a prudent retreat from these public and prominent excesses).[1] Similarly, Arendt's lifelong disapproval of the Frankfurt School 'Critical Theorists' is clearly due in part (other personal reasons aside) to the preparedness of T. W. Adorno and Max Horkheimer to attempt to live with what she felt they should already have considered unendurable. Adorno's readiness to be what she called contemptuously an 'exception Jew', to fashion for himself an acceptable identity around his mother's Italian family name rather than his father's German Jewish name of Wiesengrund, would not be forgotten; nor, following Heidegger's enthusiastic welcoming of the Jew Notice, would Adorno's forlorn attempt at Frankfurt to find some accommodation with Nazi policy towards the universities (Young-Bruehl, 1982:109).

Arendt learnt well but hard her lesson that intellectuals may be compromised, and betray their calling, by their vulnerability to the appeals of social acceptance, the chimera of respectability and influence. Better to be the pariah, the outsider, than the parvenu, the *arriviste*: the one whose exorbitant need to belong stems directly from a refusal to accept the fact of being an outsider, from an inability to embrace and value it; and who therefore remains ever hostage to the hope of acceptance, and susceptible to manipulation by those whose belonging the outsider envies and whose approval is craved.

Events in Germany culminating in the Reichstag fire prompted in Arendt a twofold response: to resist, and to rethink in an effort to understand. The latter she first pursued through a study of the late 18th century intellectual salon figure Rahel Varnhagen (see Kaplan in this volume). In quoting at the outset of her study Rahel's dying words—that, after all, she would not wish to have missed what so long had seemed the misery and misfortune of having been born a Jewess—Arendt was not merely reaffirming vicariously, despite all its burdens and contradictions in the modern German context, her own Jewish identity. She was also affirming the grounds of her repudiation of the 'exception Jews'—of Adorno and later, for example, in a devastating dismissal of what is in its own terms a superbly crafted and representative book, Stefan Zweig's *World of Yesterday* (Zweig, 1943; Arendt, 1943). She was also therefore asserting what was to become a central tenet of her subsequent mature thought: an insistence upon the inescapable fatefulness of natality.

This was a remarkable conviction in so single-minded and self-conscious an intellectual, one who valued thought and thoughtfulness above virtually all else as the grounds of keeping faith with the truth. For the assurance that modern society with its liberal ideology encourages that we may choose, by choosing our convictions, to become whatever we want is especially prevalent among intellectuals. Arendt knew better than to capitulate to the intellectualist fallacy—the illusion that one simply is what one thinks. Against this Enlightenment legacy she came to value the truths of history above the truths of dislocated reason. She knew that, while what one thinks is deeply tied up with who one is, the two are by no means the same. One is not simply the mere aggregate of one's thought or the self that is fashioned around the formulation and refinement of any ensemble of beliefs and convictions.

Perhaps things should be otherwise, perhaps one ought to be able to be the unconstrained, autonomous author of one's own being in history. But in a world where what one is—by birth—matters, matters in fact so greatly, and so decisively shapes one's orientation towards and access to the political realm of public affairs in which alone one can fully become oneself and give expression to one's dictinctive personality, what one *is* has a reality, a givenness, beyond any personal choice, beyond any simply voluntaristic election of identity.[2] For Arendt it was 'an injunction laid on all of us to follow the trajectory chance and fate have launched us on' (McCarthy 1985:36).

Arendt's full recognition of the fateful force of natality came from her relation to her friend and mentor, the German Zionist leader Kurt Blumenfeld, a former student at Königsberg's university and a member of her Berlin circle who was to remain a central figure in her life. Unlike Marx who, it might be said, came to a precocious political consciousness in his essay 'On the Jewish Question' by, so to speak, un-Jewing himself, the hitherto formidably intellectual but fundamentally apolitical Arendt ('I was interested neither in history nor politics when I was young', she later somewhat ruefully allowed [Arendt, 1964:53]) came into political awareness, largely through her relationship to Blumenfeld, as a Jew.[3]

If the rise of Nazism prompted in Arendt the dual impulsion both to understand and to resist, her friend Blumenfeld was central in catalysing both endeavours. He not only convinced her of Zionism's political reading of the sociocultural situation of Germany's Jews, of Mendelssohn's now dispossessed legatees; he also introduced her to a career of activist resistance. Because she was a scholar, and as a recent Zionist convert had no previous record in this area, she was, Blumenfeld recognised, suitable for enlistment in an important project: that of documenting in detail, from the very outset, the Nazi regime's anti-Jewish legislation and policies through research in official state archives and libraries. Such a study, he hoped, might shock delegates to the 1933 World Zionist Congress into a realisation of the seriousness of the situation of Germany's, and Europe's, Jews. The task was of course dangerous and required considerable courage. Arendt did important work in this area, at the same time helping various Communists and leftists to escape from Germany. But this phase of her now unfolding political career was to be only brief. Arrested by the Gestapo and detained for questioning for some days, she was able, by force of sheer intelligence and character, to secure her release, after which she fled to Paris, moving easily into Jewish *émigré* and resistance circles there.

Paris was to be the locale not only of the completion of the Rahel study, but also of the inception of a ten-year career, concluded in New York in 1940–1943, in the arena of Zionist political thought and action. For Arendt, there was no alternative to resisting Nazism nor was there any alternative to doing so as a Jew (Arendt, 1979:334).

> The only possibility [was] to fight back *as a Jew* and not as a human being... if you are attacked as a Jew you have got to fight back as a Jew, you cannot say 'Excuse me, I am not a Jew; I am a human being'. This is silly. And I was surrounded by this kind of silliness. There was no other possibility, so I went into Jewish politics (Arendt, 1979:334).

In Paris Arendt worked in French Jewish philanthropic bodies—Agriculture et Artisanat, a training programme; the Comité Nationale de Secours aux Juifs Allemands; and for Youth Aliyah, an organisation devoted to rescuing Jewish children and adolescents from Europe and preparing them for settlement in Palestine. The direction of this work was not uncontested; it was in fact deeply opposed by the *Consistoire*, the French Jewish leadership, which adamantly discouraged overt political action and urged trust in its quiet diplomacy within the upper reaches of French society. Arendt's mistrust of the well-connected and their strategies, based as they were upon a devastating amalgam of disdain and illusion, only sharpened her perception of the antagonism between parvenus and pariahs, as well as her commitment to the cause — and to the more comprehensive, penetrating, and unillusioned political vision — of the pariahs, who had no need to delude themselves or to find themselves 'exceptions' to some general fate.[4]

In Paris, Arendt also delivered a significant series of lectures, in German, to the local German branch of the Women's International Zionist Organisation (WIZO) on the origins and history of anti-Semitism in Germany. This connected the culturalist and historical preoccupations of the Rahel biography to the kinds of contemporary political documentation and analysis that she had done for Blumenfeld and the Zionist Congress immediately before fleeing Germany. Later, having observed the *Action Francaise* (and the powerlessness of the established French Jewish leadership confronted with it), she lectured the local WIZO, this time in French, on the comparative evolution of French and German anti-Semitism. These lectures were based upon what, in more developed form, were to become the core ideas of *The Origins of Totalitarianism*. Arendt was being irresistibly drawn into public polemics and overt politics centred upon devising and implementing an effective Jewish response to Nazism. That project, following the fall of France and her escape from a period of detention, was to become from 1940 to 1943 the centre of her life in New York.

Arendt's emphasis during this period was upon the political nature of anti-Semitism and the consequent need for an autonomous, explicitly political Jewish response to it. Arendt, who saw the modern world as fractured by nationalism's tearing of the fabric of tradition and the sundering of our connecting threads to it, nevertheless recognised that such a political response would necessarily be somehow national. At issue was what kind of nation and nationalism Zionism would yield, which to her was still a quite open question. Her somewhat reluctant nationalism may seem paradoxical, which it was, for it was situated within a field of quite paradoxical allegiances and identifications. These complexities were not only to encourage the exploration of strange alliances at the time among various Zionist factions; they would also create a legacy of political memories and tensions that the controversy 20 years later over her book on Eichmann would re-evoke.

There is, of course, a vast difference between recognising a fact and approving of it. Arendt accepted but did not endorse the centrality of nationalism; little as she liked its consequences, she could hardly dismiss it as a phenomenon of no significance in the first half of the 20th century. For the author of *The Origins of Totalitarianism* it was indeed central. She saw nationalism as the solvent of the world of tradition and as the direct cause of modern anti-Semitism and Jewish cultural and historical homelessness: of the denial to Jews of the grounds of any authentic standing in the public world.[5] The remedy for this condition had to be based upon an acknowledgement of its nature and origins: one had to recognise the political nature of the problem and frame an appropriately political response to it.

> It has been one of the unfortunate facts in the history of the Jewish people that only its enemies, and almost never its friends, understood that the Jewish question was a political one (Arendt, 1958a:56).

Arendt thus became a Zionist of pragmatic necessity: because the haven that movement sought to establish was an urgent imperative to which there was no alternative, not because it was the necessary realisation of any belief she held in nationalism as an ultimate value. This understanding put her at odds with both of the two main variants of Zionism at the time: the mainstream World Zionist Organisation and the breakaway Revisionist Zionist Organisation, which Vladimir (Zeev) Jabotinsky had founded in 1934 to mount an explicitly 'maximalist' political struggle for a Jewish state in Palestine as an alternative to Weizmann's Zionist Organisation, with its 'minimalist' strategy of accommodation with the British mandatory authority.[6]

Mainstream Zionists of various persuasions tended to minimise, at least in presenting their movement's public face, its fundamentally political character. Unlike them, Arendt did not disavow the movement's political nature. Whether of religious or socialistic orientation, mainstream Zionists tended to treat this nationalist dimension as, if not incidental, then secondary. Zionism was the realisation, for them, of an ancient religious yearning, a product not of the 19th century but of 19 centuries; or else of a desire to realise for Jews, since no-one else would share the venture with them, the benefits of humanist socialism or social normality. The fact that the solution proposed was a modern political and national one was not recognised or emphasised, either because it was not regarded as central or else for tactical reasons: to win non-Jewish support and allay political distrust. As Arendt was later cuttingly to put it, 'under Weizmann's leadership in foreign affairs... the Zionist Organization had developed a genius for not answering, or answering ambiguously, all questions of political consequence' (Arendt, 1945:134).

Arendt saw Zionism differently: the form it took, for some, might be religious or socialistic but its inner nature and impulse were nationalistic. It was an expression not of ancient religious yearnings or of certain progressive social impulses that happened to occur among Jews; it was a product of 19th century European nationalism and, with its urgent contemporary tasks, it was now situated on a post-World War I political terrain shaped by nationalism's empire- and tradition-shattering historical career. For the mainstream Zionists it was not fundamentally political or national; for Arendt, albeit reluctantly, it was—and therefore in need of a politics commensurate with its historical situation.

On the other hand, the Revisionist Zionists, to whom for example Prime Ministers Begin and Shamir trace their political filiation, saw the national impulse as primary, the religious or socialist as incidental or even distracting. Arendt did not care to delight in that fact, but she recognised it realistically as one. Zionism, she noted, 'fed on the very life blood of genuine political passions' (Arendt, 1945:140), and classical Herzlian Zionism, she recognised, had 'a definite tendency towards what later [were] known as Revisionist attitudes, and could escape them only through a wilfull blindness to the real political issues that were at stake' (Arendt, 1944:134).

Arendt was caught between the two tendencies. She agreed with the Revisionists concerning Zionism's centrally political character but regretted their narrow and intense, even antiquated, nationalism. Yet, while mainstream Zionism was less vehemently nationalistic, she was alienated by its diplomatic dissimulations, its disinclination fully to acknowledge its fundamentally political inner nature, impulse, and origins. This political reticence, the refusal to acknowledge that Zionism was a political movement, even a revolutionary one (Arendt, 1944:142, 149), she saw as resulting from the desire to present a good face, to pursue a politics of winning acceptance and of enlisting well-disposed protectors: from a parvenu apologetic, in short, or what the Revisionist leader Jabotinsky, referring caustically to a premodern Jewish politics of intercession and special pleading through court Jews and notables, called *shtadlanut* (from the *shtadlan* or courtier intermediary).

In the event, these differences would drive a wedge between her and both sides, leaving her with nowhere to go—other than to Judah Magnes and the proponents of a binational state, who were, however, soon overtaken by history.[7] They were not overtaken, however, until the possibilities of common understanding were first explored and exhausted: notably in the campaign for a Jewish army contingent to participate in the war, which in the New York context placed her in common cause with the Revisionists and their sympathisers such as the writer Ben Hecht and Peter Bergson, alias Kook, the rebellious nephew of the Palestinian chief rabbi. Indeed, with its arguments for authentic standing, via participation in equality and solidarity, in the anti-Nazi struggle and thereby for the transformation of Jewish character from that of a supplicant group to one capable of autonomous action, by organised military force even, in its own interest, the case she made in 1941 for 'A Jewish Army — the Beginnings of a Jewish Politics?' (see Young-Bruehl, 1982:169–171, 175–179) might well have been made by Jabotinsky himself, the founder of the Revisionists who had died suddenly in New York the previous year.

This advocacy, needless to say, was not well received by the official leaders of American Jewry, whose efforts, conducted in Washington, on behalf of those still trapped in Europe predictably required the presentation of a winningly respectable, an unthreateningly apolitical, face. In that way, for Arendt, and not unjustifiably (see Wyman, 1984), not enough would be done or quickly enough: the belief in patient diplomacy through 'responsible' intercession, she held, would cost lives, and the price of illusions, as with the Rothschilds of the Paris *Consistoire* in the 1930s, would again be tragic ineffectuality. This, too, would become part of the experiential basis for her criticism in the Eichmann book of the European Jewish leaders who, after 1942, sought by whatever dealings they had with the German authorities to avoid the worst, or make the best of an impossible situation (just as the contrast between Heidegger's craven complicity and Jaspers's unswayable refusal to become complicit became, for her, personal archetypes of modes of dealing with evil). Yearning for acceptability and prey to illusions concerning the effectiveness of their access politics, parvenu leaders, Arendt was convinced, can always be co-opted, manipulated. Access politics, intercession politics, was for her no politics at all because it was the antithesis of autonomous action, that grounded in a full entitlement of all those affected to participate in the public realm of identifiable human affairs.

If Arendt in some sense had certain affinities with the Revisionist approach, the possibilities of agreement with them were limited. Everything in her life impelled her away from any exclusivist parochial nationalism of the kind the Revisionists were championing within Zionist and Jewish circles (even though she admired and would continue to appreciate, sometimes fearfully, their *élan*). And as both the defeat of Germany and, from the very horror of the war, the success of the Zionist endeavour came to be real possibilities, Arendt was drawn less into dialogue with the internal Zionist opposition than into a polemical struggle with the dominant trend over the future of the Zionist movement itself. Despite the Revisionists' minority status in world Zionism, she saw them as articulating the inner nationalist impulse and hence the authentic nature of the movement: 'serious, honest and intransigent in their nationalism' (Arendt, 1945:132).

They, like it or not, were the true Herzlians—while her own preferred Jewish politics was more that of the figure she had contrasted with Herzl in a significant essay (Arendt, 1942) i.e. Herzl's fellow Dreyfusard Bernard Lazare, who had called for a national Jewish mobilisation, but not on the narrow, territorialist political and geographical foundation Herzl and the Zionists generally were to propose.

Her farewell, as it were, to the Zionist movement, was the essay 'Zionism Reconsidered'. In it she argued that, with the territorialist emphasis of the 1944 American Zionist Orgnisation's new demand for 'a free and democratic Jewish commonwealth... [which] shall embrace the whole of Palestine, undivided and undiminished', the 'Revisionist movement, so long bitterly repudiated [within the Zionist movement itself]... proved finally victorious'. It had conquered the Zionist movement generally, despite its numerical minority and outcast status, by eliciting from the movement a fully explicit declaration of its Herzlian and implicitly Jabotinskian political character. In this Arendt now saw seeds of tragedy: the leaving of the Arabs with the choice between voluntary emigration and second-class citizenship, a deadly blow to all those who had pursued in Palestine the cause of reconciliation between the two peoples (Arendt, 1945:131, 136).

This was the cause to which, in concert with J. L. Magnes, founder-president of the Hebrew University, she now devoted herself, expressing her hopes and fears in essays such as 'The Jewish State: Fifty Years After—Where Have Herzl's Politics Led?' (1946) and, forlornly, 'To Save the Jewish Homeland: There is Still Time' (1948)—all to no avail. She was left to witness what she now considered a reversion to 19th century nationalism in the formation of a state (a pariah state, even!) whose existence necessarily displaced Jewish homelessness onto another people and made them refugees.

This, for Arendt, was the end of her Zionist road—or was it? She continued to give generously to Israeli and Zionist causes and, when the Middle East war broke out in 1967, she confessed to her close friend Mary McCarthy that 'any real catastrophe in Israel would affect me more deeply than anything else' (Young-Bruehl, 1982:391; cf. also ibid., 361 and Arendt, 1946:177 and 1948:185). When the 1973 war erupted and, like many others, she realistically feared that just such a catastrophe was at hand, she averred that 'the Jewish people are united in Israel', for Judaism was a national religion! (Young-Bruehl, 1982:455–456). Despite herself or, rather, despite her own political convictions that made her critical of what Zionism had itself become and created, she remained ineradicably Jewish, caught up in the processes of the historical remaking of Jewish identity in the public postwar political world. She believed, after all, that one could not reject the identity one was born with—the basis of one's being, bestowed by fateful natality, in a politically fractured world — without sacrificing personal integrity and authenticity. That the demise of a former 'worldlessness' had in her time engendered a Jewish politics other than that she would herself have chosen was a fact, she had to accept, that could not simply be wished away (see Feldman, 1978).

Arendt's withdrawal from the Zionist political arena did not, however, end her services to significant Jewish causes or her involvement in the processes of Jewish history of her time. Rather, the form of her action changed: from the activist to the elegiac, one might say; from the political, with its concern to link present and future, to the conservationist, permitting the past to address and to inject its content into the present.

She was by now estranged from the official Jewish, including Zionist, leadership — as well as severed from a past that, it was clear by 1944, was no more. That past, its salvaging, the preservation of its surviving connecting strands to the present now became the central preoccupation informing her life. Though that past was now, in its entirety and in its own European context, irretrievable, its surviving shreds mattered; they had, she felt, to be saved and, to the extent possible, restored. The past as past had been ravaged; but the homelessness of the present as a habitation for history's orphans, her contemporaries, might be reduced by a properly mindful conservation of its surviving remnants.

Arendt thus became involved in the Conference of Jewish Relations — later the Conference on Jewish Social Studies (Young-Bruehl, 1982:184–188). Initiated in 1936, this group had by 1939 founded the journal *Jewish Social Studies*. During the darkest war years those associated with the journal came to recognise the need to compile an inventory of, and if possible to recover, whatever books and other items of the European Jewish cultural heritage might survive the war. This led to the creation of the Commission of European Jewish Cultural Reconstruction, where Arendt was to serve as research director and later executive director. Under her, a four-part 'Tentative List of Jewish Cultural Treasures in Axis-occupied Countries' was prepared and published, and some 1.5 million volumes of Judaica and Hebraica, thousands of ceremonial objects, and over one thousand *sifrei torah* (biblical scrolls) were recovered. Homelessness, the severing of tradition, could be mitigated, both as a way of giving content to the otherwise disconnected present and also as a quite personal act of fidelity (*Treue* — or *pietas*, even) towards the past itself.

The same spirit also informed her work as editorial adviser with Schocken, the Jewish publishers (formerly of Berlin, now of New York), for whom she saw to light in English works of such figures as Bernard Lazare, Franz Kafka, and her ill-fated friend Walter Benjamin. Yet this preservation of the remnants of the past and of the present's tenuously surviving connections to it was a far from morbid or dispiriting undertaking. For Arendt it was animating: in his memoir *New York Jew*, Alfred Kazin has written of Arendt at this time as 'a blazing Jew...obsessed with genocide...yet...brimming over with enthusiasm' for the work of Jewish Cultural Reconstruction (Kazin, 1978:195–196). As some picking up of the pieces, this work was the exact artifactual counterpart of the documentary and thematic piecing together that she was at the same time engaged upon—that was to become *The Origins of Totalitarianism*.

This picking up the pieces, fragments—eschewing daily politics for this documentary memorialism—was, then, not a break in her activist Jewish career, a retreat, but a reversion to original character: it was the postwar analogue of the research in the Prussian State Archives that Blumenfeld had persuaded her to conduct in 1933. Now, however, the task was to fill the present with the orienting traces of a ravaged past rather than to build a feasible future upon a diminishingly possible present. The purpose too was similar: then it had been to help shock the world into realising, from precisely documented sources, what had been set in motion to happen; now it was to enforce a shocked and also grieving recognition of what, despite all warnings, had been allowed to happen.

Found throughout her works of this time, Arendt's abstract theme of the homeless, dislocated state of her contemporaries, ourselves, in a world from which tradition had been eradicated had this quite concrete basis in her own life and undertakings. What she said of her friend Walter Benjamin applied equally to herself: that there was a deep connection between his fastidious, even obsessive, collecting of objects and his own personal formation on the terrain of the rupture of past; she speaks of 'the close affinity between the break in tradition and the seemingly whimsical figure of the collector who gathers his fragments and scraps from the debris of the past'. Now 'the transmissibility of the past had been replaced by its citability' (Arendt, 1968b:201, 193).

It is evident that the work Arendt did in active support of Jewish causes in the 1930s and 1940s informed and infused her subsequent writings of the 1950s and beyond: on totalitarianism, politics, and freedom; the demise of tradition and the culturally orphaned condition of the modern world; on the tensions between autonomous politics and the anti-politics of intercession and supplication. All these concerns shaped her thinking up to *Eichmann in Jerusalem* and beyond. Arendt remained preoccupied with the past: hers and ours. Not, as she readily admitted, an actor by nature, hers rather was to understand. Her leaving the political arena for the scholarly—her shedding of the role of the activist that only the most extreme circumstances had imposed on her, a role she had assumed against her own nature and in which from the mid-1940s she could no longer function effectively—was thus a return to character as researcher and recorder, a questioner and warner.

Arendt, the Jew, the Zionist, was a conundrum, a person not readily accommodated within the categories of the times and politics she inhabited. She was, despite her writings regretting the ravages unleashed upon the modern world by narrow and rampant nationalisms, a nationalist, but a reluctant and unhappy nationalist. Like it or not, history had made her such, for a while at least; and also a Zionist, but again an uneasy one who defied conventional categories. By historical circumstance and necessity a Zionist, she recognised that, after years of political 'worldlessness', Zionism had at last provided Jews in the modern world 'not only a guide to reality but reality itself; not simply a key to history but the experience of history itself' (Arendt, 1946:168). It positively restored politics, an authentic politics of their own, to them and thus restored them through a reaffirmation of politics, for it had stemmed from a 'desire to do something about the Jewish problem... to act and solve the problem in political terms'. Zionism 'placed the whole question on a political level from the very beginning... it tried to teach the Jews to solve their problems by their own efforts, not by those of others' (Arendt, 1946:166, 169, 170).

Arendt was thus—temperamentally and by historical circumstance —not simply a Zionist but a Herzlian, even a Jabotinskian, Zionist: one who insisted upon the inherently political nature of the movement, and that its programme and action should be commensurately and unequivocally political. Yet she was too fastidious intellectually and morally, too aware politically and historically, to be one of them: to be a political Zionist when that meant to contract into any narrow nationalism; to be a Herzlian Zionist, when the world Zionist leadership was seeking to pursue Zionist objectives through accommodation with Britain, thereby tying the Zionist project's fate to a retreating imperialism in an emerging postcolonial world; to be a Jabotinskian Zionist when that meant the imposition of Jewish nationalism upon a Mediterranean land and population by sheer military force. Arendt clearly applauded, amidst all the unrealism and illusion, the political Zionists' unabashed recognition of the political nature of their movement and their proclaimed intention therefore of situating their movement in the world of action upon absolute political realism. For Arendt, the intention was correct, but its actualisation tragically limited and defective.

Why? Because its political analysis was flawed, impaired by a fatal blindness: to the fact that the terrain for the political realisation of the Zionist project was not an uninhabited land. The often asserted conviction that Zionism was the project 'of a people without a land for a land without a people' entailed a blindness that would prove fatal:

The erection of a Jewish State within an imperial sphere of interest may look like a very nice solution to some Zionists, though to others something desperate but unavoidable. In the long run, there is hardly any course imaginable that would be more dangerous ... only folly could dictate a policy which trusts a distant imperial power for protection, while alienating the good will of neighbours ... what program have Zionists to offer for a solution of the Arab–Jewish conflict? (Arendt, 1945:162).

Political realism, on the other hand, required Zionists to recognise that 'the only permanent reality in the whole constellation' of Middle East politics was not the continuing availability of imperial protectors or great power guarantors of the Zionist endeavour, of Jewish security, but 'the presence of Arabs in Palestine, a reality no decision could alter—except, perhaps the decision of a totalitarian state, implemented by its particular brand of ruthless force' (Arendt, 1948:185). Thus, she went on to argue:

> The idea of Arab–Jewish cooperation, though never realized on any scale and today seemingly farther off than ever, is not an idealistic day dream but a sober statement of the fact that without it the whole Jewish venture in Palestine is doomed (Arendt, 1948:186).

The alternative was clear:

> There is very little doubt about the final outcome of an all-out war between Arabs and Jews. One can win many battles without winning a war... And even if Jews were to win the war, its end would find the unique achievements of Zionism in Palestine destroyed. The land that would come into being would be something quite other than the dream of world Jewry, Zionist and non-Zionist. The 'victorious' Jews would live surrounded by an entirely hostile Arab population, secluded inside ever-threatened borders, absorbed with physical self-defence to a degree that would submerge all other interests and activities. The growth of Jewish culture would cease to be the concern of the whole people; social experiments would have to be discarded as impractical luxuries; political thought would centre around military strategy; economic development would be determined exclusively by the needs of war. And all this would be the fate of a nation that—no matter how many immigrants it could still absorb and how far it extended its boundaries... would still remain a very small people greatly outnumbered by hostile neighbours. Under such circumstances ... the Palestinian Jews would degenerate into one of those small warrior tribes about whose possibilities and importance history has amply informed us since the days of Sparta (Arendt, 1948:187).

Arendt therefore experienced a dismay at the spectacle of:

> a nationalist movement that, starting out with such an idealistic élan, sold out at the very first moment to the powers-that-be—that

felt no solidarity with other oppressed peoples whose cause, though historically otherwise conditioned, was essentially the same (Arendt, 1945:152).

Thus:

> the Jews ignored the awakening of colonial peoples and the new nationalist solidarity in the Arab world from Iraq to French Morocco. In hope or in hate both peoples ... focused their attention so exclusively upon the British that they practically ignored each other: the Jews forgot that the Arabs, not the English, were the permanent reality in Near Eastern policies and the Arabs that Jewish settlers, and not British troops, intended to stay permanently in Palestine (Arendt, 1950:195).

Yet:

> even a Jewish majority in Palestine—nay, even a transfer of all Palestinian Arabs, which is openly demanded by Revisionists— would not substantially change a situation in which Jews must either ask protection from an outside power against their neighbours or effect a working agreement with their neighbours (Arendt, 1945:133).

In sum, 'the thought that "the people without a country need a country without people" so occupied the minds of Zionist leaders that they simply overlooked the native population' (Arendt, 1950:203). This tragic blindness[8] stemmed originally not from any hard-headed political ruthlessness or ethnic chauvinism towards the inconveniently resident Palestinian Arabs, but from the pathetically apolitical character of simplistic Zionist settlement idealism:

> The national aim of the socialist Zionists was attained when they settled in Palestine. Beyond that they had no national aspirations. Absurd as it may sound today, they had not the slightest suspicion of any national conflict with the present inhabitants of the promised land; they did not even stop to think of the very existence of Arabs. Nothing could better prove the entirely unpolitical character of the new movement than this innocent obliviousness... Thus the social-revolutionary Jewish national movement, which started... with ideals so lofty that it overlooked the particular realities of the New East and the general wickedness of the world has ended—as do most such movements—with the unequivocal support not only of national but of chauvinist claims—not against the foes of the Jewish people but against its possible friends and present neighbours (Arendt, 1945:140).

The difference between the self-deluding unworldliness of the apolitical dreamers and the stark realism of a Jabotinsky—who, addressing the British Royal Commission on Palestine (the Peel Commission) in the House of Lords in 1937, could bluntly state that 'a nation with your colossal colonizing past experience surely knows that colonization never went on without certain conflicts with the population on the spot' (Jabotinsky, 1937:564)—was to Arendt a clear and vital one. She could never be or follow a Jabotinsky, but she might have argued with him.

Why Arendt could not remain, in any conventional sense, a Zionist and why the Zionist political establishment could not forgive her for her 'turning' (and would still remember her 'desertion' when they found her critique of parvenu leadership in *Eichmann in Jerusalem* offensive) are clear. Meanwhile, the position for which she argued when her break with organised Zionism came—the compelling necessity of Jewish–Arab conciliation—is no easier to argue today, but certainly no less urgent. It is nonetheless important to recognise that Arendt's arguments, however insightful and discerning, do not make her a unique figure. That others, some from similar premises and others from quite different points of departure, have argued similarly emphasises that hers was no visionary, idiosyncratic, or perverse stance but part of a more general intellectual and political movement that warrants serious consideration. Arendt's views need to be systematically compared with, from the left, those for example of Isaac Deutscher (1968)[9] and Noam Chomsky (1983; and also the interview with his editor James Peck in 1987:3–55, esp. 6–14), as well as with the views of those intellectually close to her: not only Judah Magnes himself (Brinner & Rischin, 1987) but also, nearer to her German–Jewish philosophical roots, Martin Buber. Like her, Buber —whose *bona fides*, even saintliness, to Zionists are beyond impugning—saw the Palestine of his time, and ours, as 'a land of two peoples' (Buber, 1983). Much aware, like Arendt, of the moral dimension of Zionism and of the Zionist enterprise's evolution, especially in its relation to its Arab neighbours, as a test of Jewish humanism and morality, he was 'grieved to think', as his editor Mendes-Flohr has recently noted (in Nevisky, 1988:18), 'that Jewish liberation might come at the expense of another people'. Arendt's concern was not a solitary one in her time, nor is it a quixotic one in ours.

Notes

1 With unduly protective euphemism, Gadamer (1985:51) would later refer to this period as Heidegger's 'political interlude'!
2 An excellent exposition of Arendt's understanding of 'natality', applied to her own life, is to be found in Minnich (1984), who says of Arendt that she 'lived what she was given' (181).
3 On Blumenfeld's influence on Arendt's thinking, see Young-Bruehl (1982:70–74, 90–92, & 105–106).

4 One cannot help wondering whether, despite Arendt's lack of regard for Hegel, there is not to be found here some influence of his analysis of the master-slave relationship: that, contrary to appearances, the slave is more autonomous than the master who needs him, and by necessity has an understanding that is more comprehensive.
5 For a clear outline of Arendt's notion of the 'worldlessness' of the modern Jew — of how Jews were rendered powerless by their lack of any sufficient concept of the 'political', especially following the collapse of Shabbatai Tzevi's messianic movement of the 17th century — see Feldman (1978:esp.20–28).
6 A critical analytical history of Zionism has yet to be written. For brief overviews, see Cohen (1951) and Sachar (1958: chaps. 13, 18, & 22, pp. 261–283, 369–393, & 460–488). On Jabotinsky and the Revisionists, the most detailed source is the hagiographic two-volume biography by Schechtman (1956 & 1961).
7 On Magnes, see Brinner & Rischin (1987). Magnes himself, moreover, died within months of Israel's independence in 1948.
8 As Mendes-Flohr makes clear in his introduction (1983:3–33, esp.4–12) to Buber's writings on the subject of Arab–Jewish relations, the leading Zionists were from the outset blind neither to the existence of the Palestinian Arabs nor to the fact that their existence had immediate and fundamental intellectual consequences; what was to prove tragic was that Zionist ideology and programmes would remain impervious, or blind, to these facts. Zionism was not able to assimilate an awareness of these facts into its own political self-understanding and agenda. One recalls here the possibly apocryphal story (see, for example, Buber 1983:86) that, upon learning that there were Arabs in Palestine, the Zionist leader Max Nordau rushed excitedly to Herzl declaring: 'I didn't know that! If that is the case, then we are doing an injustice.'
9 See especially the essays on 'Israel's Spiritual Climate', 'Israel's Tenth Birthday', and 'The Arab–Israeli war, June 1967' (Deutscher, 1968: chaps. 5, 6, & 7, pp. 91–117, 118–125, & 126–152): e.g. the view that: 'The Jews are still too deeply intoxicated with their newly-acquired nation-state and the Arabs are too fully obsessed with their grievance to look very far ahead. Any supranational organization, like a Middle East federation, is sheer *Zukunftmusik* to both. But sometimes it is only the music of the future to which it is worth listening' (117).

Sondra Farganis

8 The chosen people: *the historical formation of identity*

The status of being a Jew is one that must be situated within a specific epoch. Even West European anti-Semitism Arendt argues in *The Origins of Totalitarianism* (Arendt, 1958a) can be explained historically and is to be understood as an historical entity, set against the backdrop of Jewish financiers with varying degrees of political access to the political officers of the state. In the context of European history, Jewishness is an ascribed status; that is, irrespective of one's views on Judaism, the ties of blood to family have been used to determine if one is or is not Jewish. Jewishness is a social category into which one is born, and which is not subject to rejection in the way that the religious tenets of that category — Judaism — are. Jewish identity as either pariah or parvenu becomes part of the social or cognitive map by which one defines oneself and is defined by others. It involves what Daniel Bell has called coming 'to terms with the past' (Bell, 1980:315). For Arendt, holding onto one's humanity involves protecting that social map, that sense of who one is and how one has come to be this and not otherwise.

In the midst of World War II in her essay on 'The Jew as Pariah: A Hidden Tradition', Arendt would write, in a manner anticipating her *The Origins of Totalitarianism*:

> Man is a social animal and life is not easy for him when social ties are cut off. Moral standards are much easier kept in the texture of a society. Very few individuals have the strength to conserve their own integrity if their social, political and legal status is completely confused... A man who wants to lose his self discovers, indeed, the possibilities of human existence, which are infinite, as infinite as is creation. But the recovering of a new personality is as difficult — and as hopeless — as a new creation of the world (Arendt, 1944:62–63).

Changes of identity—what sociologists call the playing of a multiplicity of social roles—can leave one with no clear understanding of who one is or what one considers to be of value. In political terms, one is left without that sense of self which is essential to understand the incursions of the administered society into the very recesses of the lifeworld. History, as played out in Germany, made all Jews outsiders, placing parvenus and pariahs alike 'in the same boat, rowing desperately in the same angry sea' (Arendt, 1944:90). The Nazis made Jewish identity an inescapable reality, even for those who would negate it. The gaze of the other, when that other had power, wrote one's identity: how one is regarded is social, and how one is viewed is both a lived and a theoretical question. As Arendt writes of Jews, Simone de Beauvoir writes of women: 'the situation of women is that she—a free autonomous being like all human creatures—nonetheless finds herself living in a world where men compel her to assume the status of Other' (de Beauvoir, 1968:xxix). Identity is socially constituted: through others I learn who I am. As Peter Berger later argued: 'Identity... is always identity within a specific socially constructed world' (Berger, 1966:iii).

Hannah Arendt recognised the full importance of the fact that modern Jewish identity had been historically produced. It is within this context that one can trace her ideas between ethnicity and nationalism, especially in the case of the Jews. As a graduate student, Arendt had become close with Hans Jonas and Kurt Blumenfeld, both of whom helped to shape her ideas on the culture of Judaism and its relationship to Zionism. Blumenfeld had argued that the starting point for any discussion on 'the Jewish Question' was the knowledge of how others defined and regarded Jews. Unable to assimilate, Jews had to recognise the extraordinary limitations imposed on them within states hostile to their very existence. From this recognition came that call for a Jewish community in which those defined as outcasts could experience a positive shared identity.

In all of Arendt's writings—her biography of Rahel Varnhagen is a case in point—she stresses the importance of consciously recognising that one's sense of self is social, that one is a part of history even as one consciously seeks to distance oneself from it. She emphasises that kind of social distancing or social 'bracketing' that was to be fundamental to the phenomenological perspective of Schutz, Berger, and Luckmann.

The question that Arendt had to face was whether Blumenfeld was correct in seeing Zionism—emigration out of Europe—as the only feasible means of sustaining an autonomous Jewish identity. For her, Zionism was not a set of eternal verities but a set of political principles around which individuals could reasonably act *at that time*. Just as she would later denounce the idea of a national or collective guilt which made no allowances for human action, so too was she repelled by those Zionists who spoke of all Jews as 'the chosen people'. Both made abstractions out of flesh-and-blood social actors, substituting theoretical categories for the actions of concrete individuals. What impressed her about the Blumenfeld-Jonas position was its historicity, its emphasis on the value of and need for a Jewish homeland once the rationale of anti-Semitism had played itself out on the European stage. She would write in *The Origins of Totalitarianism*: 'To be uprooted means to have no place in the world, recognized and guaranteed by others... Uprootedness can be the preliminary condition for superfluousness' (Arendt, 1958a:475).

The burning of the Reichstag in 1933 drastically reshaped the terms of all debate about the future of the Jews and, in particular, whether there was any longer any alternative to Zionism. What the Nazis made clear, in their laws as well as in their legally constituted and functionally operative extermination centres, was just how alien the Jews were. Certainly the holocaust was the attempted Final Solution to the 'Jewish Question', but it was also more. It was the obverse of the humanistic reason that had been generated by the Enlightenment; it was also dehumanisation and de-individuation on a scale that defied comprehension.

Insofar as the primary object of annihilation was the Jew, the holocaust made real the need for a homeland, a political community, where Jews could find a place not merely to be themselves but to assure their physical survival. Before the holocaust one could debate with the Zionists whether theirs was the most reasonable solution to the treatment accorded Jews in Europe; after Hitler there was no longer a place in the debate for the assimilationists and those who wished for a position for Jews within European society. The question facing Jews, as actors in history, was not whether to be Zionists but how best to realise the Zionist dream of a homeland in Palestine. From this a further consequence was to follow: with the realisation of that dream, Jews would have to include a new component in their reconstructed identity—the reality of that new homeland.

Arendt was opposed to the notion of the Jews as a 'chosen people'. She urged that the creation of a Jewish homeland be seen not as predestined by Judaic text but required by the ravages of the holocaust; and that, moreover, it be situated within the geo-political context of a world historically and legitimately inhabited by the Arabs. History had created Jews, and history had created Israel. Concrete historical events has made it impossible for Jews to assimilate into European society—certainly this is the sub-text of *Rahel Varnhagen* and the import of her writings on the fate of pariahs.

Arendt argues that Jews are construed and constructed by the attitudes of others toward them and are shaped by the historical treatment of the past—by the 19th century legacy of anti-Semitism, by the holocaust, by the political factors which led to the creation of the state of Israel. Jewish sensitivity on behalf of Israel is based on Jewish consciousness of having been for so long a homeless, stateless people. As Wallerstein has argued:

> Pastness is a mode by which persons are persuaded to act in the present in ways they might not otherwise act. Pastness is a tool persons use against each other. Pastness is an essential element in the socialisation of individuals, in the maintenance of group solidarity, in the establishment of or challenge to social legitimation. Pastness therefore is preeminently a moral phenomenon (Wallerstein, 1987:381).

If Israel had to exist, Arendt wanted a homeland, not a national state. The latter implied disregard for the Arabs, either by reconstituting them as a minority within a political state or by excluding them from the new political context. Her argument was for a Palestinian confederation incorporated into the British Commonwealth, formed and jointly administered by Arabs and Jews, where inter-racial and inter-religious cooperation would parallel the economic attractions of the kibbutz and the participatory political values of the 'council system'. This distinction between a homeland and a state is essential to understanding subsequent events in the Middle East. But a homeland was never a real possibility. Yet Israeli statehood was one generation's ill-conceived plan that, as Arendt foresaw, would require later generations to pay in blood.

Arendt did not reject the nation-state categorically. But she did appreciate that nationalism emphasises exclusivist claims and is super-particularistic in nature. She further recognised that ethnic diversity poses a potential threat to the solidarity of the nation-state. Though aware of the American success in achieving a degree of ethnic pluralism, Arendt recognised that even in the United States, materially privileged a community as it was, there was debate over the psychic price paid for the integration and assimilation of ethnically diverse groups.

Yet precarious though it may be, the state remains essential as the arena of citizenship. Persons must be allowed to live and act in the polis; for it is through our citizenship that we give meaning to our lives, that is, we make them worthwhile. The political world is the distinctively human world: 'Through making and shaping of the political realm we make for our freedom. It is this which gives us our humanness' (Arendt, 1961:146). While Arendt recognised the need for a state, a place where people would have a home in which they could engage in the highly prized activities of citizenship—the political life of the polis—she abhorred the fusing of the historical necessity of a

Jewish homeland with the propaganda of a 'chosen people'. She was horrified by those Zionists who lacked sufficient concern for the Arabs on whose soil their own historical solution had found a political resting place.

Timerman, some 25 years later, reports on the consequences of those particular Zionist policies. On one level, *The Longest War* (Timerman, 1982) is a succinct chronicle of Israel's invasion of Lebanon. On another, it is a form of historical analysis, evaluating, as it does, the actions of the Israeli government against the background of the idea of a Palestinian homeland. Timerman argues that the invasion of Lebanon by Israel closed a chapter in Jewish history. Created as a national homeland for holocaust victims, Israel had turned the table in the name of national security and had set out to destroy those Palestinians who laid claim to Israeli territory.

Conceived as a moral solution to a political problem, or, conversely, a political solution to the moral dilemma of a victimised, stateless people, Israel had now become like any other nation-state. Arguing that its power must be defended at all costs, that order and stability must prevail, it had moved from a moral stance to the demands of sovereignty. This *realpolitik* informed Ariel Sharon's demand that the invasion be judged by standards of politics, not by those of an archaic morality—although it may be pointed out that there have been those (Abba Eban is a spokesperson for their position) who have used just those political standards to assess Israeli political interventions in Lebanon, Gaza, and the West Bank as foolhardy and suicidal as well as immoral (Eban, 1986).

For his part, Timerman would hold Israel to high moral standards because its very right to exist is based on a moral contract. Trying not to recast the Jews in but another form of the 'chosen people' role, Timerman nonetheless demands a moral stance from a state whose creation was based on an international recognition that Jews needed a place to call home:

> With painstaking honesty, the Israelis have worked out the role of victim that the Jews fulfilled and continue to fulfill to this day in certain regions of the Diaspora. By necessity, this led to vindications and justifications... Yet despite this philosophical framework, which has served to maintain a certain mental balance, the Israelis never traded on the Jewish blood spilled in Europe. Strict moral limits were kept because, as a popular saying put it, 'We cannot do to others what was done to us' (Timerman, 1982:15).

Such a position resembles that of the New Jewish Agenda, a contemporary organisation of primarily secular American Jews who want to read from history a Jewish mission to resist oppression, a Jewish sensitivity to and for those who suffer. This is similar to the way in which other groups — contemporary feminists come immediately to mind — have also tried to show the ways in which social constructions develop attitudes, affinities, ways of being-in-the-world, at the same time being careful to avoid any biological and moral essentialism.

Timerman understands how the holocaust shaped an emerging military spirit among Jews and how the ideograph of 'Never again' has become part of the contemporary Jewish character. He cannot, however, condone Tyre because of Coventry, Sidon because of Dresden — dead Lebanese children because of gassed Jewish children. Mordantly, but with a profound sensitivity to its historical origins, Arendt had exposed this disastrous logic when she wrote that:

> only outmoded liberals believe in compromises, only philistines believe in justice, and only *shlemiels* prefer truth and negotiation to propaganda and machine guns ... in sum — we are ready to go down fighting, and we will consider anybody who stands in our way a traitor and anything done to hinder us a stab in the back (Arendt, 1948:181).

Timerman takes issue, as Arendt would, with those who treat the memory of the atrocities as an ongoing enterprise that provides moral entitlement for whatever may be done in its name. Timerman is appalled by this politicisation of the holocaust for the purpose of legitimating the militarism of the Israeli government. Can the holocaust possibly excuse the victims from all future accountability? Does it tie all Jews to Israel? Does it limit what Diaspora Jews can and cannot say about Israel? It is the historical peculiarity of the state of Israel that it allows for both internal and external debate over the formation of national policy. It has political, economic, and moral ties to the Jews of Europe and the United States. But Israel now has an indigenous population including not only a variety of Jews but also Druzes, Muslims, Armenians, and Greek Orthodox, who do not always see the world in the same way as do Diaspora Jews.

Most emphatically, there is that special relationship which Jews have had with Israel. Timerman believes that Diaspora Jews should be allowed a say in Israeli politics. Underlying this view, however, is a failure to see Israel as a national entity with the sovereignty that accompanies statehood. How has this come about? The novelist Amos Oz speaks of this tie to the Diaspora as reflecting, in effect, an earlier moment in Israel's history: 'The old Israel was formed on the basis of a marriage between the Yiddishkeit mentality of the ghetto and Russian inspired ideas. It was this that formed the culture of the

Israeli Labor movement that originally built Israeli society' (Oz, 1986:24).

While most Diaspora Jews will not settle in Israel—in fact, the West has begun to attract Israelis, some of whom are understandably war-weary—there remains that sense of Israel as 'home' to Jews everywhere, a view which Israelis themselves, and their government, encourage and reinforce. This not only raises the question of Jewish identity but also that of national loyalties. The Pollard Affair is a case in point. Jonathan J. Pollard, an American Jew who had worked for the United States Navy, had been recruited by Israel and had sold to it certain information on nuclear weaponry. He defended his actions on the grounds of his loyalty to Israel. Most American Jews—certainly most spokespersons for American Jewish organisations—were visibly and vocally angered by Pollard's actions and motives. And yet, Pollard may simply have played out the dual loyalty to which Timerman appealed.

Arendt's work details the concrete ways in which Jewishness is a social construction. Like being feminine or masculine, it is to be understood in terms of that dialectical relationship between a socially objective definition (*of* a Jewish mother, *of* Jewish parentage) and the ways in which that status is held, esteemed, and regarded by others.

Israel was founded and carved out of Palestinian land because of Nazi anti-Semitism. Historically, the 'Jewish question' asked whether one's ties were to one's Jewishness or to one's country. Israel became a way to resolve that inherent tension, a place where Jewishness was esteemed; yet that solution created in turn new problems of its own. The very existence of Israel as a state now complicates the world of Diaspora Jews, as in its extreme form the Pollard case indicates. Meanwhile, the Israeli Declaration of Independence reads: 'In the land of Israel the Jewish people first arose ... Exiled, the people remained faithful to it in all the lands of their dispersion.' Following directly from it, the Jewish state's first enactment, the Law of Return, automatically awards Israeli citizenship to Diaspora Jews upon their migration to Israel, although it needs also to be added that it is Israel or rather, the designated rabbis of the moment who decide who dare the government of the day to contest their exercise of this right—which decide who is a Jew and what constitutes Judaism.

Arendt and Timerman make us aware of how the moral idea of a Jewish homeland became something different once that idea was realised in the creation of a national state; for a state in practice is different from a moral idea in theory. Israel is now a state with a national interest, able to use physical force to extract compliance with its orders. It is not a moral construct but a legal–rational association and, as such, uses history as an ideology to legitimate its existence while making *realpolitik* accommodations with the Germans, South

The chosen people 115

Africans, and Argentinians. Critics of Arendt and Timerman write as if the Jews' relation to Israel is an impossible one, at least, politically. Jews are of Israel; but by not being in Israel, they have excluded themselves from determining, or at least questioning, its political direction. It is only Jews in Israel who may raise voices of support for alternative policies and of censure of those that have been adopted. Jews outside are just that, outsiders in a self-imposed exile; only by the political act or relocation can they become Israeli Jews, a status fused from lineage and location. Outside one is not inside and one cannot pretend or act as if that state speaks in one's name. Yet Jews can become Israelis and in this they have a potential for reconstructing their identity which non-Jews do not have.

Timerman was reviled for morally questioning in *The Longest War* the state that had provided him with a haven from his Argentinian prison cell and torturers. Arendt, having criticised from its inception the state of Israel as 'a deadly blow to those ... who have tirelessly preached the necessity of an understanding between the Arab and the Jewish peoples' (from 'Zionism Reconsidered' Arendt, 1945:131–132), could yet write during the 1967 Middle East War that 'Any real catastrophe in Israel would affect me more deeply than almost anything else'. She came actually to fear, at the outbreak of the 1973 war, that Israel's destruction was imminent—a fear that impelled her into intense public activity on Israel's behalf (see Young-Bruehl, 1982:455–456). Of such ambiguities and ambivalences is the situation of the reflective contemporary Jew, indissolubly linked by history to Israel but disquieted at the actions prompted by its pragmatic *raisons d'état*, composed.

IV
Feminism and anti-feminism

Maria Markus

9 The 'anti-feminism' of Hannah Arendt

One of the strengths of contemporary feminist theory is its readiness to rethink, re-evaluate, reinterpret, or simply to learn from, a variety of theoretical contributions offered by men. Yet feminist theory has also displayed a disturbing tendency to persistently ignore women thinkers unless they openly declare their allegiance to feminism. Works lacking such declarations are generally considered unworthy of serious critical examination. They may be dismissed either as having 'next to nothing' to say about women, or else for advancing unsound views about women that are intended merely to enable the author to 'sneak into the men's club'. This problematic demand for 'loyalty' is dangerously self-limiting, and also inconsistent with feminist theory. For if the experience of being a woman is of the importance feminist theory ascribes to it (and I think it is), then that experience informs women's theoretical work regardless of whether or not it is explicitly feminist. Ignoring such contributions cannot but impoverish feminist theory by depriving it of valuable perspectives.

The treatment feminist scholarship has accorded Hannah Arendt's work is a case in point. Taken seriously by philosophers, especially political philosophers, Arendt has been largely ignored by feminists. Only very recently has there been some feminist rethinking of her work, a rethinking that has yielded interesting results and introduced new perspectives into feminist analysis.[1]

Arendt's ideas, especially those with a direct relevance to feminist theory, are often as stimulating as they are problematic. They cannot be ignored, for they yield insight into the 'human condition' in general and 'women's condition' in particular, and afford new understanding of pressing problems as well as possible solutions to them. Christopher Lasch rightly points out that while Arendt 'raised some of the most important questions that can be raised about modern history... she rejected easy answers' (Lasch, 1983:v). This is sufficient reason for feminist theory to engage with Arendt's thought.

This paper seeks neither to praise Hannah Arendt nor to defend her, but to stimulate an interest in her ideas and to demonstrate their continuing relevance. The issues raised here do not exhaust what feminists may find interesting in her writings nor will this discussion provide a feminist reinterpretation of these questions. Attention is instead restricted to three particular issues: Arendt's view on the question of 'difference' that remains central to feminist debates; her concept of the 'conscious pariah' as it may be applied to women; and finally, her attitude to the so-called 'woman problem' and the women's movement and its connection with her concept of solidarity. Although nowhere elaborated in detail, this concept recurs persistently in her analysis, and appears to be one of the key ideas of her social-political theory. From the point of view of feminism, 'solidarity' seems to be much more telling and also more fruitful—both theoretically and practically—than the currently favoured concept of 'sisterhood'. Such an analysis can also provide a portrait, however sketchy, of Hannah Arendt as philosopher, rebel, and woman.

The problem of 'difference'

In her letter to Gershom Scholem—written in the midst of the controversy over her book *Eichmann in Jerusalem*, and explaining her attitude toward her own Jewishness—Hannah Arendt writes:

> The truth is I have never pretended to be anything else or to be in any way other than I am, and I never even felt tempted in that direction. It would be like saying that I was a man and not a woman... that is, [to deny] indisputable factual data of my own life, and I have never had the wish to change or disclaim facts of this kind. There is such a thing... as a basic gratitude for everything that is as it is; for... what has been *given* and was not, could not, be *made*, for things that are *physei* and not *nomos* (Arendt, 1964:53–4).

In the course of her further elaboration elsewhere, it becomes clear, it is not 'gratitude' and certainly nothing like 'pride' that she is speaking about here. Her attitude is rather one of *acceptance* of what is given to us, acceptance of our 'destiny', which the world presents us with as a part of our human condition of natality. 'Natality' refers both to the contingent quality and also to the fatefulness, for the person concerned, of the circumstances of his or her birth. One grows from but never altogether beyond the identity that is bestowed by the historically circumstantial conditions of one's birth (cf. Minnich 1984).

Natality, its constant and universal character notwithstanding, has also a historical, geographical, or some other social dimension, and in this sense is accidental. The specific characteristics resulting from these dimensions of natality 'pluralise' us and define 'what' we are in society, but they do not exhaust the human condition of plurality which refers also to the uniqueness of each personality.

'What' we are creates a framework within which 'Who' we are is formed and realised, but it never conditions us absolutely. 'Plurality is the condition of human action', says Arendt, because it means that 'we are all the same, that is, human in such a way that nobody is ever the same as anyone else who ever lived, lives, or will live' (Arendt, 1958:8). Without this condition, *action* would be not only meaningless but also impossible. Society, however, not only defines the concrete dimensions or content of 'what' we are; it also hierarchises or differentially values the identities encompassed within this plurality. Some it accepts and recognises as members; to others it ascribes the status of 'outsider' or even 'outcast', the *pariah*. Such a hierarchisation prevents these outsiders from fully 'acting out' their intrinsic possibilities and potentialities. For it is only in action that a person discloses her or his 'Who' nature: it is only in action that we come to know ourselves, and are able to let ourselves be known to others. And it is just this type of human activity—action, which can be performed only in relation to others, that is, above all in public—from which the pariah is excluded.

The characteristics given to us in 'what' we are undoubtedly restrict us. The possibilities, however, which they open up and foreclose are not only historically and socially specific; we are not simply passively 'exposed' to them, but can relate to them in a number of ways. According to Arendt, this is so even in the case of a 'pariah'. For example, one can accept 'exclusion' as the fate of the pariah without resistance and thus remain 'invisible', unable to influence the community in which one lives. Alternatively, one can attempt to assimilate, to deny, or to hide 'what' one is, and thus to gain some access to community affairs. By taking this second option one becomes what Arendt termed a 'parvenu', a social type toward which she can only display, perhaps not always justly, either contempt or pity.

Pity, because such a life-strategy must lead to a struggle against oneself and, in consequence, to a continuous *denial of oneself*. 'The possibilities of being different from what one is, are infinite', writes Arendt in describing Rahel Varnhagen's attempts at assimilation. Once one has negated oneself, however, there are no longer any particular choices: 'There is only one aim: always, at any given moment, to be different from what one is: never to assert onself' (Arendt, 1957:9).

Contempt, because whoever denies 'what' she or he is must also deny their solidarity with those to whom she or he really belongs. For it is solidarity, according to Arendt, and not love or other 'personal' emotions, which one owes to one's own kind, especially to those with whom one shares discrimination, oppression, or exclusion. This is an unwritten moral code for Arendt.

Yet for her, it is important to note, 'solidarity' never implies uncritical acceptance or total identification. On the contrary, it presupposes an ability to be independent in one's own judgements, to be oneself. Only by accepting in this way 'what' we are can we learn 'who' we are.

This leads Arendt to identify yet another possibility, a third alternative in our relationship to what we are: the 'conscious pariah'. The person who really wants to be assimilated cannot pick and choose among the elements to which she or he would be willing to assimilate, cannot decide what she or he likes and dislikes. By contrast, the conscious pariah insists upon her or his rights to be not only 'What' but also 'Who' she or he is, and is therefore able to maintain an independence, a certain distance towards both communities—the one she belongs to by the fact of natality and the one in which she lives.

The conscious pariah

Hannah Arendt chose to adopt in her own life the stance of the conscious pariah, which she first described in telling the painful story of Rahel Varnhagen. This same attitude she also found in the life and work of Heinrich Heine, Sholem Aleichem, Franz Kafka, and Walter Benjamin, all of whom 'affirmed their pariah status together with their right to a place in European culture, all of whom were and remained, above all, themselves'. No less important, these individuals rejected all attempts to treat them as exceptions; they were 'themselves' and therefore unique, just as every human being is a particular somebody and a unique someone. Refusing any exceptional status, they were also rebels and as rebels they did more than just arrange their personal lives and make personal choices: they provoked. Thus when Hannah Arendt herself was offered a professorship by Princeton University she considered rejecting it because the university had presented her case as that of an 'exception woman'. Arendt, however, wanted to be treated not as an exception but as 'what' and 'who' she was—as a woman, a philosopher, a Jewess. Conscious pariahs, writes Arendt:

> were those bold spirits who tried to make of the emancipation of Jews what it really should have been—an admission of Jews *as Jews* to the rank of humanity, rather than a permit to ape the gentiles or an opportunity to play the *parvenu* (Arendt, 1944:68).

It can be argued, of course, that the ability to choose the stance of the conscious pariah is not open to everybody and is therefore elitist in

'Anti-feminism' 123

nature. Every example of a conscious pariah offered by Arendt—Rahel Varnhagen, for example—was in some way an 'exceptional' person. Arendt, however, insisted that Rahel found her place in the history of European humanity only because she remained after all a Jew and pariah, that is, she *remained what she really was*.

There were several reasons for Rahel's failure to 'become one human being among others'. Partly it was due to the discrepancy in her time between 'what men expected of women "in general" and what women could give or wanted in their turn, a gap that virtually could not be closed' (Arendt, 1957:xiii). It was also due partly to her discovery that, for a pariah, entrance into society was possible only at the price of lying, of sacrificing every natural impulse, of concealing all truth, misusing all love (Arendt, 1957:169), something that she was not prepared nor able to do because of 'who' she was. Finally, she had to recognise that 'if one wishes to be a normal person precisely like everybody else, there is scarcely any alternative to exchanging old prejudices for new ones' (Arendt, 1957:182). It was only from this recognition (for she was not a naturally courageous person) that her courage, a courage to return to herself, emerged. Although she clearly felt that this self of hers was just 'nothing', it still meant a great deal more to her than to be 'nothing more than her husband'. It still was *herself*. This process of recognition made Rahel Varnhagen a rebel. To be a rebel and to be isolated were the two characteristics common to almost all the 'conscious pariahs' described by Arendt. Neither characteristic was sought. Rather, each ensued from the much more basic choice made by those individuals—to remain what they were.

Among Arendt's heroes there is, however, a conscious pariah of a different type, exemplified by Rosa Luxemburg. 'She was an outsider not only because she was and remained a Polish Jew in a country [Germany] she disliked and party she came soon to despise, but also because she was a woman', writes Arendt of Luxemburg (Arendt, 1966:44-5). Her situation thus resembled Rahel's. Both, as Jews and women, were cast as outsiders and above all, both claimed their right to be what they were, even if in Rahel's case she arrived at this decision late in life and only after much hesitation. Despite the fact that an entire century separated the two women, and despite the differences in their social milieu, education, and personal qualities, a number of parallels connect them to each other, as well as to Hannah Arendt herself. They all shared a 'longing for happiness', an enjoyment of 'simple things', of the 'true realities' such as nature, poetry, and music.

Rahel and Rosa also shared loneliness, though they were lonely in different ways. Rahel's loneliness had to do with extreme insecurity and vulnerability. She never aspired, and in her time could not really aspire, to become involved in public issues. All she really wanted was to define herself, to affirm herself, to find out 'Who' she really was: through her purely personal relations, through her loves, through her friendships, through her literary salon. Although the disclosure of who we are always demands the presence of others, it is possible not only in the public sphere 'out there' but also, in different ways, in our most intimate relationships.

By contrast Rosa Luxemburg was a doer, a revolutionary, a leader and a theoretician of a mass-movement, and this represented for Arendt a conscious pariah of a different type than Rahel. Rosa was a rebel by choice from the very outset. She also enjoyed a self-confidence often misjudged by others as arrogance and conceit (a trait shared by Arendt). This self-confidence of Luxemburg's had two sources. First, the 'essentially simple experience of a childhood world in which mutual respect and unconditional trust, a universal humanity and a genuine, almost naive contempt for social and ethnic distinctions were taken for granted' (Arendt, 1966:41), provided by her family. The second source was the extraordinary peer group that surrounded her in her native Poland, a group whose most notable characteristic was not so much shared moral principles as, in Arendt's words, shared 'moral taste'.[2] This peer group and its standards, which were 'uniquely their own', provided Luxemburg with strength and the will to act and hence the will to endure not just her social position as a pariah but a lack of recognition even in her own world of revolutionaries.

'Success', writes Arendt, 'was withheld from Rosa Luxemburg in life, death, and after death' (Arendt, 1966:34), but it was not success or acknowledgement that she sought. Yet some, including her excellent biographer Nettl, not to mention her 'quasi-peers' from the German Social Democratic Party, considered her overly ambitious. In a man with similar gifts and comparable opportunities, the ambition displayed by Rosa Luxemburg would have been considered natural. But in a woman, and one so consciously a woman as her, it appeared objectionable.

Her own life demonstrates, however, that it was not ambition nor even a concern with herself which propelled her into political action, for 'if she had been concerned with herself, she would have stayed on in Zürich after her dissertation and would have pursued certain intellectual interests' (Arendt, 1979:311). Or having made the mistake of 'engaging' herself in the socialist movement, she could have lived quite comfortably in the pariah society of German socialists, itself a reassuring miniature of German society at large. Her entry into political activity, was motivated, not by her concern with herself, but by the fact that 'she could not stand the injustice *within the world*' (ibid., see also Arendt, 1966:38). When one is concerned with the world and not with oneself one acts politically, whatever the character of this action otherwise may be, Arendt emphasises (ibid). Such action is not guided by pity or even compassion but by *solidarity*. Solidarity may be aroused, but is not guided, by suffering. Solidarity can inspire and guide political action because 'it partakes of reason, and hence of generality' and therefore 'is able to comprehend a multitude conceptually'. It is out of such solidarity that humans 'establish deliberately and, as it were, dispassionately a community of interest with the oppressed and exploited' (Arendt, 1979a:88).

This was Hannah Arendt's view of Luxemburg, one with which she could easily identify even though her own passion was for thinking, not acting. She was not a doer, unless the circumstances provided no morally acceptable alternative. Her interest and concern, however, had always been *in* and *for the world*. Therefore, although the Rahel Varnhagen book is considered by many as an 'autobiographical biography' of Hannah Arendt, it was Rosa Luxemburg who was Arendt's real heroine — not the much more passive, self-centred, and vulnerable Rahel. To deny the existence of fundamental historical and, above all, political differences between Luxemburg and Arendt would be absurd. Yet on some basic issues Arendt totally agrees with her, and even in cases where she does not, she justifies Luxemburg's choices and solutions within her own specific situation.

Arendt accepted a number of principles that Luxemburg expressed. Like Luxemburg, she was convinced that 'the organisation of revolutionary action can and must be learned in revolution itself' and that the political instruments fashioned by the people in spontaneous participatory action are also the most appropriate instruments of government. Like Luxemburg she shared Heine's view that a 'deformed revolution' is much more dangerous than an unsuccessful one. Like Luxemburg, Arendt too stressed the absolute necessity of both individual and public freedom under all circumstances. She too supported the idea of the republic. Above all, she resembled Luxemburg in her courage to represent the most unorthodox standpoints whenever they expressed her genuine opinion and judgement, regardless of the consequences.

The 'women's problem'

The parallel between Rosa Luxemburg and Hannah Arendt extends to their common understanding of the so-called 'women's problem' and its solution. Neither of them, and certainly not Arendt, expected these very real problems to be solved automatically as the result of other social–political transformations. They shared the conviction that women's issues cannot and should not be divorced from larger political concerns and broader political struggles, instead insisting that they be pursued jointly with other political goals in coordinated political activities.

Arendt gave expression to her understanding of the women's problem as early as the 1930s in her review of A. Ruhle-Gerstel's *The Contemporary Women's Problem* (Young-Bruehl, 1982:96–97) and in her study of Rahel Varnhagen. Her formulation contained in the latter is not only more original but also reflects quite clearly both the insights and the inconsistencies of Hannah Arendt's views concerning women. As has already been noted, Arendt here emphasises that as far back as in Varnhagen's time, the 'woman problem' appeared as 'the discrepancy between *what men expected* of women "in general" and *what women could give or wanted* in their turn'. Her contrasting, or identifying this tension between what men expected of women and what women really were and wanted thus evokes one of Arendt's central convictions: that we can only realise our 'sameness', our common humanity, by being faithful to 'What' and 'Who' we are, that is, only by upholding the plurality of our individual and collective identities. This clearly suggests that personal as well as collective identities are dynamic, that they are historically formed and also *transformed*; and that this transformation is not a process external to or independent from us but instead one that we actively take part in ('what women wanted').

To speak of our wanting or expecting something must refer somehow to our needs. One might conclude from this that a solution to the 'woman problem' is achievable only through a *re-negotiation* of the needs and, related to them, of the collective identities of men and women alike. Neither of these is, however, Arendt's own conclusion. For one, she does not connect collective identities with needs, at least not explicitly. Moreover, though she does not openly deny the changing nature of needs, she is inclined to treat them as 'given' rather than 'negotiable' characteristics. It is for this reason, according to her, that needs are non-political issues and hence not worthy of being talked about in public.

Yet undeniably—and this is an outstanding characteristic of modernity—needs have been brought into the public sphere. In order to take account of this process, Arendt distinguishes between 'social' issues, which are not genuinely 'public', and political issues, which are. With its 'quasi-public' character the emergence of the social has blurred the important distinction between the private and the political and has also led to the atrophy of both spheres.

Arendt agrees that social issues are not irrelevant to society or even to the successful operation of the political. In *On Revolution* she writes that: 'while it is true that freedom can come only to those whose needs have been fulfilled, it is equally true that it will escape those who are bent upon living for their desires' (Arendt, 1979a:139). For the concern with the 'political' orients us toward the world and towards those with whom we share it, while it is simply ourselves and our own desires that we represent in our 'social' discourses. Arendt herself is unable to sustain a consistent distinction between the 'social' and the 'political'. She nevertheless insists that it is possible to separate them by distinguishing between 'things that are debatable and worthy of debate' and matters which 'we can figure out with certainty, and which therefore are not the proper subject for public talk' (Arendt, 1979:315-320).

This distinction between the 'social' and the 'political' is one of the reasons for Arendt's ambivalence towards the women's movement, since she considers most of the issues it raises to be basically social and not political. They are concerned with liberating women economically and not with their freedom as citizens. Although this characterisation may have been more applicable to the movement Arendt knew than to its present-day variants, the distinction remains problematic.

At the same time, as several writers have emphasised, this is not a pointless distinction, although it clearly requires further elaboration and perhaps reinterpretation. It is perhaps possible, as Hanna Pitkin suggests, 'to conceptualise the public [in a way that] recognises its roots in human need and its consequences for power, privilege, and suffering, without incurring the dangers Arendt fears' (Pitkin, 1981:343). This may involve a reconceptualisation of 'needs' themselves. Nancy Fraser's recent writings pose the question in just this fashion. She distinguishes between different aspects and levels of 'needs-talk'. Notably, she distinguishes the 'struggle over the interpretation of needs' from the institutionalised talk of experts and from the 'needs-definitions' provided by different state apparatuses. In this way she both affirms Arendt's distinction and demonstrates not just the possibility but the reality of the discourse about needs attaining a truly political character within contemporary feminist and social movements.

Arendt's ambivalence towards the women's movement, however, is not exhausted by this point, but is embedded much deeper in her social–political theory. She was concerned that the women's movement often promotes a form of emancipation that resembles the assimilation of the parvenue, and which therefore is not a real emancipation at all. For to be really emancipated, women have to be emancipated *as women*; that is, not to accept the existing structures but to pluralise them and change them to a degree that suits their own identities. For 'man and woman can be the same, namely human, only by being... different from each other' (Arendt, 1957a:89). Although this argument may now seem a familiar concern, by making it when she did Arendt demonstrates both her perspicacity and also the inconsistency in her treatment of 'needs' and the 'social'.

The grounds of her ambivalence went even further. Arendt feared that should women as a group enter the sphere of politics concerned primarily with their own 'women's problems', they would face up neither to the plurality of opinions and judgements among women themselves nor to the plurality of opinions confronting them. Such a shortcoming would necessarily lead to a deformation of the movement itself and to a further destruction of the political sphere. Though not quite consistent with her commitment to the idea of participatory politics—which should be open to all—she really would have preferred the way to be led not by 'the oppressed and degraded' but 'by those who were not oppressed and not degraded but could not bear that others were' (Arendt, 1973a:167).

This, according to her, would ensure genuinely political action, action led by those with a *concern for the world* and not merely their own particular interests. For Arendt, politics is not primarily about 'making claims' but above all about learning what it means to 'share the world with others'. To bring about change (which is also a task of politics) claims obviously have to be made. But to maintain the interest in others which identifies the political, Arendt would have preferred claims to be raised not self-interestedly but on behalf of others. Thus her approval for the movements of the 1960s was almost without exception directed towards actions undertaken in the name and for the sake of others (ibid:165).

This again underlines the centrality of the concept of 'solidarity' for Hannah Arendt. This concept, which she sometimes equated with a non-intimate understanding of 'friendship', she contrasts with that of 'fraternity' or brotherhood. Promoted to the political sphere by the French Revolution, 'fraternity' is considered by Arendt as the natural bond between pariahs, between the 'repressed and persecuted, the exploited and humiliated' (Arendt, 1968a:14), but not between citizens. Fraternity for Arendt is only a 'psychological substitute ... for the loss of the common, visible world' (ibid:16) and is therefore irrelevant to politics. Friendship or solidarity, on the other hand, 'makes political demands and preserves reference to the world' (ibid:25). It constitutes a possible basis for an exchange of opinions about this world, and thus for political discourse and political action. How the *transition* from the status of the 'pariah' to that of the 'citizen' is to be made is a question that Arendt does not address clearly, and this constitutes a primary problem for contemporary feminism.

The success of the feminist movement today depends largely upon its ability to generate social solidarity across boundaries. For, as historical experience has demonstrated, women's emancipation is not purely a question of appropriate legislation. Rather, it depends upon the ability of the movement to renegotiate some of the most vital definitions and norms with the other half of humanity in order to truly universalise them. To do this will require an ability to generate support for a programme of social change that promotes liberation, the recognition of diverse human potentialities and ways of life, the renegotiation of value-hierarchies, and the constitution of new meanings.³ For such a programme Hannah Arendt's ideas remain relevant.

Notes

1 See e.g. Riot-Sarcey & Varikas' (1986), 5, iv (1986); Nancy Fraser (1987) and Nancy Hartsock (1983), London, Longman.
2 I do not intend to enter here into a debate with this evaluation of Luxemburg's peer-group, which Arendt herself took partly from Nettl and partly from her own family's tales. It was undoubtedly an extraordinary group, even if one cannot insist without qualification upon its high 'moral taste'.
3 I have attempted to elaborate upon this point in some detail in M. Markus, 'Women, success, and civil society: submission to, or subversion of, the achievement principle', *Praxis International*, 5, iv (1986), and in a paper delivered to an International Symposium on New Perspectives on Democracy and Civil Society, London, February 21-22, 1986: 'The Antinomies of Civil Society and the Feminist Movement' (manuscript).

V
Philosophy

Elizabeth K. Minnich

10 To judge in freedom: *Hannah Arendt on the relation of thinking and morality*

> I will admit that I am, of course, primarily interested in understanding. This is absolutely true. And I will admit that there are other people who are primarily interested in doing something. I am not. I can very well live without doing anything. But I cannot live without trying at least to understand what happens.
>
> (Arendt, 1979:303)

Hannah Arendt spent her life trying to understand what was happening, but her intense involvement with the problems posed by the dangerous and dramatic times in which she lived was not the result of any original taste for politics. As a student, she planned to lead the exalted life of the mind that, following the dominant Western tradition, she understood to be quite separate from the sordidness of action. But the dark times in which she lived would not allow her to remain in the ivory tower. She chose to try 'at least to understand'. Despite the mildness of that phrase, it names a passionate choice, a deep commitment.

With that choice, she expressed her difference from, and profound disillusionment with, those 'professional thinkers' (Arendt, 1979:303) who refused to face what was happening as Hitler came to power — with those who retreated into the academic version of the 'inner emigration'[1] of many Germans of the time as well as with those who, horrifyingly, turned into apologists and even collaborators. Watching friends, students, professors fail to comprehend what was happening, she learnt in no uncertain terms that the academic life of the mind, as she said later, is no protection against culpable political stupidity.[2]

Later in her life, in a similarly quiet statement, she noted that 'it may even be nice that we lost the monopoly of what Kant once very ironically called the professional thinkers. We can start worrying about what thinking means for the activity of acting' (Arendt, 1979: 303). And that, indeed, is what she 'worried' about for the rest of her life. The question that was basic to Hannah Arendt's work came into being then, and remained. She set out to discover if there is a life of the mind that does not unsuit us for good political judgement, if in thinking itself there might be a basis for a morality adequate to action.

As a contemporary of the creation of totalitarianism (about which she wrote her classic study), Arendt came to believe that thinking is one of our most vulnerable, not one of our most persistent, abilities. It is not only true, she decided, that freedom requires thought: thought also requires freedom. She would say, with a sigh, that Spinoza's belief in the freedom of the mind was possible to him as a thinker only because totalitarianism had not yet been invented. Totalitarianism proved, to her, that few can go on thinking when all around them have ceased to do so.

In an utterly characteristic move, she turned upside down the centuries-old assumption that the one thing over which we do have complete control is our own minds. She considered that in at least some of its functioning, the human mind may well *require* publicness, hence the freedom of public communication. (In this as in so many things she learnt from or found corroboration in Kant, in this case in his political writings where he argues for the essential nature of freedom of the pen).[3]

It is important to notice here, from the beginning, that *freedom* is a critical consideration. As Arendt thought about thinking and whether it provides a basis for a morality adequate to action, she was thinking about freedom. As part of that emphasis on freedom, she early thought about how to *comprehend* reality—not how to know it, not how to explain it, but how to remain, as a thinker, open to it.

In *Rahel Varnhagen: The Life of a Jewish Woman* (written in 1933, published first only in 1957), Hannah Arendt created an unusual biography that suggests, at least, the kind of understanding she continued to seek. She set out to find a way to uncover the meaning of Varnhagen's life, not the truth about it. She writes of her method:

> [I do not use] interpretations according to the psychological standards and categories that the author introduces from the outside; nor about her position in Romanticism and the effect of the Goethe cult in Berlin, of which she was actually the originator; nor about the significance of her salon for the social history of the period; nor about her ideas and her 'weltanschauung', [world view] in so far as these can be reconstructed from her letters. *What interested me solely was to narrate the story of Rahel's life as she herself might have told it* (Arendt, 1957/1974:xv; emphasis added).

Arendt wanted to understand from within, not to know about. She stood within the centre of the circle with her subject, rejecting all the viewing posts around the perimeter from where the experts might have claimed to speak knowingly about the gazed-on subject. Arendt sought some act of mind that could move her both in and out of Varnhagen's life in a way that neither Rahel, caught within her own story, nor others, standing outside of it, could achieve. She decided to think *with* Rahel Varnhagen, and neither *as* nor *about* her.

She chose not to think *about* Rahel, because of her conviction that to turn a subject, and individual, into an object violates the freedom that only makes sense for subjects — for people, not things — and, at the same time, falsifies reality. People are not simply things. Arendt held it to be a given about human beings that 'nothing entitles us to assume that [humans have][4] a nature or essence in the same sense as other things' (Arendt, 1958:10). To know our own individual or collective nature or essence would be a trick akin to 'jumping over our own shadow' (ibid); therefore only some sort of god could know us as we know things. For Arendt, humans are subjects always, and must not be understood as objects — not, that is, if we value freedom.

Hannah Arendt used to say that the real problem with strict behaviourism (or any social 'science' that mimics knowledge about things) is not that it is not accurate but that it could become so. She would then note that those who take the proof of their theories to lie in their ability to predict human behaviour have a very dangerous stake in increasing predictability — that is, in reducing freedom — in the real world.[5]

The idea that knowledge needs to be 'above' change, to be of the realm of Being rather than that of Becoming (as Plato put it in *The Republic*), is, Arendt said, one of the basic reasons why 'political philosophy' would have seemed to the ancients to be a contradiction in terms.[6] The turn to thinking rather than to knowing when she set out to write about Rahel Varnhagen was Arendt's early way of working through such problems. In this biography she was beginning to re-think thinking, to break loose from the notion that thinking has its end, its termination or purpose or justification, in knowing. After all, insofar as knowledge is made up of answers to questions, it is not appropriate to humans who are, as Arendt liked to say (paraphrasing Augustine), questions to themselves.[7]

That we cannot *know* ourselves was, according to Arendt, no cause for despair; quite the contrary. This realisation frees us to consider what it means that we can *think*. Arendt's work on thinking is most evidently engaged in conversations with Kant — whose 'maxims of common human understanding' in *The Critique of Judgement* (Kant, 1964:136) include 'to put ourselves in thought in the place of everyone else', as Arendt tried to do with Rahel — and with Socrates, whose metaphors for the thinker (midwife, electric fish, gadfly) and for thinking (a wind that blows everything down, a conversation between me and myself) recur throughout her writings.

Thinking stings us awake—as Socrates, the Athenian gadfly, stung with his questions anyone who claimed to know something about humans and how we ought to be. When we are stung into thought, we awake from the bemusement of our certainties and are thus thrown back into the world, back into genuine, open converse with others. We no longer have anything to teach; we have only the kind of questions Socrates learnt to ask from his brilliant teacher, Diotima (whom he credits in 'the Symposium'). The Diotemic method uses questions motivated by Eros, the yearning for that which we do not *and cannot* possess. Thinking, like love, effects a kind of propulsion out of ourselves toward others. This is one way in which it is related to the political.

However, while thinking is related to the political, it is not sufficiently so. It does throw us out into the public and require our engagement with others, but it also requires that we have solitude (even in the midst of others). When we are actually caught up in thinking, we pursue our own internal conversation. The wind of thought can throw us suddenly out of the very public realm into which it has propelled us. Socrates, we remember, was renowned not only for his presence in the market place but also for the 'trances' to which he was subject. Sometimes, he would stand absolutely still for great stretches of time, oblivious to all around him. Thinking is like a wind that blows everything down, a stinging fly that wakes us up—but it is also, Socrates was careful to tell us, like an electric fish that paralyses.

'Stop and think', Arendt often said, with delight at the aptness of the cliché. Furthermore, when we have stopped to think and so removed ourselves from those around us, we also 'move among invisibles', as Arendt liked to put it (Arendt, 1971: passim). With the use of memory that 'makes present what is absent'[8] and imagination that can change what is really unchangeable, we leap above the stubborn here/now/thisness of this world.

Is thinking, then, finally non- or even anti-political, despite the fact that it propels us into the company of others and prepares us to comprehend them? The answer to this for Arendt is no: that in thinking lies the basis for political virtue.

Arendt wrote:

Reason itself, the thinking ability which we have, has a need to actualize itself... We have forgotten that *every* human being has a need to think, not to think abstractly, not to answer the ultimate questions of God, immortality, and freedom, nothing but to think while... living (Arendt, 1979:303).

Thinking is a basis of human being, a *common* virture. It is not an ability belonging only to the few; it belongs to us all. It is, then, a basis for our being 'political animals', creatures who live together, even though it also throws us out of company when we actually do it. It is from thinking that we develop that critical political virtue, common sense.[9]

In addition to grounding our commonality with others such that we can, if we will, develop common sense, thinking also relates us to reality, the realm of action. Arendt wrote: 'The task of the mind is to understand what happened, and this understanding, according to Hegel, is [the human] way of reconciling... with reality; its actual end is to be at peace with the world' (Arendt, 1961:8). Understanding, emerging from thinking not as a product, not as knowledge, but as reconciliation with reality, expresses not just the ability and the need of all human beings to think but the link between thinking and reality. For Arendt, thinking is an antidote not just to a notion of the life of the mind that scorns the messiness of reality, not just to the whatness of knowledge, but to the despair of those for whom reality has been more than they can bear. It is a faculty we need if we are to be able to live *with* others, with ourselves in our real world.

In 1944 in her essay 'The Jew as Pariah' she wrote: 'A true human life cannot be led by people who feel themselves detached from the basic and simple rules of humanity nor by those who elect to live in a vacuum, even if they be led to do so by persecution. [People's] lives must be nominal, not exceptional.' And she goes on to note that for Kafka, whom she greatly admired, his

> whole genius, his whole expression of the modern spirit, lay precisely in the fact that what he sought was to be a human being, a normal member of human society. It was not his fault that this society had ceased to be human, and that, trapped within its meshes, those of its members who were really [people] of goodwill were forced to function within it as something exceptional and abnormal—saints or madmen (Arendt, 1944:89).

In such a world, to seek to be normal is, like the effort to understand, a terrible struggle. We remain beings who *can* think but that does not mean that we will do so, or that we will do so well. Our ability to think does not deny us the capacity to lie to ourselves. We are many within ourselves. Our thinking actualises the split between 'me' and 'myself' and invokes the voices of others within us with whom we think. In so doing, it creates conscience from consciousness[10] —but we are always free to choose to silence those voices that say what we do not want to hear.

Indeed, Hannah Arendt worried that 'thoughtlessness—the heedless recklessness or hopeless confusion or complacent repetition of "truths" which have become trivial and empty' (Arendt, 1958:5)—is 'among the outstanding characteristics of our time'. And, as she saw it, such thoughtlessness is an aspect of, or makes possible, human evil. That, too, marks thinking as a basis for political virtue: it gives us our commonality and common sense, calls us to think and so speak together, awakens conscience from consciousness, allows us to reconcile ourselves with reality, *and so*, when we turn from it, allows us to be politically very dangerous indeed.

It was while covering the Eichmann trial in Jerusalem that she 'found herself with a concept', as she liked to say (cf. Arendt, 1971:419)—that of 'the banality of evil'. Eichmann, the consummate bureaucrat who was as well-behaved a prisoner as he had been a Nazi, stood before her as the incarnation of the evil of thoughtlessness. Arendt found herself with the question that is basic to all her work now crystallised:

> Could the activity of thinking as such, the habit of examining and reflecting upon whatever happens to come to pass, regardless of the specific content and quite independent of results, could this activity be of such a nature that it 'conditions' [humans] against evil-doing? (Arendt, 1971:418).

The phenomenon of Eichmann, as well as the other aspects of thinking we have noted, might well suggest that this is the case. But being 'conditioned' against evil-doing does not guarantee anything at all about being able to do good. We have not yet answered her question.

Arendt summed up the problem along with her main propositions as follows:

> *First*, if such a connection [between the ability or inability to think and the problem of evil] exists at all, then the faculty of thinking as distinguished from the search for knowledge, must be ascribed to everybody; it cannot be a privilege of the few.

We have seen that she assented to this proposition, and why. She held that all humans have the ability to think and a need to do so. Not all will develop that ability, but that does not change its givenness.

> *Second*, if Kant is right and the faculty of thought has a 'natural aversion' against accepting its own results as 'solid axioms', then we cannot expect any moral propositions or commandments, no final code of conduct from the thinking activity, least of all a new and now allegedly final definition of what is good and what is evil.

This, too, she accepted. Thinking, in actualising the split between me and myself and drawing in all the others with whom we have thought, is resultless. There is always another perspective, another question. The wind of thought blows everything down.

Third, if it is true that thinking deals with invisibles, it follows that it is out of order because we normally move in a world of appearances in which the most radical experience of *dis*appearance is death... hence, *the question is unavoidable: How can anything relevant for the world we live in arise out of so resultless an enterprise?* (Arendt, 1971:425-426; emphasis added).

This, then, is the problem: our ability and need to think make it possible for us to prepare for moral action and yet give us no positive guidance on what to do. But that does not mean that thinking changes nothing. It actualises and develops certain basic human abilities — it has, not results-as-products, but *effects*. What, then, are the effects of thinking? From the perspective of the person, the particular 'who' that thinks, the 'who' that lies at the heart of all human being, the effect is far from negative. Thinking opens us to the unmediated experience of the subject. And that, the experience of being human in the essential mystery of the unknowable subject–self, is in itself moral. It is an experience Eichmann did not have. Eichmann needed to know the rules to know himself, and from a self so constituted, monstrous deeds — far beyond his own limited capacity to conceive, to intend, to feel — were possible. Eichmann killed indirectly, just as he lived, and finally died, indirectly — playing a role, not enacting himself. He did not actualise himself through thinking; he did not realise his own common humanity; and so he could not comprehend that of others. They were 'whats' not 'whos' to him.

In a culture that has held up to us as models of courage those willing to be martyred — and far too often, to kill — for their certainties, it is worth comparing Eichmann and Socrates very carefully. Socrates, the thinker, died rather than renounce his uncertainties, his need to talk with others because he himself did not know anything. On his death bed, after refusing an offer to help him escape, Socrates discussed with his friends his utter lack of fear of death, which sprang not from his certainties but from his uncertainty as to whether death should be feared or desired. In our frustration that thinking prepares us for morality without giving us positive guidance on what we should do, we should not overlook the critical effects it does have: it undoes certainties that are inappropriate and so threatening to action, and it actualises a self that is able freely to act well with others understood to be subject–selves.

Still, if we have no rules, no principles, no maxims to apply, are we not left vulnerable to the worst sort of relativism, the kind that slides quickly into nihilism, or utter egocentricity, or unaccountable particularity of the most eccentric sort?

It is here that Arendt turned to the human faculty of judgement. She writes: 'The purging element in thinking, Socrates' midwifery, that brings out the implications of unexamined opinions and thereby destroys them — values, doctrines, theories, and even convictions — is political by implication'. We have seen some of the reasons she had for so saying, but in this late essay on 'Thinking and Moral Considerations' she is ready to add something important:

> For this destruction has a liberating effect on another human faculty, the faculty of judgement, which one may call, with some justification, the most political of [our] mental abilities. It is the faculty to judge *particulars* without subsuming them under those general rules which can be taught and learned until they grow into habits (Arendt, 1971:446).

Thinking, then, does not give us directions on what to do. It prepares us for, precisely as it makes us aware that we need to turn to, a different faculty — judgement.

Arendt drew on Kant's *Critique of Judgement* to explore the faculty that enables us to change realms, as it were, to move from principle to particular — from thought to world and back, not deductively and not inductively, but as thinkers.

Deduction asks us to apply principles to the world without taking the world into account: what is right is right, regardless of circumstance, of history, of motive. Induction takes the world into account without regard for principle: what is right is what I decide I need to do here and now. A purely inductive judge is like the Queen in Alice in Wonderland, making up rules to suit each new occasion.

But a thinker, having found that all principles can be questioned and that particular situations can be comprehended if we think them through — think *with* them — is free to bring non-determinate judgement to bear, to ask which principle might illuminate this situation, to see how this situation illuminates that principle.[11]

The thinker understands that, in the realm of human action in which freedom is fundamental, neither the tyranny of principle nor the tyranny of random individual will is acceptable. S/he is like the (rare and wonderful) judge who is able to honour both principle and individual, struggling to bring them together such that neither is violated but both are illuminated, both are better understood.

What we need to exercise good judgement is knowledge of relevant principles or laws; an understanding of what we know; experience that can give us a sense of what knowledge, what principles, rules, laws, might be relevant and helpful — and the ability to see, to hear, to comprehend the individual or particular situation as Arendt tried to understand Rahel Varnhagen. Judgement does not stand alone, or enter as a kind of mental *deus ex machina*. What it does is move between what we know and understand and what, in the moment, we comprehend as *this* that is before us.

But how are we to learn judgement? Arendt accepts from Kant that judgement emerges as a 'peculiar talent which can be practised only and cannot be taught' because 'judgement deals with particulars, and when the thinking ego moving among generalities emerges from its withdrawal and returns to the world of particular appearances, it turns out that the mind needs a new "gift" to deal with them' (Arendt, 1971:215).

How then is it done, the movement from principle to particular, from rule to person such that both are comprehended and taken equally into account? We have arrived at the key, and the trick, question: 'How is it done?' sounds as if it is a question to be responded to with directions, with a method codified and so reproducible. For Arendt, the correct response is: 'It is done in freedom'. That is essential, for as soon as it is not done freely, judgement has become something else, has been collapsed back into deduction or induction.

We cannot be taught how to think or exercise good judgement, but that does not mean that we cannot learn. If we are thinkers, we are developing a self capable of being good in action among others. Then, to develop the capacity to judge well so that we may make sound moral judgements about what we should do in the realm of action, of *praxis*, we must *practise*. No code, no principles, no training will suffice or substitute for practice, which must then be thought through, learned *with*. To practise living well, it is necessary to exercise all our human faculties within our particular reality, comprehended insofar as we are able so that we may be reconciled to it and will not be tempted to flee it, to except ourselves from the great struggle to understand what happens. We must think as ourselves, with others, in an effort to think what we are doing, as Arendt put it in the Prologue to *The Human Condition* (1958:5).[12]

Finally, Arendt's question 'Is there a ground for morality adequate for action in thinking itself?' has to be answered. In any ordinary sense the answer is no. But in the sense that the life of thought prepares us for judgement which gives us guidance without allowing us to give up freedom, the answer is yes. Thinking, and all it actualises in us, not only liberates us from dogmatism but develops in us the common sense on which judgement relies as the ground on which to bring together principle and individual in the real world we share.

As we practise thinking, judging, and acting, we become who we are. If we do so well, we remain our own friends, we achieve reconciliation with ourselves, the others we think with, and with reality. On this Arendt agreed with Plato: the just person, the one who makes good judgements, is one who acts so as to be able to go on being her/his own friend. When we fail, we fail in reconcialiation with others, with the world we share with them, and in so doing we fail ourselves. For Arendt, finally, the life of the mind *of the thinker* in itself constitutes a reason for caring about the life of action.

In a poem Arendt particularly liked, W. H. Auden wrote of himself:

> You hope, yes,
>   your books will excuse you,
> save you from hell:
>   nevertheless,
> without looking sad,
>   without in any way
> seeming to blame
>   (he doesn't need to,
> knowing well
>   what a lover of art
> like yourself pays heed to),
>   God may reduce you
> on Judgment Day
>   to tears of shame,
> reciting by heart
>   the poems you would
> have written, had
>   your life been good.
>
> (quoted in Arendt, 1966a:207)

Notes

1 The phrase 'inner emigration' was used often by Hannah Arendt in her lectures and conversation. For an instance of its usage in print, see Arendt (1968a:19).
2 Throughout this paper, I am drawing not only on Hannah Arendt's published works but on my recollections of our conversations and the courses I took with her when I was a graduate student and her teaching assistant at the Graduate Faculty of The New School for Social Research.
3 See the collection of Kant's political writings listed, edited by Hans Reiss (1970).
4 I have substituted the parenthetical '[humans have]' in this line to avoid the distraction of Arendt's use of 'man', as I have changed her use of 'he' and 'mankind' elsewhere in the paper. In general, I consider correcting authors' usage of exclusive language a very tricky business, and never do so without considerable care and thought. In many cases, changing 'mankind' to 'humankind', for example, succeeds only in hiding the genuine exclusiveness of the text: its author may actually have intended to refer only to males, and often only to a particular group of males, such as literate upper-class Western males at that. To change the language of such a text so that it appears that its author was being inclusive when such was not the case only further mystifies that tradition within which the classification of some human subjects into a group of objects was so fully accepted that it passed without notice. In this case, however, I have corrected Hannah Arendt's language for several reasons. She genuinely

intended to be inclusive when she spoke on a general level about humankind. That her language, and more importantly the dominant tradition within which she was educated and lived, may sometimes have betrayed her intention may also be true—but that is another story.

5 I am here recalling comments she made to me in conversation that are, I believe, borne out by her written work: cf. her essay on Lessing in *Men in Dark Times* (Arendt, 1968a:3–31).
6 This is a comment with which she liked to begin her lectures at The Graduate Faculty of The New School for Social Research.
7 See, for example, her comment in *The Human Condition* (1958:10).
8 I am paraphrasing a comment that Arendt made frequently in her lectures and seminars; cf. her lecture on 'Thinking and moral considerations' (1971:424) as well as her discussion in *The Life of the Mind* (1978, I: esp. 85, 133, & 201).
9 This is a critical notion that has been given far less than due consideration in this paper. For some of its background in Arendt, see the lecture on 'Thinking and Moral Considerations' (1971:425); 'Willing', the appendix on 'Judging' (1978, II:267–271); and, of course, Arendt's source, Kant's *Critique of Judgement*, para. 40, 'Of taste as a kind of sensus communis' (Kant, 1964).
10 This is also an important notion that begs further elaboration. For some of its background in Arendt, see (1978, I:190) and (1971:418 & 442).
11 Obviously, I am not here following Kant's definitions of the different forms of judgement closely, but trying to suggest what I take to be an understanding closer to Arendt's.
12 The preceding points in the sentence are paraphrases of two of Kant's 'Maxims of common human understanding' in his *Critique of Judgment*, 1964, para. 40.

Agnes Heller

11 Hannah Arendt on the 'Vita Contemplativa'

The Life of the Mind was planned as the culmination of Hannah Arendt's lifelong preoccupation with fundamental questions of the human condition. As is well known, of the whole work only the volumes on 'Thinking' and 'Willing' were concluded and published posthumously. Arendt died suddenly before she could commence work on the third volume dealing with 'Judging'. Some of Arendt's lectures on Kant's *Critique of Judgement* have now been published in a volume entitled *Lectures on Kant's Political Philosophy*, and her preliminary remarks on judging are scattered all over the first two volumes of *The Life of the Mind*. Even so, a reconstruction of the whole project demands unusual interpretive sensitivity.

Perhaps the deepest problem to be faced by those who wish to attempt such a reconstruction is the fact that the second volume (on 'Willing') was written impatiently, visibly in a hurry. No doubt there are in all philosophies inconsistencies which are difficult, if not impossible, for the authors themselves to eliminate. Nonetheless it is clear that certain inconsistencies, both within and between the first and second volumes of *The Life of the Mind*, would have been eliminated had Arendt had the time to complete the third volume. Since the oeuvre remained incomplete, an interpreter is presented with two options. She can either take the text as it now stands or she can try to eliminate those inconsistencies she believes the author would herself have eliminated. The second option is riskier, though certainly more fecund.

Let me illuminate the dilemma with reference to an issue of major importance. Hannah Arendt often refers to *thinking, willing*, and *judging* as the fundamental faculties at work in *bios theoreticos* while, she suggests, other mental faculties are operative in a life of 'action'.

In other contexts, however, she refers to thinking, willing and judging as the only three 'mental faculties'. She accepts the traditional division of the human self into *mind, soul* and *body* while relegating emotions to the soul and the aforementioned three faculties to the mind. The gist of the matter is that in Arendt the category 'thinking' stands for *nous* or reason (as *Vernunft*) and she emphatically stresses that 'cognition' (as *Verstand*) is not 'thinking' and that, moreover, it has nothing to do with thinking.

Of the merits and demerits of this theoretical proposal more will be said later. In this context, however, the following consideration is important: if 'thinking', 'willing' and 'judging' exhaust the faculties of the mind, where can 'cognition' or 'intellect' be located, if only metaphorically? The same question arises with regard to 'imagination', to which Arendt otherwise assigns a pre-eminent role in contemplative life. Is imagination, one might ask, simply inherent in the three faculties of the mind? If so, it has nothing to do with cognition; if not, it must be an additional faculty.

These, and similar, problems can be eliminated at the outset if one decides to argue with Arendt against Arendt. In this account the whole idea of a mind–soul–body trichotomy as well as the theory of the three 'mental faculties' are brushed aside. It assumes that Hannah Arendt intended to assert the following: there is one 'mental faculty' termed 'thinking' which is tantamount to speculation–meditation. There are two further mental faculties ('willing' and 'judging') which are, *in one of their interpretations*, mobilised in the 'vita contemplativa' alone. Cognition or 'intellect' (*Verstand*) pertains to the 'vita activa', as do 'willing' and 'judging' in another interpretation.

One further preliminary remark is required here. Arendt defines 'thinking' as the faculty dealing with the 'invisible', but she sometimes refers to 'thinking' as the attitude of 'the spectator'. Since the two metaphors are obviously at cross purposes, the attitude of the 'spectator' will in this discussion be confined solely to the faculty of 'judging'.

A brief reconstruction

Human beings labour, work, and act; yet they also withdraw from labouring, working, and acting. Togetherness *and* solitude comprise the 'human condition'. We constantly switch from togetherness to solitude and back again. We keep our own company when thinking, willing, and judging. This life of the mind, so Arendt argues, though solitary, is by no means passive. On the contrary, mental life is *energeia*, just like action. The mind's activity is an end in itself. Among the three faculties of contemplative life, thinking stands for the general–universal, willing for the individual, and judging for the particular (*das Besondere*). Thinking takes place in the absolute present, willing is future-oriented, whereas judging is past-oriented.

Except for a few subchapters in the first volume, Arendt elucidates the categories of the life of the mind by presenting and interpreting philosophies she regards as *representative*. We would be misled by this way of elucidation, should we fail to pay due regard to the author's intention. In Arendt's view, it is not only philosophers who practise thinking, willing, and judging in the first place; we all do. Moreover, pure thinking, as Arendt understands it, is rather under-represented in the history of philosophy. Indeed, with the sole exception of Socrates, no philosopher adequately satisfies her criteria of 'pure thinking'. The history of philosophy consists of footnotes to Plato, and not to Socrates, for the simple reason that where there is no text, there can be no footnotes.

Yet, even if philosophers were not paragons of 'pure' thinking, philosophy as *metaphysics* always included 'pure thinking' as well. More important, philosophy makes us think about thinking, willing, and judging. Thus philosophies are arsenals of a variety of ideas we should rely on, however critically, in embarking upon the discovery of the life of the mind. Arendt had a further reason for elucidating her categories through interpretations of philosophies rather than from the material of everyday life and poetry. As we shall see, one of her main concerns throughout *The Life of the Mind* is to address the problem of 'the end of philosophy and the task of thinking' and to provide an alternative answer to Heidegger's.

In order to understand why philosophers cannot be regarded as 'pure' thinkers, one need only glance briefly at Arendt's concept of thinking. We already know that thinking arises from an intentional withdrawal from the 'vita activa' and that it is preoccupied with the 'invisible'. It is a process which can be elicited by anything which induces a state of 'wonderment' (*thaumazein*). While thinking, we detach ourselves from our surroundings: we are no longer 'here' but are 'absent', in another and unshared world, in the absolute present; that is, in an eternity where we neither will nor judge. In elucidating her own concept of thinking, Arendt takes as her point of departure the Aristotelian concept of *nous*, the Kantian notion of 'pure reason', and the Heideggerian notion of thinking, and pushes all three notions to their limits.

Thinking, according to Arendt, is *the quest for meaning*, yet it is not a quest for truth, nor is it the quest for knowledge. In an even more extreme formulation, thinking, as a quest for meaning, has absolutely nothing to do with a quest for truth or with a quest for knowledge. She even adds that thinking has nothing whatsoever to do with *logos* either. The latter thesis appears in both a strong and a weak version, but in the main current of Arendt's train of thought the weaker version prevails. Thus the thesis reads as follows: there is no consistency in thinking. Reasoning and argumentation are alien to thinking. Finally, what is thought cannot be taught. Socrates is interpreted by Arendt in just this fashion. Socrates did not 'know' anything, he made no case for truth, he did not teach anything, nor did he reason.

Arendt takes both the Aristotelian notion of *nous* and the Kantian notion of 'pure reason' to their logical extremes. Not so obvious is how she also pushes the Heideggerian notion of 'thinking' to its extreme. Like Arendt, Heidegger also insists that philosophy since Plato has ceased to be 'pure thinking'. He too refers to Socrates as the model of pure thinking: Socrates stood in the 'draught' of Being and it is Being which calls for thinking. This is, however, not so with Arendt. First, if it is Being that 'calls for' thinking, then thinking is not absolutely autonomous. Second, if it is Being which calls for thinking, then one has to subscribe to the identification of Meaning with Truth (for Heidegger, the Meaning of Being is the Truth of Being). With Arendt, the main characteristic of thinking is *absolute autonomy*: thinking is *Selbst-denken*, and nothing but *Selbst-denken*. After Socrates, philosophy ceased to be pure *Selbst-denken*. Yet, it thematises *Selbst-denken* and can make a case for it. This is why a model of pure thinking can emerge through an elucidation of representative philosophies.

Absolute autonomy is, however, not only characteristic of thinking; it is also characteristic of willing and judging. The life of the mind as such is completely autonomous and, furthermore, all three faculties of this life are completely autonomous with regard to one another. Put bluntly, the Aristotelian thesis that *energeia* is an activity which is an end in itself is also taken to its extreme, far beyond Arendt's own interpretation of Aristotle in *The Human Condition*. There, in contradistinction to labour and work, action was understood as that activity which is an end in itself. It was autonomous in its relation to work and labour. Yet it was not regarded as autonomous in *itself*. Arendt now restates this crucial difference. Liberty, or rather liberties, not freedom *per se*, are the central categories of action. As actors, humans can never be completely free, but in thinking, willing, and judging they certainly can. This is why the *solitary* character of the life of the mind is so frequently emphasised.

Of the three so-called faculties of the contemplative mind, thinking was previously characterised as the general faculty, willing as the individual, and judging as the particular. These distinctions require further elaboration. The sequence in which the three faculties are discussed by Arendt is an ontologico-historical one. Thinking has both an ontological and historical priority, for there is simply no human life without thinking. In this respect, 'thinking' is the mirror image of 'labour'. Thinking, like labour, *is living*. By contrast, neither 'willing' nor 'judging' is conceived as an ontologico-historical universal.

According to Arendt, the first person to thematise 'willing' was the Apostle Paul and, to the amazement of her interpreters, she argued that no one prior to Kant had ever thematised the faculty of judging. In other words, the faculty of 'willing' established itself, or to speak with Hegel, 'came to its notion' in the Roman world, in particular with Christianity, whereas the faculty of 'judging' first 'came to its notion' in modernity. Needless to say, the faculty of thinking is not the *cause* of the faculty of willing, for thinking does not stand in a cause–effect relationship with anything, and willing is as autonomous as thinking. Yet thinking is the precondition of willing in exactly the same manner that labour is the precondition of work (*techne*).

What, then, is 'willing'? It is the faculty of full personal autonomy. It is freedom understood as the autonomy of the person. It is the *fiat* of the life of the person qua person. Willing has no cause but itself and no objective but itself. In practical life, there are *volitions* but no 'willing'. Will is future-oriented for we will to become pure willing, we will to become fully autonomous *personalities*. Thus willing is a constant activity, yet not the kind of activity we perform in the 'world' in our togetherness with others, but an activity striving for absolute *independence* from that world. This is why 'willing' is a faculty of the *mind*; it is thus inherent in the 'vita contemplativa' and not in the 'vita activa'. It is for this reason that Arendt criticises Kant's notion of 'practical reason' for undercutting the autonomy of willing for the sake of the autonomy of 'pure reason'. Yet she is also quick to claim Kant for her own theoretical endeavours. In the final analysis the faculty of willing was a contemplative one for Kant as well, as his notion of 'practical reason' has nothing to do with action. The term 'practical' refers to the activity of the mind, and not to praxis. However, Arendt here does not face the crucial difference between Kant's concept of pure practical reason and her own concept of pure willing. 'Pure practical reason' defines autonomy as a *moral* autonomy, whereas Arendt's concept of pure willing is tantamount to *personal* autonomy as such and it is, finally, devoid of *moral* imperatives of any kind.

Willing is the faculty in the realm of the contemplative life which corresponds to *techne* (work) in the life of action. Although 'willing' is an end in itself which *techne* is not, both are instances of human self-assertion and both are *creative*. *Techne* creates things exterior to activity whereas 'willing' creates itself. The autonomous personality, in this sense, is the one which defies all external constraints.

Judging as a faculty of the life of the mind is past-oriented. This faculty has nothing to do with *phronesis*, ethical or political. Judging is not tantamount to *primary* judgement in any respect. Primary judgement can be understood as an independent faculty, in this sense also as an autonomous one, but it cannot be practised fully autonomously. The faculty of judging discussed by Arendt relates to *secondary judgement*. It is not the kind of judgement we pass *in* action but the one we pass *on* action. We can pass a secondary judgement on actions if the action has already terminated or, at least, we pass secondary judgements on actions *as if* the actions had already terminated. The person who mobilises the faculty of judgement is not the actor but *the spectator*. Judgement is certainly activity (*energeia*), an end in itself: judging has no other end but judging.

The faculty of judging is a 'particular' one (*das Besondere*) on three counts. Judging as an autonomous faculty is, in a manner of speaking, the synthesis of thinking and willing. It *is* thinking for we mobilise our faculty of pure thinking in judgement, yet it is willing as well, for we perforce detach ourselves as persons from all externalities in order to be in the position of judging. The second aspect is made clear by Arendt repeatedly, and invariably in conjunction with Kant's judgement of the French Revolution, which he passed from the position of the onlooker, and not from that of the actors. Judging is the only mental faculty which *mediates* between the 'vita contemplativa' and the 'vita activa'. Although judgements are passed *by spectators* they are passed *on actors*. The faculty of judgement judges political actions. This is why Arendt argues that Kant's 'real' and 'hidden' political philosophy must be deciphered from *The Critique of Judgement*. And there is more to this mediation than is apparent at first glance.

First, although judgement is passed by the spectator (and judging here is every bit as solitary as thinking and willing), it is passed from the vantage point of the '*sensus communis*'. Kant's remarks concerning the onlookers who followed the actions of French revolutionaries — that he disapproved morally of the revolutionary actors themselves, but approved of those who empathised with them — serve as a model. The onlookers express the *sensus communis*, their own political taste, and they are ready to suffer the consequences of this particular political taste. Thus in the process of judging, the person (like Kant) is still solitary, yet he/she also shares the *sensus communis*.

Second, mediation has yet another aspect which is implied in the notion of 'taste'. Because judging also mediates between the life of the mind and our senses, including our soul, it thus includes pleasure and displeasure. Third, judgement, though past-oriented, transforms the past into present and future. Put simply, whereas solitary thinking is coterminous with life and hence dies with the thinker, and whereas solitary willing is a pronouncement of the human subject which dies along with the subject, judgement does not die. Rather, it immortalises those who are judged, or, to use Kant's words, an event like this cannot be forgotten (*lässt sich nicht vergessen*).

Hence, with its dual message, the motto Arendt chose for her never-to-be-written book on judging: *Victrix causa deis placuit sed victa Catoni* (the victors' cause pleased the gods, that of the vanquished pleased Cato). The word *placuit* (pleased) emphasises the dimension of taste in judgement. The gods who are pleased by the cause of the victors are the rulers, and they are in the plural. Cato, who was pleased by the cause of the vanquished, was a Stoic (a man of willing) and a single individual. The sentence quoted here is a typical 'spectator sentence'. Cato is both an actor and a spectator. He is a spectator like those supporters of the French Revolution to whom Kant referred, a spectator filled with enthusiasm and commitment. When asserting that the cause of the vanquished pleases him, Cato *raises a claim* to a *sensus communis* and he addresses those who pass secondary judgements, judgements upon actions. 'Tell the story from this viewpoint, immortalise those who have been vanquished, the cause of the vanquished must not be erased from human memory': so his claim reads.

One should not draw hasty conclusions from this particular interpretation of Cato's dictum. The unsentimental Arendt did not press the point that judgement should invariably side with the vanquished and never with the victors. Her message was different: she stressed the plurality of the world of judgement. Judging, like thinking and willing, is a quest for meaning and not a quest for knowledge. Meaning is pluralistic. Meaning constituted by judging, though pluralistic, can be shared, contrary to the meanings constituted by the processes of thinking and willing. This is why judging, as the faculty of the contemplative life, corresponds to political action in the *vita activa*. In the final analysis, then, the political dimension gains the upper hand even in *bios theoreticos*.

Failures through virtues

Hannah Arendt thus presented a philosophical system, neither a pedantic nor a closed one, but a system all the same. The system is constructed retrospectively, as it were, from the vantage point of the end result. Arendt's whole system can be seen as the ontologico-historical foundation of a *political philosophy*, because it is the faculty of judging that synthesises the two other faculties of the life of the mind. Moreover, judgement mediates between the theoretical and practical life, and is thus pre-eminently a political faculty. Yet the intrinsic norms and rules of philosophical language denied Arendt's own postulates. She was intent on *proving something*; she embarked on *making a case for something*; she made preparations for the *solving of a problem*; she *argued*. In short, she was engaged in precisely those mental operations which she herself had excluded from the contemplative life proper. She thus wrote her own footnote to Plato, and a very original one, nor would she have denied that this was exactly what she had done.

At any rate, pure thinking and pure willing cannot be committed to paper but in Arendt's view pure judging can, and Arendt often engaged in such pure theoretical judgements. And yet, she herself came to the conclusion that the Kantian *quaestio juris* could not be answered through pure acts of judgement. Indeed, it was this very problem which gave her the impetus to write a book on the life of the mind. In the introductory remarks to the volume on 'Thinking' she refers back to her book *Eichmann in Jerusalem* and to the view developed there that 'evil is banal'. Her remarks here would seem to indicate that she is now fully aware that she had not answered the *quaestio juris* required of such statements. But now, she contends, she is equipped to furnish an answer. Her intention is not to demonstrate that the statement concerning the 'banality of evil' carries meaning, which it certainly does, but that *it is true*.

Later discussion will return to the merits and demerits of her argumentation, but at this point the issue is a different one. As a work, *The Life of the Mind* is fundamentally at odds with its own principal thesis: that the quest for meaning has absolutely nothing to do with the quest for truth or the quest for knowledge. Arendt, however, might well have responded to this objection by arguing that philosophy is neither pure thinking nor pure willing or judging, and with this one would not quarrel. Yet it is philosophy—and not pure 'thinking' or 'willing' or 'judging'—which contends that thinking, willing, and judging do *not* represent quests for truth or knowledge. It is, further, philosophy, even Arendt's own philosophy, which raises the *truth claim* that thinking/willing/judging etc. make no such contentions. The person engaged in the activity of 'pure thinking' does not make such distinctions. If in the process of 'wonderment', regardless of what may have prompted it, a meaning is revealed, then a truth is revealed, an insight is revealed, a 'secret' is revealed, knowledge is revealed.

Persons engaged in such an act of pure thinking do not necessarily have to read the *Critique of Pure Reason* and may be entirely unfamiliar with positivist philosophies. Even if they happen to be familiar with all the limits of pure theoretical reason, involvement in the process of pure thinking would lift the barriers and the safeguards erected by philosophy against *transcensus*. Kant never claimed that pure theoretical reason does not seek after truth or knowledge. Rather, he argued that although the quest for knowledge is present as well as the quest for truth, neither can ever achieve its goals, can ever be satisfied. It is this which constitutes the 'scandal of reason'. From this one might draw the conclusion that 'pure thinking' is also a quest for knowledge and a quest for truth to the same extent that it is a quest for meaning; and further, that it is an end in itself precisely because the quest for truth and knowledge do not result in true knowledge of a type one could term 'scientific knowledge'.

Why was it so crucial for Hannah Arendt to 'liberate' the life of the mind from the quest for truth and from the quest for knowledge? Why was it so important for her to deny any meeting point, contact, or connection whatsoever between thinking, willing, and judging on the one hand, and *Verstand* (cognition), argumentation, and problem-solving on the other? There are three distinct answers to this question which, however, coalesce.

First, Arendt accepted without the slightest reservation the post-Kantian positivist interpretation of truth, knowledge, cognition, and problem-solving. Truth is understood by her as 'true scientific knowledge'. Truth consists of statements of facts and conclusions drawn from these facts. Cognition achieves 'true knowledge' and proceeds from it to achieve yet further 'true knowledge'. Cognition is by definition *Verstand* (translated as 'intellect'), it is *instrumental*; it is never an end in itself for we cogitate *in order* to come to know something. We come to know things in an infinite chain of progression. Although Arendt was familiar with Kuhn's discoveries, she did not want to follow such recent developments in the philosophy of science—as far as the exigencies of her own philosophy were concerned, for good reason.

Second, after having subscribed to a post-Kantian positivist conception of knowledge and truth, Arendt makes a strong case for a kind of thinking which is not instrumental but autonomous, which is an end in itself—a kind of thinking that *knows no progression*. To speak of 'progress' in the quest for meaning, she argues, makes no sense at all. It is obvious, as it would have been to Arendt herself, that the *positivist concept* of thinking has nothing whatever to do with rendering meaning. Indeed, to hail as the paragon of thinking this positivist kind that yields no meaning is to degrade thinking and strip it of its dignity. And yet, because she subscribes so strongly to the post-Kantian positivist interpretation of truth, she must completely isolate the quest for meaning from the quest for truth and the quest for knowledge. If 'truth' is nothing other than true scientific knowledge, then indeed the 'quest for meaning' has nothing to do with the 'quest for truth'. If knowledge is but an end result external to cognition, then in no way can knowledge partake of, be embedded in, or result from pure thinking.

Third, it should be remembered that Arendt is attempting to construct a philosophical system: the theoretical image of the life of the mind must reconfirm and reinforce her conception of the *vita activa*. As György Markus and other critics have pointed out, Arendt drives the Aristotelian polarisation between *poiesis* and *praxis* to an almost absurd point. She is led to draw an absolute, unbridgeable line of division separating the 'political' from 'the social'. For her, political life is an end in itself whereas social life consists of a series of 'means–ends' relationships. There is liberty in the political realm, and this is why only opinions can reside there, not 'truth'. Where there is truth there is no liberty, for truth compels. There can certainly be truth, though it belongs only in the social realm; this is the truth of professional knowledge which aims at problem-solving. Now, with her concern to see the life of the mind as analogous to the *vita activa*, it is this model of the political realm which is applied by Arendt to the life of the mind. Since the life of the mind is autonomous—that is, free in the ontological sense of the word—the quest for truth should be excluded from it: as we have seen, truth compels, and what is autonomous cannot be compelled. The quest for knowledge and for truth are attributed by Arendt to cognition understood as a kind of *techne*. Because cognition is defined as science and science is defined as *techne*, knowledge and truth have to be *completely* excluded from thinking, willing, and judging. This is where Arendt reaches the extreme position of having to exclude intellect, cognition, argumentation, even *logos*, from the realm of 'mental faculties'.

All three aspects of Arendt's argumentation converge in an attack upon progress. The idea of progress, she asserts, is the idea of instrumentalisation. If we stand for the idea of progress, then everything we think or do is but some *means* to future ends. *Techne* (including knowledge, truth, and cognition) 'progresses', but we should not let ourselves be instrumentalised by it. Against its progress we should juxtapose all those activities which are ends in themselves and are thus completely autonomous (such as the life of the mind) or which are autonomous when contrasted to *techne* (such as political action). The pure 'quest for meaning' clearly cannot be conceived in terms of the category of 'progress'. Thinking cannot be conceived of as 'progressive' even within the life span of a single individual. If we withdraw into our 'inwardness', in the activity of thinking, some meaning or other will be disclosed. Yet these meanings cannot be accumulated over time. And even if such accumulations of meaning were conceivable within the life of an individual (as they can be in future-oriented willing), they could certainly not result in anything that might be either taught or mediated. That which cannot be taught can not be learned; it cannot accumulate, nor can it progress.

The practical message of this conclusion is clear. Here Arendt takes a stand as a citizen against two fashionable positions: against that which measures development or progress by quantitative yardsticks;

and also against any progressivist dismissal of the present as having no value of its own, as some secular 'vale of tears', in relation to some mundane 'paradise' supposedly yet to come. Arendt eloquently insists that our worldly existence is *not* a yoke, nor is it the prison of consciousness, nor again is it a rung on the ladder to eternity, to the future, or to the realisation of anything which we are not. The present is what we receive when we are born. Heidegger toyed with the words 'thinking–thanking' and for Arendt, too, thinking is thanking, and so are willing, judging, and acting. For her 'life is good', since life is an end in itself, and whatever is an end in itself is good.

Even were we to agree completely with Arendt's philippics against progress, her own philosophy would leave us with some residual doubts. As mentioned, Arendt discusses thinking as the general faculty of the mind, whereas she contends that the second (individual) faculty, willing, emerged (or 'came to its notion') in Roman times, while the third, the particular, the synthetic and mediating faculty of judging, was first discovered by Immanuel Kant. Even if, with Arendt, we were to accept that all three faculties of the contemplative mind are equally autonomous—that none is superior or inferior to the other two, even though judging is still the synthesis of both thinking and willing—it still *must* be the case that progress of a kind *has already taken place*: a progressive step first and foremost with Christianity (by the Apostle Paul) in ancient Rome, and a second progressive step in modernity. However, a qualification here might be that this progress is limited and already complete: since there are only three autonomous faculties of the contemplative mind and since, with modernity, *all three* have made their appearance in full and have come to occupy their autonomous position in the life of the mind, *there will be no further progress*.

By such argumentation, however, we put ourselves in the place of the owl of Minerva. But what then, is it that we are looking back upon? Are we facing the end of progress alias the end of philosophy; or rather, the end of philosophy alias an end of progress?

The Banality of Evil revisited

Hannah Arendt begins *The Life of the Mind* with a commitment to answering the *quaestio juris* about her thesis on the 'banality of evil'. Indeed, she takes up the problem at the end of the volume on 'Thinking' as well as in the volume on 'Willing'. In what follows, one may venture a guess as to the line of justification Arendt might well have adopted in her unwritten book on judging.

First, however, the two justifications that she did proffer, both of which are arguably quite inadequate, need to be considered. Not even her culture, eloquence, her sense of the unique, and her imagination suffice to cover up the tentativeness and theoretical meagreness of her argument.

There is first the answer given at the end of the volume on 'Thinking', that pure thinking can take the form of a dialogue a person conducts with himself. There are 'two in one': the person withdraws into solitude and keeps himself–herself company as Socrates did. While thinking, one is one's own best friend. Yet, Arendt adds, who wants to be the best friend of a murderer? Obviously no one and this is why, while thinking, one cannot be evil. She concludes from this that evil is merely the absence of thinking, and therefore banal. This is, however, an unconvincing conclusion on at least three counts. The first of these is stressed by Arendt herself. She had argued that thinking is dangerous and that non-thinking is equally dangerous. Yet, if both thinking and non-thinking can be equally dangerous, then a kind of thinking can be as evil as non-thinking. Put simply: both parties to a discussion concerning a murder can be murderers, and they can also be each other's best friend, as thugs often are. Second, *thaumazein* (wonder) is not necessarily ignited by matters of moral relevance. Third, since Arendt emphasises that everyone thinks (since thinking is life), how can non-thinking exist and how can she possibly attribute evil in general to non-thinking? She ought to have attributed evil to non-thinking *in matters of good and evil* whereby she should then have come to the conclusion that thinking on matters of good and evil cannot be 'pure' in her own definition of pure thinking, for it cannot be completely *autonomous*. One must have some preliminary knowledge about good and evil, there must be at least a single value or a single norm which compels (the truth of good), so that thinking can reject evil thoughts and evil deeds.

A second but still unsatisfactory answer is given in the volume on 'Willing', where the discussion of 'the banality of evil' is deeply embedded in concrete analyses, in particular in the 'redeeming critique' of Epictetus, Augustine, and Duns Scotus. What can be distilled from these critiques is that the will cannot be evil. Since every *beginning* and *new beginning* requires willing (in the individual), the individual cannot be positively evil. Evil is pure negation, and as such it is a 'lack', it is nought, it does not exist. Arendt appears to subscribe uncritically to the concept of willing as presented in Christian philosophy, just as she uncritically subscribes to the concept of knowledge and truth as presented in post-Kantian positivist philosophies. Yet she seems to do so intentionally, precisely because she wants to make a case for the banality of evil. This is one of the reasons, albeit not the major one, for Arendt's inability to address moral problems proper as they appear in the contemporary world.

To turn now to guesswork; how might Hannah Arendt have addressed the issue of 'the banality of evil' in conjunction with the faculty of judging? Judging, as we have seen, is the faculty of the *spectator*. Indeed, Arendt several times quotes Goethe's famous aperçu: 'The actor is always guilty, only the spectator is innocent'. She certainly held doubts about the first half of the sentence, but never about the second. There is no doubting this affirmation of the innocence of the spectator, for this is how Arendt interpreted Kant's remark on the French Revolution. Arendt emphasised that there is no contradiction whatsoever between Kant's moral disapproval of the revolutionary actors and his moral approval of those who felt empathy for them. Without becoming so himself, the spectator can even feel empathy with the acts of those who are guilty. The guesswork starts at this point. One might argue that there are kinds of guilt with which no pure (impartial) spectator can and would feel empathy, acts which must generally and necessarily 'displease'. It is these actions which we term 'evil'. The 'pure' judging faculty is not even secondary; it is tertiary. It is the faculty of mind mobilised if stories are told 'departing from a *sensus communis*'. Since evil never 'pleases', it will never be the *sensus communis* in secondary judgement, nor can such evil be immortalised by tertiary judgement (in story-telling). In all representative stories which we tell about histories, evil will appear as mere negation, as nought, as insubstantial and irrelevant. Good is immortalised, even guilt not amounting to evil may be, though evil itself will never be. If this guesswork is correct, we could readily subscribe to the probable result of Arendt's reasoning.

Yet, while the thesis (if well reconstructed) is a forceful argument against the concept of 'radical evil', it is not an argument for the banality of evil. One can assert that evil is not ineradicably embedded in so-called human nature, nor, for that matter, in human 'willing', without asserting that it is therefore 'banal'. One need not say that everyone is born evil to contend that there are evil maxims, that there are actors who are evil, and that people can be infected with evil and so become *positively* evil. When innocent spectators recount stories of evil, these stories implicitly assume, by virtue of their being recounted, that evil exists. Furthermore, in such stories evil is not immortalised in the same way as other actions may be. For example, it cannot be immortalised as a model for a new beginning. It is kept in our memory so that we should never forget it. It is also immortalised as a warning: even if humans are not 'by nature' evil, evil is in the world, watch out and discover it before it is too late!

The spectator is innocent so long as he/she is not guilty in a positive sense. Yet even the spectator can be guilty of forbearance if he/she fails to detect evil whenever and wherever it makes its appearance. Although evil does not please, if we fail to detect it, the *sensus communis* might play a nasty trick on us and implicate us in it. The faculty of judging cannot be conceived as absolutely autonomous in matters of moral taste. Here too we need to be *compelled* by true and good norms. Knowledge and also the quest for knowledge are prerequisites for the proper use of the faculty of judging.

The 'end of philosophy' and the task of thinking

Arendt usually put the phrase 'the end of philosophy' in inverted commas. She refused to believe that philosophy had come to an end; rather, her contention was that there was a 'new beginning' in modern philosophy. As she so often argued, modern philosophy has become *political philosophy*. In her book on the life of the mind, Kant's *Critique of Judgement* is seen as its moment of 'foundation'. Of course, one must be extremely cautious in identifying a 'new beginning'. As Arendt remarked, every footnote written to Plato is in fact such a new beginning. Philosophy is *Selbst-denken*, 'personal thinking', to the extent that anything, once it comes to be written, can be. Every 'ism', 'tendency', trend, school represents a degradation of the proper *function* of philosophy which is now, as it has always been, the satisfaction of the need for metaphysics, which is as close to 'pure thinking' as is possible.

Interestingly, this confession of faith does not prevent Arendt from showing a sympathy, sometimes explicit, for the late-flying owl of Minerva, Philosophy, which once satisfied the need for metaphysics by thinking on thinking and which later satisfied the same need by thinking on willing, and which now satisfies this need, from Kant onwards, as thinking on judging. This is not tantamount to the statement that philosophy ceases to think on thinking and willing; it only means that philosophy does so from the standpoint of thinking on judging. Philosophy becomes past-oriented, since the capacity of judging is past-oriented.

Put simply, modern philosophy satisfied the need for *meaning* while telling *representative stories of the past*. 'Past' stands here both for the past-of-the-present and for the 'bygone'. In the first case, philosophy puts to use the pure faculty of judging by telling stories of things which occurred only yesterday, the stories of political action. In the second case, philosophy puts to use the pure faculty of judging by telling the stories of pre-modern times, but not only, nor even primarily, political stories. The stories which need to be told are the stories of the footnotes written to Plato. Arendt does not have in mind a 'history of philosophy'. Even less does she aspire to good philology or the precise reconstruction of ancient texts, however brilliant she indeed is in such undertakings. Rather, she asserts that a philosopher should recount the stories of the footnotes written to Plato as *representative* stories, as she sees and understands them in their capacity of being representative.

We know that Arendt rejected the idea of progress. Yet she did so not in order to accept the idea of regression or that of an eternal recurrence. There is no world history, she contends, there never was and there never will be. However, there is always a *new beginning*. The birth of every infant is such a new beginning, so is the act of founding a new city or even the revolution if it becomes a 'foundation'. Every new beginning needs the stories of philosophies, which for their part are the stories of new beginnings. The fact that philosophy has become past-oriented does not indicate 'the end of new beginnings'; rather, it reconfirms human freedom and liberty (freedom in the life of the mind and liberty, or liberties, in the political realm). It is the actor as well as the thinking, willing, and judging person who begins anew. In telling representative stories of the past, philosophy can become the 'midwife' of such new beginnings. The philosophy which thinks thinking, willing, and judging from the vantage point of judgement is *closer* to the founding father of philosophy, Socrates, than any other footnotes written to Plato have ever been. Philosophy thus returns from heaven to earth, deals with human matters, with opinions, and it does not treat actors as ignorant fools.

What is the adequate term for *the representative stories* recounted about the footnotes written to Plato or of the representative stories recounted about matters of 'moral, political, and aesthetic taste'? The adequate term is 'culture'. What is the adequate term for the representative stories recounted about events of yesterday, and, in particular, about actions for a 'new beginning' irrespective of success or failure? The adequate term is 'political culture'.

If we follow Arendt all the way through, we must come to the conclusion that modern philosophy becomes perforce 'the philosophy of culture'. It is for this reason that it takes its beginning with Kant's *Critique of Judgement*. Arendt will not assert that philosophies which follow in the footsteps of the ancients have become 'impossible', 'obsolete', or 'irrelevant' in the modern age. Since for her, philosophy is *Selbst-denken*, 'personal thinking', no form or manner of *Selbst-denken* can in principle be excluded from the realm of contemporary philosophy. She argued no more than that the main current of modern philosophy is, or irreversibly becomes, 'judgemental'.

Perhaps in this spirit, however, she makes a strongly 'judgemental' statement. In her view, 'positivism' is not philosophy since authentic philosophy is always metaphysics. Once we strip philosophical categories of their *metaphysical aura* they cease to be philosophical categories. In noting this retreat from metaphysics, Arendt gave quite an apposite picture of the main trend in contemporary philosophy. Yet this trend, conceived of by others as decline without remedy, as collapse, or at least as pathology, appears in a completely different light in her presentation. The evaluative signs are reversed. Far from coming to an end, philosophy has just commenced to live up to its promise in full.

Arendt is the last to venture into predictions. While she believes that there always was, there is, and that there will be new beginnings, she does not pretend to possess intuition, even less knowledge, of any new beginnings which lie in the future. No one can tell whether such new beginnings will turn out to be blessings or disasters. Nor does Arendt make predictions about the *future* of philosophy. She only states (and no more) that so long as people live up to the task of philosophy, which is also a task of thinking, so long as the representative stories of the 'past-of-the-present' and of the 'bygone' continue to be recounted by innocent spectators, and so long as culture is kept alive, there is always a possibility for new beginnings.

Modern philosophy is indeed the owl of Minerva in that it is past-oriented, yet it is not the owl of Minerva in the Hegelian sense of the term, since there is no single philosophy which can legitimately claim to be the true one. All philosophies, diverse as they are, provide meaning, or rather different meanings, and they together, *as culture*, immortalise what is good in us. Thus Arendt's work on the life of the mind conveys to us the norm that reads as follows: do not let political actions pass into oblivion; do not let philosophy pass into oblivion! Even those who believe that philosophy may have additional tasks to perform should nevertheless subscribe to this norm and live up to it.

References

Allen, W. S. (1984) *The Nazi Seizure of Power. The Experience of a Single German Town*, rev. edit. New York: F. Watts

Arendt, Hannah (1942) 'Herzl and Lazare', reprinted in H. Arendt, *The Jew as Pariah: Jewish Identity and Politics in the Modern Age*, ed. & introd. by R. H. Feldman, New York: Grove Press, 1978, pp. 125–130

Arendt, Hannah (1943) 'Portrait of a period' [Review of Stefan Zweig, *The World of Yesterday*], reprinted in Arendt, *The Jew as Pariah*, pp. 112–121

Arendt, Hannah (1943) 'We refugees', reprinted in Arendt, *The Jew as Pariah*, pp. 55–66.

Arendt, Hannah (1944) 'The Jew as Pariah: A Hidden Tradition', reprinted in Arendt, *The Jew as Pariah*, pp. 67–90

Arendt, Hannah (1945) 'Zionism reconsidered', reprinted in Arendt, *The Jew as Pariah*, pp. 131–163

Arendt, Hannah (1945a) 'Organized Guilt and Universal Responsibility', reprinted in Arendt, *The Jew as Pariah*, pp. 225–36

Arendt, Hannah (1946) 'The Jewish state: fifty years after: where have Herzl's politics led?', reprinted in Arendt, *The Jew as Pariah*, pp. 164–177

Arendt, Hannah (1948) 'To save the Jewish homeland: there is still time', reprinted in Arendt, *The Jew as Pariah*, pp. 178–192

Arendt, Hannah (1948) 'Jewish history, revised', reprinted in Arendt, *The Jew as Pariah*, pp. 96–105.

Arendt, Hannah (1950) 'Peace or armistice in the Near East?' reprinted in Arendt, *The Jew as Pariah*, pp. 193–222

Arendt, Hannah (1951) *The Origins of Totalitarianism*, New York: Harcourt Brace and Co

Arendt, Hannah (1953) 'Understanding and politics', *Partisan Review*, 20, 5, pp. 377–392

Arendt, Hannah (1957) *Rahel Varnhagen: The Life of a Jewess*, New York: East and West Library

Arendt, Hannah (1957a) 'Karl Jaspers: Citizen of the World?' reprinted in *Men in Dark Times*, pp. 81–94

Arendt, Hannah (1958) *The Human Condition*, Chicago: University of Chicago Press

Arendt, Hannah (1958a) *The Origins of Totalitarianism*, 2nd ed. Cleveland: Meridian/World Publishing Company

Arendt, Hannah (1961) *Between Past and Future*, London: Faber and Faber

Arendt, Hannah (1963) *Eichmann in Jerusalem: A Report on the Banality of*

Evil, revised edit. New York: Viking Press

Arendt, Hannah (1964) Letter to Gershom Scholem of 23 June 1963, published in G. Scholem & H. Arendt, 'Eichmann in Jerusalem: an exchange of letters', *Encounter*, 22, i, January 1964, pp. 51–56 reprinted in Arendt *The Jew as Pariah*, pp. 240–51

Arendt, Hannah (1964a) 'Personal responsibility under dictatorship', *The Listener*, 6 August, pp. 185–187 and 205

Arendt, Hannah (1965) *Eichmann in Jerusalem: A Report on the Banality of Evil*, revised enlarged edition New York: The Viking Press

Arendt, Hannah (1966) 'Rosa Luxemburg: 1871–1919' reprinted in *Men in Dark Times*, pp. 33–56

Arendt, Hannah (1966a) 'Bertolt Brecht: 1898–1956' reprinted in *Men in Dark Times*, pp. 207–49

Arendt, Hannah (1966b) 'Introduction' in B. Naumann, *Auchwitz*, New York: Frederick A. Praeger

Arendt, Hannah (1966c) *The Origins of Totalitarianism*, 3rd edition, New York: Harcourt, Brace, World

Arendt, Hannah (1968) *Men in Dark Times*, New York: Harcourt Brace Jovanovich

Arendt, Hannah (1968a) 'On Humanity in Dark Times: Thoughts about Lessing', in *Men in Dark Times*, pp. 3–31

Arendt, Hannah (1968b) 'Walter Benjamin: 1892–1940', reprinted in Arendt, *Men in Dark Times*, pp. 153–206

Arendt, Hannah (1971) 'Thinking and moral considerations: a lecture', *Social Research*, 38:417–446

Arendt, Hannah (1972) 'Lying in politics' in *Crises of the Republic*, Harmondsworth: Penguin

Arendt, Hannah (1973) *On Revolution*, 2nd ed. Harmondsworth: Penguin Books

Arendt, Hannah (1973a) *Men in Dark Times*, Harmondsworth: Penguin

Arendt, Hannah (1973b) *Crises of the Republic*, Harmondsworth: Penguin

Arendt, Hannah (1974) *Rahel Varnhagen: The Life of a Jewish Women* rev. ed., trans. R. and C. Winston, New York and London: Harcourt Brace Jovanovich

Arendt, Hannah (1977) *Eichmann in Jerusalem: A Report on the Banality of Evil*, rev. ed. New York: Penguin

Arendt, Hannah (1978) *The Life of the Mind*, New York: Harcourt Brace Jovanovich

Arendt, Hannah (1978a) *The Jew as Pariah: Jewish Identity and Politics in the Modern Age*, ed. and introd. by R. H. Feldman, New York: Grove Press

Arendt, Hannah (1979) 'On Hannah Arendt' [A Conversation] in M. A. Hill ed. *Hannah Arendt: The Recovery of the Public World*, New York: St. Martin's Press, pp. 301–339

Arendt, Hannah (1979a) *On Revolution*, Harmondsworth: Penguin

Arendt, Hannah (1982) *Lectures on Kant's Political Philosophy*, London: Harvester Press

Aristotle (1932 edn.) *The Politics*, trans. H Rackman, London: Heinemann, Loeb Classical Library

Aristotle (1956 edn.) *The Nicomachean Ethics*, trans. H Rackman, London:

Heinemann, Loeb Classical Library
Aristotle (1981 edn.) *The Politics*, trans. T. A. Sinclair & T. J. Saunders, Harmondsworth: Penguin
Aron, R. (1968) *Democracy and Totalitarianism*, London: Weidenfeld and Nicolson
Auerbach, E. (1953) *Mimesis*, Princeton: Princeton University Press
Bach, H. I. (1984) *The German Jew: A Synthesis of Judaism and Western Civilisation 1730–1930*, London: Oxford University Press
Banks, R. (1983) 'The vocation of the public servant', in *Private Values and Public Policy*, ed. Banks, Sydney: Lancer
Barker, E. (1957) *Social and Political Thought in Byzantium*, Oxford: Clarendon Press
Bauer, Y. (1978) *The Holocaust in Historical Perspective*, Canberra: Australian National University Press
Beatty, J. (1976) 'Thinking and moral considerations', *Journal of Value Inquiry*, 10, pp. 266–278
Beauvoir, Simone de (1946) 'Oeil pour Oeil', *Le Temps Modernes*, 1, 5, pp. 813–830
Beauvoir, Simone de (1968) *The Second Sex*, trans. by H. M. Parshley, New York: Modern Library
Beiner, R. (1982) 'Interpretive essay', in Hannah Arendt, *Lectures on Kant's Political Philosophy*, London: Harvester Press
Bell, D. (1980) *The Winding Passage: Essays and Sociological Journeys, 1960–1980*, New York: Basic Book
Benjamin, J. & Rabinbach, A. (1984) 'Germans, Leftists, Jews', *New German Critique*, no. 31, pp. 183–194
Berger, Peter L. (1966) 'Identity as a problem in the sociology of knowledge', *European Journal of Sociology*, 7, pp. 105–115
Bettleheim, B. (1963/64) 'Eichmann', *New Republic*, 148, pp. 23–33
Bieber, Leon E. (1979) 'Ich bin Bestandteil deutscher Wirklichkeit', in H. M. Broder and R. Lang *Fremd im eigenen Land* (see below), pp. 48–56
Bondy, F. (1961) 'On misunderstanding Eichmann', *Encounter*, November, pp. 32–54
Bourriot, F. (1976) Recherches sur la nature du Genos: étude d'histoire social Athenienne—periodes archaique et classique, diss. 2 vols, Lille: Universite Lille III
Bracher, K. D. (1973) *The German Dictatorship: The Origins, Structure, and Consequences of National Socialism*, trans. Jean Steinberg, Harmondsworth: Penguin
Brandt, L. (1979) 'Ein anormales Miteinander, ein Zustand ohne Zukunft', in H. M. Broder and R. Lang *Fremd im eigenen Land*, pp. 69–75
Brinner, W. M. & Rischin, M. (1987) *Like All the Nations?: The Life and Legacy of Judah L. Magnes*, Albany: State University of New York Press
Broder, H. & Lang, M. R. (eds.) (1979) *Fremd im eigenen Land. Juden in der Bundesrepublik*, with a foreword by B. Engelmann, Frankfurt/M.: Fischer Verlag
Bronsen, D. (ed.) (1979) *Jews and Germans from 1860–1933: The Problematic Symbiosis*, Heidelberg: Carl Winter Universitätsverlag
Broszat, M. (1981) *The Hitler State: The Foundation and Development of the*

Internal Structure of the Third Reich, trans. John Hiden, London: Longman
Broszat, M. (1985) 'Hitler and the genesis of the "Final Solution" an assessment of David Irving's theses', in H. W. Koch, ed. *Aspects of the Third Reich*
Brzezinski, Z. (1956) *Permanent Purge: Politics in Soviet Totalitarianism*, Cambridge: Harvard University Press
Buber, M. (1983) *A Land of Two Peoples: Martin Buber on Jews and Arabs*, ed. & introd. by P. R. Mendes-Flohr, New York: Oxford University Press
Bullock, A. (1962) *Hitler, A Study in Tyranny*, rev. ed. Harmondsworth: Penguin
Burch, B. (1964) *Dictatorship and Totalitarianism: Selected Readings*, Princeton: Van Nostrand
Bury, J. B. (ed) (1920) *The Hellenistic Age: Aspects of Hellenistic Civilization*, New York: Norton
Canovan, M. (1974) *The Political Thought of Hannah Arendt*, New York: Harcourt Brace Jovanovich
Canovan, M. (1974) *The Political Thought of Hannah Arendt*, London: Dent
Canovan, M. (1978) 'The Contradictions of Hannah Arendt's Political Thought', *Political Theory*, 6:5–26
Carroll, B. (1968) *Design for Total War: Armaments and Economics in the Third Reich*, The Hague: Mouton
Childers, T. (1983) *The Nazi Voter*, Chapel Hill: University of North Carolina Press
Chomsky, N. (1983) *The Fateful Triangle: The United States, Israel, and the Palestinians*, Boston: South End Press
Chomsky, N. (1987) *The Chomsky Reader*, ed. James Peck, New York: Pantheon Books
Cochran, C. E. (1982) *Character, Community and Politics*, University: University of Alabama Press
Cohen, I. (1951) *A Short History of Zionism*, London: Frederick Muller
Cooper, Leroy A. (1976) 'Hannah Arendt's political philosophy: an interpretation', *Review of Politics*, 38:145–176
Coser, L. A. (1984) 'Hannah Arendt (1906–1975): self-proclaimed pariah' in Coser, *Refugee Scholars in America. Their Impact and Their Experience*, New Haven and London: Yale University Press
Chorover, St.L. (1979) *From Genesis to Genocide: The Meaning of Human Nature and the Power of Behavior Control*, Cambridge, Mass. and London: The MIT Press
Craig, G. A. (1978) *Germany, 1866–1945*, New York: Oxford University Press
Crick, B. (1977) 'On reading The Origins of Totalitarianism', *Social Research*, 44:106–126
Crossman, R. (1963) *The Observer*, 13 October
Crozier, M. (1964) *The Bureaucratic Phenomenon*, Chicago: University of Chicago Press
Cumont, Franz (1956) *The Oriental Religions in Roman Paganism*, New York: Dover
Dawidowicz, L. (1975) *The War Against the Jews*, Harmondsworth: Penguin
Denhardt, R. B. (1981) *In the Shadow of Organization*, Lawrence: University of Kansas Press

Dennehy, M. (1979) 'The Privilege of ourselves', in M. Mill ed. *Hannah Arendt*, New York: St Martin's Press
Deutscher, I. (1968) *The Non-Jewish Jew and Other Essays*, ed. & introd. by T. Deutscher, London: Oxford University Press
Dicey, A. V. (1905) *Law and Public Opinion in England*, London: Macmillan
Dicks, H. V. (1972) *Licensed Mass Murder*, New York: Basic
Donovan, J. (1960) *Eichmann: Man of Slaughter*, New York: Avon
Dossa, Shiraz (1980) 'Human status and politics: Hannah Arendt on the holocaust', *Canadian Journal of Political Science*, 13, 2:309–323
Dostal, R. J. (1984) 'Judging human action', *Review of Metaphysics*, 37, pp. 725–755
Draenos, S. (1982) 'The totalitarian theme in Horkheimer and Arendt', *Salmagundi*, 56, pp. 156–169
Duerrenmatt, F. (1961) *The Quarry*, trans. E. H. Moreals, New York: Grove
Eban, Abba (1986) 'The central question', *Tikkun*, 1:19–22
Elias, N. (1982) 'Scientific establishments', in Elias, H. Martins & R. Whitley eds. *Scientific Establishments and Hierarchies*, Hague: Nijhoff
Elshtain, J. B. (1982) 'Aristotle, the public–private split...' in Elshtain, ed. *The Family in Political Thought*, Amherst: The University of Massachusetts Press
Ethics and Conduct (1976) Didactic Systems, Cranford: N. J
Feher, F., Heller, A. & Markus, G. (1983) *Dictatorship over Needs: An Analysis of Soviet Societies*, Oxford: Basil Blackwell
Feldman, R. H. (1978a) 'Introduction: the Jew as pariah: the case of Hannah Arendt (1906–1975)', in Arendt, *The Jew as Pariah*, pp. 15–22
Ferguson, W. S. (1910) 'The Athenian Phratries', *Classical Philology*, 5, 3:257–84
Ferguson, W. S. (1938) 'The Salaminioi of Heptaphylai and Sounion', *Hesperia*, 7:1–74
Fest, Joachim C. (1974) *Hitler*, trans. Richard & Clara Winston, Harmondsworth: Penguin
Fleischauer, I. & Klein, H. (1978) *Uber die jüdische Identität: Eine psychohistorische Studie*, Frankfurt/M.: Jüdischer Verlag
Foote, M. (1978) *Resistance*, London: Paladin
Fraser, N. (1987) 'Women, Welfare and the Politics of Need Interpretation', *Thesis Eleven* 17, pp. 88–106
Friedlander, S. (1969) *Counterfeit Nazi: The Ambiguity of Good*, trans. C. Fullman, London: Weidenfeld and Nicolson
Friedrich, C. and Brzezinski, Z. (1961) *Totalitarian Dictatorship and Autocracy*, New York: Praeger
Friedrich, C. and Brzezinski, Z. (1966) *Totalitarian Dictatorship and Autocracy*, 2nd edition, New York: Praeger
Friedrich, C., Curtis, M. and Barber, B. (1969) *Totalitarianism in Perspective: Three Views*, New York: Praeger
Fromm, E. (1941) *Escape from Freedom*, New York: Holt
Fustel de Coulanges, N. D. (1873) *The Ancient City*, reissued New York: Anchor Doubleday
Gadamer, H. G. (1985) *Philosophical Apprenticeships*, trans. R. R. Sullivan, Cambridge, Ma: MIT Press

Galbraith, J. K. (1980) *Annals of an Abiding Liberal*, London: Deutsch
Gamm, H. J. (1979) *Das Judentum: Eine Einführung*, Frankfurt/M., New York: Campus Verlag
Giddens, A. (1985) *The Nation State and Violence*, Cambridge: Polity Press
Glock, Y., Selznick G. J. & Spaetch, J. L. (1966) *The Apathetic Majority: A Study Based on Public Responses to the Eichmann Trial*, New York: Harper and Row
Glotz, G. (1904) *La Solidarité de la famille dans le droit criminel en Grèce*, Paris: Librarie des Ecoles Françaises d'Anthenes
Goral, Ariel (1979) 'Ich bin Jude, also bin ich', in Broder & Lang *Fremd im eigenen Land*, pp. 203-221
Grab, W. (1984) 'The German way of Jewish emancipation', *The Australian Journal of Politics and History*, vol. 30, no. 2, pp. 224-235
Hall, R. (1963) 'The concept of bureaucracy: an empirical assessment', *American Journal of Sociology*, 69, 1, pp. 32-40
Hartstock, N. C. M. (1983) *Money, Sex and Power*, London: Longman
Hasluck, P. (1981) *Diplomatic Witness*, Melbourne: Melbourne University Press
Hausner, G. I. (1966) *Justice in Jerusalem*, London: Nelson
Heather, G. P., & Stolz, M. (1979) 'Hannah Arendt and the problem of critical theory', *The Journal of Politics*, 41:1-22
Hill, Melvyn A., (ed.) (1979) *Hannah Arendt: The Recovery of the Public World*, New York: St. Martin's Press
Hirschman, A. O. (1970) *Exit, Voice, and Loyalty*, Cambridge: Harvard University Press
Hodgkinson, C. (1983) *The Philosophy of Leadership*, Oxford: Blackwell
Hood, C. H. (1983) *The Tools of Government*, London: Macmillan
Hont, I. & Ignatieff, M. (eds) (1983) *Wealth and Virtue: The Shaping of Political Economy in the Scottish Enlightenment*, Cambridge: Cambridge University Press
Hughes, C. (1981) 'Administrative ethics' in Curnow G. R. & Wettenhall, R. L. eds. *Understanding Public Administration*, Sydney: Allen and Unwin
Hume, D. (n.d.) 'Of the first principles of government' in T. H. Greene & T. H. Grosse eds. *Essays*, London: Cadell
Humphreys, S. C. (1977) 'Public and private interests in classical Athens', *The Classical Journal*, 73, 2:97-104
International Military Tribunal (1950) *Trial of German Major War Criminals*, XXII London: HMSO
Isaacs, Harold R. (1975) 'Basic group identity: The idols of the tribe' in Nathan Glazer & Daniel P. Moynihan, eds. *Ethnicity: Theory and Experience*, Cambridge: Harvard University Press, pp. 29-52
Jabotinsky, V. (1960) Evidence submitted to the Palestine Royal Commission (1937) [excerpt] in A. Hertzberg ed. *The Zionist Idea: A Historical Analysis and Reader*, New York: Meridian Books & Jewish Publication Society of America: Philadelphia, pp. 559-570
Jackson, M. W. (1986) *Matters of Justice*, London: Croom Helm
Jaspers, K. (1947) *The Question of German Guilt*, trans. E. Ashton, New York: Capricorn
Jay, Martin (1979) 'Hannah Arendt: opposing views', *Partisan Review*,

45:348-380
Jonas, H. (1977) 'Acting, Knowing, Thinking: Gleanings from Hannah Arendt's Philosophical Work', *Social Research*, 44, pp. 25-43
Juden in Deutschland 1983 - integriert oder diskriminiert? Ein Symposium, Reihe Frankenthaler Gespräche 1983
Jung, C. G. (1957) *The Undiscovered Self*, trans. R. Hull, New York: Mentor
Kagan, Donald (1963) 'The enfranchisement of aliens by Cleisthenes', *Historia*: 41-46
Kamenka, Eugene & A. E. S. Tay (1979) 'Freedom, law and the bureaucratic state', in E. Kamenka & M. Krygier (eds) *Bureaucracy*, London: Arnold
Kampmann, W. (1981) *Deutsche und Juden: Die Geschichte der Juden in Deutschland vom Mittelalter bis zum Beginn des Ersten Weltkrieges* Frankfurt/M.: Fischer Taschenbuch Verlag
Kant, Immanuel (1928) *Critique of Aesthetic Judgement*, London: Oxford University Press
Kant, Immanuel (1952) *Critique of Judgement*, trans. J. C. Meredith, Oxford: Oxford University Press
Kant, Immanuel (1964) *Critique of Judgement*, New York: Hafner Publishing Co., Hafner Library of Classics
Kaplan, M. (1981) *Die jüdische Frauenbewegung in Deutschland. Organisation und Ziele des jüdischen Frauenbundes 1904-1938*, Hamburg: Hans Christians Verlag
Kaplan, G. T. (1984) The Politics of Survival, PhD Thesis, Monash University, Clayton, Melbourne
Kaplan, G. T. & Adams, C. (1988) in C. Hartung (ed.) 'The Attractions of Fascism/Traditionen und Traditionssuche des Deutschen Fascismus *Wissenschaftliche Beiträge* 55 (1988) special issue fasc. 83, Halle/Salle, pp. 3-25
Kateb, G. (1983) *Hannah Arendt: Politics, Conscience, Evil*, Oxford: Martin Robertson
Kazin, A. (1978) *New York Jew*, New York: Knopf/Random House
Kent, B. (1973) 'Bureaucracy in Nazi Germany', *Public Administration (Sydney)*, 32, pp. 56-61
Kershaw, I. (1981) 'The persecution of the Jews and German popular opinion', *Leo Baeck Yearbook*, 26, pp. 261-289
Kershaw, I. (1981a) 'The Führer image and political integration: the popular conception of Hitler in Bavaria during the Third Reich', in G. Hirschfeld & L. Kettenacker, eds. *Der Führerstaat. Mythos and Realität*, Stuttgart: Klett-Cotta: 133-161
Kershaw, I. (1985) *The Nazi Dictatorship: Problems and Perspective of Interpretation* London: Edward Arnold
Kettenacker, Lothar (1985) 'Social and psychological aspects of the Führer's rule', in H. W. Koch, ed. *Aspects of the Third Reich*, pp. 96-132
Koch, H. W. (1985) 'Introduction', in H. W. Koch, ed. *Aspects of the Third Reich*, pp. 181-195
Koch, H. W. (ed.) (1985) *Aspects of the Third Reich*, London: Macmillan
Kogan, E. (1978) *The Theory and Practice of Hell*, trans. H. Norden, New York: Octagon

Kramer, S. N. (1963) *The Sumerians*, Chicago: University of Chicago Press
Kwiet, K. & Eschwege, H. (1986) *Selbstbehauptung und Widerstand. Deutsche Juden im Kampf um Existenz und Menschenwürde 1933-1945*, Hamburg: Christians Verlag, 2nd ed
Kwiet, K. (1987) 'Judenverfolgung und Judenvernichtung im Dritten Reich. Ein historiographischer Überblick', in Dan Diner ed. *Ist der Nationalsozialismus Geschichte?* Frankfurt/M.: Fischer Verlag, pp. 237-264
Kwiet, K. (1988) 'Gehen oder bleiben', in *Die deutschen Juden am Wendepunkt. Der Judenpogrom 1938. Von der Reichskristallnacht zum Völkermord*, Frankfurt/M.: Fischer Verlag, pp. 132-145
Lang, Von J. (ed.) (1984) *Eichmann Interrogated*, London: Bodley Head
Lasch, C. (1983) 'Introduction' [to special Hannah Arendt issue], *Salmagundi*, 60, pp. iv-xvi
Lenz, S. (1968) *The German Lesson*, trans. E. Kaiser and E. Wilkens, London: MacDonald
Less, A. W. (1983) 'Interrogating Eichmann' *Commentary*, 75, 5, pp. 45-51
Lewis D. M. (1963) 'Cleisthenes and Attica', *Historia*, 22-40
Livy (1971 edn.), *The Early History of Rome*, trans. Aubrey de Sélincourt, Harmondsworth: Penguin
Lord Russell of Liverpool (1962) *The Trial of Adolf Eichmann*, London: Heinemann
Louthan, W. C. (1981) *The Politics of Managerial Morality*, Washington, D.C.: University Press of America
Machiavelli, Nicolo (1950) *The Prince and The Discourses*, New York: Random House
MacIntyre, A. (1967) *A Short History of Ethics*, London: Routledge and Kegan Paul
Mann, Thomas (1945) 'Deutschland und die Deutschen' in *Reden und Aufsätze*, vol. 3 of *Thomas Mann. Gesammelte Werke in Dreizehn Bänden*, Fischer Verlag: Frankfurt/M., second ed., 1974 pp. 1126-1148
Mann, M. (ed.) (1983) *The Macmillan Student Encyclopedia of Sociology* London: Macmillan
Marx, Karl (n.d.) *Capital*, vols. 1 & 3 Moscow: Progress Publishers
Marx, Karl (1953) *Grundrisse*, Berlin: Dietz Verlag
Marx, Karl (1973) *The Grundrisse*, trans. Martin Nicolaus, Harmondsworth: Penguin
Marx, Karl (1974) *The Ethnological Notebooks*, Assen: Van Gorcum
Marx, Karl (1975) *Collected Works*, vol. 3, London: Lawrence and Wishart
Mason, T. R. 'Labour in the Third Reich', *Past and Present*, 1966:33
May, D. (1986) *Hannah Arendt*, Harmondsworth: Penguin
Meerloo, J. A. M. (1969) 'Eichmannism', *Psychoanalytic Review*, 56, pp. 609-614
Merson, A. (1985) *Communist Resistance in Nazi Germany*, London: Lawrence and Wishart
McCarthy, M. (1985) 'Saying good-bye to Hannah (1907 [sic]-1975)' in *Occasional Prose*, San Diego: Harcourt Brace Jovanovich, pp. 35-42
Mendes-Flohr, P. R. (1983) 'Introduction' in M. Buber, *A Land of Two Peoples: Martin Buber on Jews and Arabs*, New York: Oxford University Press, pp. 3-33

Merz, K. (1979) 'Die toten Juden werden zum zweiten Mal umgebracht', in Broder and Lang eds.: pp. 289–291
Miale, F. & Selzer, M. (1975) *The Nuremberg Mind*, New York: Quadrangle
Milgram, S. (1974) *Obedience to Authority*, New York: Harper and Row
Millar, F. (1977) *The Emperor in the Roman World*, London: Duckworth
Minnich, E. K. (1984) 'Hannah Arendt: thinking as we are', in C. Asher, L. de Salvo, & S. Ruddick eds. *Between Women: Biographers, Novelists, Critics, Teachers and Artists Write about Their Work on Women*, Boston: Beacon Press, pp. 171–185
Moravia, A. (1961) *The Conformist*, trans. A. Davidson, New York: Signet
Morgan, L. H. (1877) *Ancient Society, or Researches into the Lines of Human Progress from Savagery through Barbarism to Civilization*, Chicago: Charles H. Kerr and Co.
Morgenthau, Hans (1977) 'Hannah Arendt on totalitarianism and democracy', *Social Research*, 44:127–131
Morony, M. G. (1984) *Iraq After the Muslim Conquest*, Princeton: Princeton University Press
Mosse, G. L. (1978) *Rassismus: Ein Krankheitssymptom in der Europäischen Geschichte des 19. und 20. Jahrhunderts*, Königstein/Ts.: Athenäum Verlag
Mosse, G. L. (1985) *German Jews beyond Judaism*, Bloomington: Indiana University Press, Cincinatti: Hebrew Union College Press
Nash, H. T. (1980) 'The bureaucratization of homicide', in E. P. Thompson & Dan Smith eds. *Protest and Survive*, Harmondsworth: Penguin
Neave, A. (1978) *Nuremberg*, London: Hodder and Stoughton
Nelson, John S. (1978) 'Politics and truth: Arendt's problematic', *American Journal of Political Science*, 22:270–301
Neumann, F. (1942) *Behemoth*, London: Oxford University Press
Nevisky, M. (1988) 'Martin Buber today' [An Interview with Paul Mendes-Flohr], *Jerusalem Post International Edition*, 1. iv, p. 18
New York Times (1971) *The Pentagon Papers*, New York: Bantam
Nietzsche, Friedrich (1966) *Beyond Good and Evil*, trans. Walter Kaufmann, New York: Vintage Books
Nock, A. D. (1933) *Conversion: The Old and the New in Religion from Alexander to Augustine of Hippo*, Oxford: Clarendon Press
Nock, A. D. (1944) 'The cult of heroes', *Harvard Theological Review*, 37, 2:141–73
Oakeshott, M. (1962) *Rationalism in Politics*, New York: Basic
O'Brien, Mary (1981) *The Politics of Reproduction*, London: Routledge and Kegan Paul
O'Donovan, P. (1961) *The Observer*, 23 April
Okin, S. M. (1977) 'Philosopher Queens and private wives: Plato on women and the family', *Philosophy and Public Affairs*, 6:345–69
Oppenheim, A. L. (1969) 'Mesopotamia—land of many cities', in Ira M. Lapidus, ed. *Middle Eastern Cities*, Berkeley: University of California Press
Oppenheim, F. (1976) *Moral Principles in Political Philosophy*, (2nd edition) New York: Random House
Orwell, G. (1984) *Nineteen Eighty-Four*, London: Oxford University Press
O'Sullivan, Noel (1973) 'Politics, totalitarianism, and freedom: the political thought of Hannah Arendt', *Political Studies*, 21:183–198

O'Sullivan, Noel (1975) 'Hannah Arendt: Hellenic nostalgia and industrial society', in Anthony de Crespigny and Kenneth Minoque, eds., *Contemporary Political Philosophers*, New York: Dodd, Mead, and Co., pp. 228-251

Oz, Amos (1986) 'An interview with Amos Oz: David Twersky', *Tikkun*, 1, pp. 23-27

Phillips, D. L. (1983) 'Normative theorizing in the social sciences', *Kennis en Methode*, 12, 3, pp. 170-189

Phillipson, N. (1983) 'Adam Smith as civic moralist', in Istvan Hont and Michael Ignatieff *Wealth and Virtue*, Cambridge: Cambridge University Press

Pitkin, H. F. (1981) 'Justice: on relating private and public', *Political Theory* 9, pp. 327-352

Plato, *The Laws* trans. R. G. Bury, (1926 edn.) Loeb Classical Library, London: Heinemann

Pocock, J. G. A. (1975) *The Machiavellian Moment: Florentine Political Thought and the Atlantic Republican Tradition*, Princeton: Princeton University Press

Pocock, J. G. A. (1983) 'Cambridge paradigms and Scotch philosophers: a study of the relations between the civic humanist and the civil jurisprudential interpretation of eighteenth century social thought', in Istvan Hont & Michael Ignatieff *Wealth and Virtue*, Cambridge: Cambridge University Press

Pocock, J. G. A. (1985) *Virtue, Commerce and History*, Cambridge: Cambridge University Press

Pomeranz Carmely, K. (1981) *Das Identitätsproblem jüdischer Autoren im deutschen Sprachraum von der Jahrhundertwende bis zu Hitler*, Königstein/Ts.: Scriptor Verlag

Quinton, A. (1983) 'Hannah Arendt' in A. Bullock & R. B. Woodings eds. *20th Century Culture: A Biographical Companion*, New York: Harper and Row

Rabinbach, A. (1985) 'Between enlightenment and apocalypse: Benjamin, Bloch and modern Jewish messianism', in *New German Critique*, no. 34, Winter, pp. 78-124

Rawls, J. (1971) *A Theory of Justice*, Cambridge: Harvard University Press

Reichhardt, H. J. (1970) 'Resistance in the Labor Movement', in H. Graml et al. *The German Resistance to Hitler* London: Batsford, pp. 149-192

Reiss, Hans (1970) (ed.) *Kant's Political Writings*, trans. H. B. Nisbet, London: Cambridge University Press

Reynolds, Q. (1960) *Minister of Death*, London: Cassell

Richarz, M. (ed) (1976) *Jüdisches Leben in Deutschland: Selbstzeugnisse zur Sozialgeschichte 1780-1871*, introd. by Monika Richarz, Stuttgart: Deutsche Verlags-Anstalt (altogether 3 vols. later vol. 1979 and 1982)

Riot-Sarcey, M. & E. Varikas, 'Feminist Consciousness in the Nineteenth Century: The Consciousness of a Pariah', *Praxis International* 5, pp. 443-65

Rogat, Y. (1961) *The Eichmann Trial and the Rule of Law*, Santa Barbara: Center for the Study of Democratic Institutions

Rohr, J. (1978) *Ethics and Bureaucrats*, New York: Dekker

Rostovtzeff, M. (1957) *The Social and Economic History of the Roman Empire* 2nd edn., Oxford: Clarendon Press, 2 vols

Roussel, D. (1976) *Tribu et cité: études sur les groupes sociaux dans les cités Greques aux époques archaïque et classique*, Paris Les Belles Lettres
Rürup, R. (1975) *Emanzipation und Antisemitismus Studien zur Judenfrage der bürgerlichen Gesellschaft*, Gottingen: Vandenhoeck & Ruprecht
Sachar, H. M. (1958) *The Course of Modern Jewish History*, London: Weidenfeld and Nicolson
Sachar, H. M. (1977) *The Course of Modern Jewish History*, updated and expanded edn., New York: Delta
Saggs, H. W. F. (1984) *The Might That Was Assyria*, London: Sidgwick and Jackson
Sallen, H. A. (1977) *Zum Antisemitismus in der Bundesrepublik Deutschland*, Frankfurt/M.: Suhrkamp
Sartre, J. P. (1956) *Being and Nothingness*, trans. H. Barnes, New York: Philosophical Library
Saxonhouse, A. W. (1980) 'Men, women, war and politics: family and polis in Artistophanes and Euripides', *Political Theory*, 8, 1, pp. 65–81
Schapiro, L. (1972) *Totalitarianism*, London: Macmillan
Schechtman, J. B. (1956) *Rebel and Statesman: The Vladimir Jabotinsky Story — The Early Years*, New York: Thomas Yoseloff
Schechtman, J. B. (1961) *Fighter and Prophet: The Vladimir Jabotinsky Story — The Last Years*, New York: Thomas Yoseloff
Schmidt, M. (1984) *Albert Speer*, New York: St Martin's Press
Schoenbaum, David (1966) *Hitler's Social Revolution: Class and Status in Nazi Germany, 1933–1939*, New York: Doubleday
Scholem, Gershom (1976) *On Jews and Judaism in Crisis: Selected Essays*, ed. by Werner J. Dannhauser, New York: Schocken Books
Scott, W. G. & Hart, D. K. (1979) *Organizational America*, Boston: Houghton Mifflin
Sealy, Raphael (1960) 'Regionalism in archaic Athens', *Historia*, pp. 155–80
Sellenthin, H. G. (1959) *Geschichte der Juden in Berlin und des Gebäudes Fasanenstraße 79/80*, Festschrift on the Opening of the Synagogue in Berlin, published by the Vorstand der Jüdischen Gemeinde, Berlin
Shaw, R. (1967) *The Man in the Glass Booth*, London: Chatto and Windus
Shklar, J. (1963) 'Review essay: Hannah Arendt, Between Past and Future', *History and Theory*, 2, pp. 286–292
Silberman, A. & Sallen, H. A. (1976) 'Latenter Antisemitismus in der Bundesrepublik Deutschland', *Kölner Zeitschrift fur Soziologie und Sozialpsychologie*, vol. 28, Cologne
Silone, I. (1960) *Fontamara*, trans. H. Ferguson, New York: Dell
Silone, I. (1962) *Bread and Wine*, trans. H. Ferguson, New York: Signet
Slater, P. (1968) *The Glory of Hera*, Boston: Beacon Press
Spiro, H. (1968) 'Totalitarianism' in D. L. Sills ed. *International Encylopedia of the Social Sciences*, Vol. 16, New York: Macmillan/Free Press, pp. 106–113
Springborg, Patricia (1984a) 'Karl Marx on democracy, participation, voting and equality', *Political Theory*, 12, 4, pp. 537–56
Springborg, Patricia (1984b) 'Aristotle and the problem of needs', *History of Political Thought*, 5, 3:393–424
Springborg, Patricia (1986) 'Politics, primordialism and orientalism: Marx,

Aristotle and the myth of the Gemeinschaft', *American Political Sciences Review* 80, 1:185–211

Springborg, Patricia (1987) 'The contractual state: reflections on orientalism and despotism', *History of Political Thought*, 8, 3:1–39

Stern, S. M. (1970) 'The constitution of the Islamic city' in *The Islamic City* ed. A. H. Hourani & S. M. Stern, Oxford: Cassirer, pp. 25–50

Syme, R. (1958) *Colonial Elites: Rome, Spain and the Americas* Oxford: Oxford University Press

Thomson, G. (1961) *Studies in Ancient Greek Society I* London: Lawrence and Wishart

Thomson, J. C. (1968) 'How could Vietnam happen?', *Atlantic Monthly*, 221, 4, pp. 42–53

Thompson, V. (1975) *Without Sympathy or Enthusiasm*, University: University of Alabama Press

Thucydides (1954) *The Peleponnesian War*, trans. R. Warner, Harmondsworth: Penguin

Timerman, J. (1981) *Prisoner Without a Name, Cell Without a Number*, trans. by Toby Talbot, New York: Alfred A. Knopf

Timerman, J. (1982) *The Longest War: Israel in Lebanon*, trans. by Miguel Acoda, New York: Alfred A. Knopf

Trevor-Roper, H. (1961) *The Sunday Times*, 23 April

Vigliero, C. (1987) 'Verlassen Sie sich nicht selbst! Zu einem ungedruckten Brief von Rahel Levin', *Bulletin of the Leo Baeck Institute* 77/87, Frankfurt/M.: Jüdischer Verlag, pp. 49–71

Vonnegut, K. (1961) *Mother Night*, New York: Avon

Wade-Gery, H. T. (1933) 'Studies in the structure of Attic society: II, the laws of Kleisthenes', *Classical Quarterly* 27:17–29

Wallerstein, I. (1987) 'The construction of peoplehood: racism, nationalism, ethnicity', *Sociological Forum*, 2:373–388

Wasserstrom, R. (1974) 'The relevance of Nuremberg' in M. Cohen, T. Nagel & T. Scanon eds. *War and Moral Responsibility*, Princeton: Princeton University Press

Weber, Max (1947) *The Theory of Social and Economic Organisation*, trans. T. Parsons, Glencoe: Free Press

Weber, Max (1958) *The Protestant Ethic and the Spirit of Capitalism*, New York: Scribner

Weber, Max (1968) *Economy and Society: an Outline of Interpretative Sociology*, 3 vols, ed. G. Goth & Claus Wittich, New York: Bedminster Press

Weldon, T. D. (1953) *The Vocabulary of Politics*, Baltimore: Penguin

Whitfield, S. (1980) *Into the Dark: Hannah Arendt and Totalitarianism*, Philadelphia: Temple University Press

Winch, D. (1983) 'Adam Smith's "enduring political result": a political and cosmopolitan perspective' in I. Hont and M. Ignatieff *Wealth and Virtue*, Cambridge: Cambridge University Press

Wood, E. M. & Wood, N. (1978) *Class Ideology and Ancient Political Theory*, New York: Oxford University Press

Wyman, D. S. (1984) *The Abandonment of the Jews: America and the Holocaust, 1941–1945*, New York: Pantheon

Young-Bruehl, E. (1979) 'From the pariah's point of view: reflections on

Hannah Arendt's life and work' in M. A. Hill ed. *Hannah Arendt: The Recovery of the Public World*, New York: St Martin's Press, pp. 3–5

Young-Bruehl, E. (1982) *Hannah Arendt: For Love of the World*, New Haven: Yale University Press, 1982

Young-Bruehl, E. (1982a) 'Reflections on Hannah Arendt's The Life of the Mind', *Political Theory*, 10, 2, pp. 277–305

Zipes, J. (1984) 'The return of the repressed', *New German Critique*, no. 31, pp. 201–210

Index

References to the works of Hannah Arendt (with date of original publication)

'A Jewish Army — The Beginnings of a Jewish Politics?' (1941), 99
'Bertolt Brecht: 1898–1956' (1966), 142
Between Past and Future (1961), 2, 31, 34, 37, 50, 52, 137
Crises of the Republic (1973), 2, 128
Eichmann in Jerusalem (1963), 31, 34–40, 43, 46, 49, 96, 99, 102, 106, 120, 151
'Jewish History, Revised' (1946), 90
'Karl Jaspers: Citizen of the World?' (1957), 127
Lectures on Kant's Political Philosophy (1982), 144
Letter to Gershom Scholem (24 July 1963), 95, 120
'On Hannah Arendt' (1979), 32, 92, 93, 95, 124, 127, 133, 134, 136
'On Humanity in Dark Times: Thoughts about Lessing' (1960/1968), 128, 142, 143
On Revolution (1963), 2, 60, 111, 125, 126
On Violence (1970), 2
'Organized Guilt and Universal Responsibility' (1945), 52
'Peace or Armistice in the Near East?' (1950), 105
'Personal Responsibility under Dictatorship' (1964), 48, 53
'Portrait of a Period' (1943), 94
Rachel Varnhagen: The Life of a Jewess (1957), 1, 71–90, 95, 96, 109, 110, 121–6, 134
Review of A. Ruhle-Gerstel, *The Contemporary Women's Problem* (1933), 126
'Rosa Luxemburg: 1871–1919' (1966), 123–4
The Human Condition (1958), 10–14, 21, 31, 32, 36, 135, 137, 141, 147
'The Jew as Pariah: A Hidden Tradition' (1944), 87, 89, 108, 109, 122, 137
'The Jewish State: Fifty Years After' (1946), 100, 103, 104
The Life of the Mind (1978), 3, 42, 48, 52, 54, 143, 144–59
The Origins of Totalitarianism (1951), 2, 18, 33, 34, 36, 39, 40, 43, 56–68, 84, 96, 97, 102, 108, 110
'Thinking and Moral Considerations: A Lecture' (1971), 53, 136, 138–40, 143
'To Save the Jewish Homeland' (1948), 100, 104, 113
'Understanding and Politics' (1953), 53
'Walter Benjamin: 1892–1940' (1968), 102
'We Refugees' (1943), 86, 90
'Zionism Reconsidered' (1945), 97–100, 104, 105, 115

General

academics, the professoriat, 2, 93, 133
Achilles, 53, 54
action, 9, 11, 64, 110, 121, 133, 144; autonomous Jewish, 99, 103; and freedom, 10–11, 67; as human agency, 28, 31, 34, 40, 63; participatory, 125, 128; and thinking, 137
actor, 156–8

Adorno, T. W., 93, 94
agonal spirit, competition, 11, 22, 28
alienation, 11
anti-Semitism, 2, 4, 18, 38–9, 59–60, 65, 78–82, 96, 108, 111, 114
appropriation of Arendt's ideas, vi, 4, 56–9, 64, 67–8
Aquinas, St Thomas, 9
Arabs, 100, 104–6, 110–12, 115
Aristotle, 9, 17, 21, 146, 147
Aron, R., 21, 26
assimilation, 19, 74, 79–81, 85–7, 109–10, 121, 122
Auden, W. H., 142
Auerbach, E., 50
authoritarian personality, 42
autocracy, 60

Bauer, Y., 84
Beauvoir, S. de, 47, 109
Begin, M., 98
beginning, 24, 25, 155, 157, 158
behaviourism, 135
Beiner, R., 54
Bell, D., 108
Benjamin, W., 80, 101–2, 122
Berger, P. L., 109
Bettelheim, B., 55
Bernstein, R., 23
Bloch, E., 80
Blumenfeld, K., 74, 83, 95, 96, 109, 110
Bondy, F., 55
Buber, M., 106–7
bureaucracy, 10, 15–17, 43, 46–9

Canovan, M., 9, 32, 45
capitalism, 22, 60
Cato, 150
Chomsky, N., 106
citizen, 21, 24, 28, 127, 128, 153
citizenship, vii, 4, 76, 111
city-state, 14–15
civil society, 10, 61
classes, 34–8, 60–1
cognition, 145, 152–3
Cold War, 2, 56, 58
colonialism, 60, 61, 105
common sense, 137, 138, 141
Communists, 35, 66–8, 95
community, 11, 35, 38, 54

competition, 11, 22, 28
Conference on Jewish Social Studies, 101
conscience, 137, 138
consensus, 26; *see also* sensus communis
consent, political support, 43–4
Consistoire, 96, 99
culture, 158, 159

Denhardt, R. B., 47
democracy, 23, 26–8
despotism, 12–13, 15–17, 63–4
Deutscher, I., 106, 107
Diaspora, Jews of, 19, 73, 112–15
Dicey, A. V., 43
difference, 92, 120–2, 127–8
Duerrenmatt, F., 46
Duns Scotus, 155

Eban, A., 112
Eichmann, A., 42–5; as bureaucrat, 47–9, 138–9; as monster, 42, 44–7; trial of, 2, 44, 54, 138
Ellsberg, D., 48
emancipation, 20; Jewish, 18, 77, 82, 85, 86; social, 19; women's, 127, 128
Enlightenment, 1, 19, 76, 94, 110
Epictetus, 155
equality, 10, 21, 26, 32, 38, 74–6, 99
evil, 4, 43, 46, 48, 99; banality of, 36, 138, 151, 154–7; lesser, 53; as negation, 155; radical, radicalisation of, 20, 64, 65; and thoughtlessness, 155
exceptions, 96, 123; 'exception Jew', 93, 94, 122; 'exception women', 122

family, 10, 13, 14
Fanon, F., 20
fascism, 11, 43, 56, 58
Fichte, J., 89
feminism, feminists, 119, 129
Foote, M. R. D., 48
Frankfurt School, 16, 93
Fraser, N., 127
freedom, 10, 21, 24–6, 31–3, 41, 75, 92, 102, 125–6, 134–5, 140–1, 158; conflict of life and, 20–1; German concept of, 85; versus liberties, 24–5, 147; *see also* liberty
French Revolution, 22–5, 32, 128;

Kant's judgement upon, 149, 150, 156
Friedrich, C. J., 57–60

gaze, 109, 135
genocide, 36, 46, 57–9, 64–5
Gestapo, 37, 95; *see also* secret police

Hecht, B., 98
Hegel, G. W. F., 12, 22, 25, 107, 137, 148
Heidegger, M., 1, 11, 16, 89, 93, 99, 106, 146–7, 154
Heller, A., 24, 68
Herzl, T., 80, 98, 100, 103
Hillel, Rabbi, 83
Himmler, H., 39, 63
Hirschmann, A., 47
history, Arendt's view of, 31–4; and identity, 109–10
Hitler, A., 37–40, 57–8, 91, 110
holocaust, 71–3, 91, 99, 101–2, 111–13
homelessness, 97, 100–3, 110
Horkheimer, M., 93
household (*oikos*), 10, 12–14, 17, 21, 22
Humboldt, W. von, 78
Hume, D., 43
Hungarian Revolution, 26, 41, 67
Husserl, E., 1

identity, 4; formation of, 73, 78, 108–11; Jewish, 91, 93, 100, 108–11; national, 86, 87; religious, 77–9, 114–15; social construction of, 109–14; *what* and *who*, 121–4, 139; *see also* natality
ideology, 33–39, 40–1, 50, 57–9, 66–7
interests, interest groups, 33–7
imperialism, 4, 22, 60–1, 103–4
instrumentalization, 153
Israel, state of, 73, 91, 110–11

Jabotinsky, V. (Z.), 97, 98, 99, 100, 103, 105–6
Jaspers, K., 1, 53, 87, 99
Jefferson, T., 9, 27
Jewish Social Studies, 101
Jew, Jews, 4, 35, 91; as pariah, 18–20; in court politics, 60, 76, 98, 108; genocide of 10–11, 59, 64–5;
German, 1, 35–40, 71–90, 95, 109; *see also* Judaism
Jodl, A., 44, 49, 55
Jonas, H., 109, 110
Judaism, 4, 77–9, 83, 108
judgement, 75, 139, 140, 150; 'reflective', 44, 47–8, 50–5; learnt in practice, 141
judging, 43, 44, 49–53, 146–50; thinking on, 157–9

Kafka, F., 81, 101, 122, 157
Kant, I., 1, 9, 27, 46–7, 51–2, 85, 134, 138, 140–1, 146–51, 154; *Critique of Judgement*, 135, 140, 143–4, 149, 157, 158; *Critique of Pure Reason*, 151
Kateb, G., 3
Kazin, A., 102
kibbutz, 14, 22
kinship, 13
kulaks, extermination of, 10–11, 65–7

labour, 32–3, 145, 148
Lafayette, Marquis de, 20
Lasch, C., 119–20
Laval, P., 47
law, laws, 31, 44, 49–51, 135
Lazare, B., 100, 101
Lenin, V.I., 66
liberty, liberties, 24–5, 86, 147; *see also* freedom
life of the mind, 49, 54, 133–4, 145–7
Luxemburg, R., 123–5

Machiavelli, N., 9, 16
Magnes, J. L., 98, 100, 106
Maine, H., 13
male, masculine, 12
Mann, T., 85–7, 90
Markus, G., 153
Marwitz, A. von der, 74–5, 78, 88–9
Marx, K., 9, 11–13, 15–16; and history, 25; on Jewish question, 19, 95; and politics of needs, 21; and state, 24
masses, 33–6, 39, 41, 61
mass society, 10, 11, 13, 16, 66
May, D., 3, 4
McCarthy, Senator J., McCarthyism, 2, 58–9, 68
McCarthy, M., 3, 94, 100

Mendelssohn, M., 1, 76, 84, 86, 93, 95
metaphysics, 146, 157, 158
minorities, 26, 111
'mob', 60–1
modernity, 11, 12, 21–5, 28, 33, 65, 67, 96, 126; and judging, 148, 154
monarchy, 10, 12, 15
Montesquieu, Baron C. de, 15
moral action, 139, 141
moral community, 52, 54; *see also* sensus communis
morality, 49, 112, 134
Morgan, L. H., 13
movement, 61–2, 64
Mussolini, B., 56, 68

natality, 67, 83, 94, 100–1, 106, 108, 120–2; *see also* identity
nation, German, 85
nationalism, 10, 35, 76, 80, 96–100, 103–4, 111
nationality, 61, 87
nation-state, 11, 14, 16, 19, 61, 111; Israel as, 112–15
Nazis, Nazism, 1, 2, 4, 34–41, 43, 58–9, 74, 93, 95
needs, 20, 21, 126, 127
Nettl, J. P., 124
New Jewish Agenda, 112
New School for Social Research, vi, 2, 3, 142
Nietzsche, F., 9, 11, 12, 15, 16, 19, 75
Nordau, M., 107
Nuremberg Tribunal, 44–5, 49

obedience, defence of, 44–5
Orwell, G. (E. Blair), 43–4, 54
outsider, 123; *see also* pariah
Oz, A., 113–14

Palestine, 2, 92, 96, 114
Palestinians, 92, 100, 104–6, 112
Parekh, B., 3
pariah, 18–21, 74–5, 88, 93–4, 108–10, 121, 128; Arendt as, 91; conscious, 122–5; pariah state, 100; pariahdom, 2
Paris Commune, 26
participation, 22, 27, 111
particulars, judging, 49–54, 140–1, 145–9

parvenu, 74, 93–4, 98, 102, 108–9, 121–2, 127; parvenu leadership, 96, 99
patriarchy, patriarchal family, 10, 12–14
patrimonialism, 12, 17
Pentagon Papers, 3
philosophers, 93, 146
philosophy, 4, 52, 93, 146–7, 151; end of, 154, 157–9; new beginning of, 159; as philosophy of culture, 158
Pitkin, H. F., 127
Plato, 135, 141, 146, 147, 151, 157
pluralism, 26, 50
plurality, 33, 92, 121, 126–8, 150; elimination of, 59, 64
pogrom, 76, 78
Polanyi, K., 23
polis, 9, 10, 12–16, 111
political action, 20, 31–7, 41, 50, 65–7, 75–7, 84; 128; and judging, 150
political community, 19, 26, 61, 110
political culture, 24, 158
political economy, 21
political issues, 126
political judgement, 134
political philosophy, 2, 135, 150, 157
political realm, 158
political, and the social, 10, 153
politics, 4, 34, 36, 93, 97, 103, 111, 126, 128; Jewish lack of, 85, 107; of parvenu, 96, 99, 102
Pollard, J., 114
positivism, 151, 152, 155, 158
power, 27, 60, 61, 63
Princeton University, 2, 52, 85, 86, 122
private, and the political, 22–4, 126
private, and the social, 21
progress, 152, 153, 154, 158
propaganda, 40, 62, 112
property, 22
public realm, space, 9–11, 32, 52, 92, 97, 99, 121, 126–8, 134–6; and private, 13–14; and social, 126–7

race, racism, 10, 36, 40, 61, 66, 80
Rawls, J., 52
rebel, rebellion, 19, 75, 122–4
relativism, 50, 139
republic, 9–17, 24–7, 125; American, 27; citizens of, 24; versus democracy,

Index

26–7; free, 26; French, 26–7 republicanism, 12, 13, 15, 16
resistance, 1, 37, 53, 90, 94, 95
responsibility, 4, 27, 44, 63
Revisionist Zionists, 97, 98, 99
revolution, 22–5, 50, 77, 85, 125, 158
revolutionary tradition, 25–6
Robespierre, M., 20, 27
Rousseau, J.-J., 20, 22, 26

St Augustine, 155
St Francis, 53
St Paul, 148
Sartre, J.-P., 20
Scholem, G., 18–19, 83, 89, 95, 120
sensus communis, 149, 150, 156
secret police, 57, 63, 67; *see also* Gestapo
Shabbetai Tzevi, 19, 84, 107
Shamir, Y., 98
Sharon, A., 112
shlemiel (shlemihl), 77, 89, 113
'Sholem Aleichem' (S. Rabinowitz), 122
Silone, I., 43
'social problems', the 'social question', 21–2, 32–5, 125–8
social, and the political, 10, 20, 21–4, 127
social realm, 9, 32
socialism, 80
socialists, German, 124
society, civil, 10, 54, 61
Socrates, 49, 50, 51, 53, 135, 136, 139, 146, 147, 155
solidarity, 77, 99, 120–2, 125, 128; of colonial peoples, 105
solitude, 55, 136, 145, 147, 149, 155
Soviet Regime, 58, 65–8
soviets, revolutionary, 26
spectator, and judgement, 145, 149, 150, 156
Speer, A., 47
Spinoza, B., 134
Stalin, J., 57, 58, 59, 65–7
Stalinism, 43
state, 23, 24, 60, 61, 63, 100; and civil society, 22; totalitarian in Palestine, 104
students, 41

taste, 51, 124, 149, 150

terror, 33–4, 36–7, 40–1, 50, 59, 63–4
thinking, 4, 43–4, 49–50, 53–5, 64, 94, 125, 136, 138–9, 144–6; distinct from knowing, 135; on judging, 157–9; and the public, 92, 134; not quest for truth, 145–6, 152
thoughtlessness, 2, 48–53, 137–8
Timerman, J., 112–15
Tocqueville, A. de, 9, 26
Toennies, F., 13
totalitarianism, 4, 10, 12, 18, 31–41, 43, 54, 56–8, 102, 134; development of, 59, 65–7; genesis of, 59, 60–5; and 'no-think', 44; and organisation, 62; and Soviet Russia, 65–7
'totalitarian syndrome', 20, 22, 28
trade unions, 33, 36
Treaty of Versailles, 35, 37
Treitschke, H., 80
Trotsky, L. D., 27, 66
tyranny, 26, 27, 36, 40, 64

uncertainty, 48, 138, 139
understanding, 134, 137
universals, 49–53, 145–6, 148

Varnhagen, R., 73–9, 94, 121–3, 135, 140
victims, 63, 64, 112
Vietnam War, 2, 43, 48
violence, 27, 61
vita activa, 39, 146, 149, 150, 152–3
vita contemplative, 144–59

Wallerstein, I., 111
Weber, M., 9, 11, 12–16; on bureaucracy, 43, 47–8; on pariah, 19, 75; on power, 27; on state, 64
Weizmann, Ch., 97
Weldon, T. D., 51
Whitfield, S., 3, 56, 58
willing, 49, 50, 148, 154
women, 4; German–Jewish, 73, 81; women's movement, 81, 127; women's question, 119, 125–6, 129
Women's International Zionist Movement (WIZO), 2, 96
work, 32, 145
working class, 34–7

Young-Bruehl, E., 3, 4, 53, 74, 79, 81, 82, 93, 99
Youth Aliyah, 2, 96

Zetkin, C., 81
Zionism, 2, 20, 80, 82, 91–107, 108–13, 115
Zweig, S., 94